ECONOMIC RESTRUCTURING AND THE
GROWING UNCERTAINTY OF THE MIDDLE CLASS

AF786511

This project has been supported by the foundation
"Vereniging Trustfonds Erasmus Universiteit Rotterdam" and the
"Koninklijke Nederlandse Academie van Wetenschappen" in the Netherlands.

Economic Restructuring and the Growing Uncertainty of the Middle Class

Edited by

BRAM STEIJN
Erasmus University Rotterdam

JAN BERTING
Erasmus University Rotterdam

and

MART-JAN DE JONG
Erasmus University Rotterdam

SPRINGER-SCIENCE+BUSINESS MEDIA, B.V.

A C.I.P. Catalogue record for this book is available from the Library of Congress.

ISBN 978-1-4613-7588-3 ISBN 978-1-4615-5655-8 (eBook)
DOI 10.1007/978-1-4615-5655-8

Printed on acid-free paper

All Rights Reserved
© 1998 Springer Science+Business Media Dordrecht
Originally published by Kluwer Academic Publishers in 1998
Softcover reprint of the hardcover 1st edition 1998
No part of the material protected by this copyright notice may be reproduced or utilized in any form or by any means, electronic or mechanical, including photocopying, recording or by any information storage and retrieval system, without written permission from the copyright owner.

Contents

Preface VII

Notes on Contributors IX

Introduction
Bram Steijn, Jan Berting, and Mart-Jan de Jong 1

1 Rise and Fall of Middle-Class Society? How the Restructuring of Economic and Social Life Creates Uncertainty, Vulnerability, and Social Exclusion
Jan Berting 7

2 Social Exclusion and Inclusion within the British middle classes, 1980-1995
Mike Savage 25

3 Women's employment, the household and middle-class heterogeneity
Rosemary Crompton 45

4 Social Exclusion and Increasing Uncertainty of the Middle Classes: The West German Case
Martin Kronauer 61

5 Proletarization of the Dutch Middle Class: Fact or Fiction?
Bram Steijn and Dick Houtman 73

6 From the logic of permanence to the logic of fragmentation: Socio-productive conditions and rearticulation of the middle-class
Eduardo Crespo Suarez, Florentino Moreno, and Amparo Serrano Pascual 93

7 Social change and the risk of social exclusion in Greece: How do the middle classes fare?
Maria Petmesidou 115

8 Notes on neocapitalism, unemployment and social exclusion: The case of Greece
Zissis Papadimitriou and George Hadjiconstantinou 135

9 Impoverishment of the Russian population and the problem of middle-class formation under market transformations
Natalia Rimashevskaya and Galina Voitenkova 145

10 Middle-class uncertainty: A synthesis and a research agenda
Mart-Jan de Jong 157

Subject Index 171

Name Index 175

Preface

Most readers will expect in the preface a short introduction to the theme of the book they are reading. This, however, is not the case with this preface. For an introduction to the theme of this book we refer to the introduction, which also contains a short history of the origins of the project that has resulted in this book. It suffices to mention here that this book is the result of a conference held in Rockanje (the Netherlands) in November 1996. Most (but not all) contributors to this volume had submitted an earlier version of their chapter to this conference.

In this preface we will limit ourselves to an expression of thanks to all the people and institutions who have made this book possible. In this respect we have first to thank the 'Vereniging Trustfonds Erasmus Universiteit', the Department of Sociology of the Erasmus University Rotterdam, and the KNAW, who have given financial support to our project.

Next, we have of course also to thank the contributors to this volume. Without them - and their patience - this book would have been impossible. As becomes clear from their chapters, they have incorporated the results of the discussions on the conference in their final versions.

Most importantly, however, we have to thank the many people who - in one way of the other - have contributed to the complex editing of this volume. In the first place we have to thank Marianne Otte, who plaid a vital part in the organisation of the conference in 1996 and was also responsible for the first editing of several chapters in this book. Betty Thiels gave important support to that task.

Nelly van Loon and Gonny Blaauw did an extremely good job in preparing the camera-ready version. The conversion problems between Word Perfect and Word drove them (and us) sometimes crazy, but - thanks to the technical support of Evelien Boshuizen and Wil Bouwman - they always found a solution for unexpected problems. Without them, the internal consistency between the several chapters would have been much lower. Next to them Jeannette van Walderveen and Nelleke Weltevreden deserve many thanks for the perfect way they prepared the index.

Finally, we have to thank Kluwer Academic Publishers, and especially Allard Winterink, for their enthusiasm for this book, and their support and advice throughout.

We are sure that - thanks to all these people - the reader will learn a lot from this book about the current situation of the middle class.

Notes on contributors

Jan Berting retired in 1995 as professor of Sociology at the Erasmus University Rotterdam. He presently lives in Southern France. He has published many books and articles on a variety of subjects (including sociological theory, social stratification, new technology, and risks in modern society). At the moment he is still active in his domain, especially with respect to the analysis of collective representations and cross-national comparisons.

Rosemary Crompton is professor of Sociology at the University of Leicester. She has published widely in refereed journals and edited volumes. She also wrote several books, mainly on social stratification. Her latest book (edited with D. Gallie and K. Purcell is *Changing Forms of Employment* (1996). She is also involved in a research project about gender relations and employment.

Eduardo Crespo Suarez is professor in Social Psychology at the Faculty of Sociology of the Universidad Complutense in Madrid. The meaning and centrality of work in modern societies and discourse analysis have been the topics of his recent work and publications. One of his recent publications (1996) is: *Introducción a la Psicologia Social*. Madrid: Editorial Universitas.

George Hadjiconstantinou is associate professor in Economics at the Faculty of Law of the Democritos University of Thrace. He has written 5 books and more than 40 articles about a variety of social and economic topics. Recently he is publishing about risks in modern industrial society.

Dick Houtman is a research fellow at the Department of Sociology of the Erasmus University Rotterdam (The Netherlands). He completed his dissertation on judgments on the rights and obligations of the unemployed in 1994. Currently, most of his publications address 1) the relationship between culture, stratification and modernity and 2) the social bases of resistance to the rationalisation of society.

Mart-Jan de Jong is associate professor of Sociology at the Erasmus University Rotterdam. For his Ph.D. thesis he studied the educational careers of immigrant children. He also co-authored a book on political issues in the Welfare State. His latest book is about the lives and work of nine masters of sociological thought (*Grootmeesters van de sociologie*, 1997).

Martin Kronauer is research associate at the Sociological Research Institute at the University of Göttingen (SOFI). He has published mainly on the fields of unemployment, social inequality and urban studies. Among others, he has published *Im Schatten der Arbeidsgesellschaft* in 1993 (together with B. Vogel and F. Gerlach).

Florentino Moreno Martin is doctor of Psychology and lector of Social Psychology at the Universidad Complutense in Madrid. His research activities has been focused essentially on the social-psychological study of social and political violence, on the one hand, and motivation at the work place, on the other hand. One of his recent publications in this field is (with B. Rey): Cooperación para el desarrollo, solidaridad y derechos humanos *Transformación social y compromiso de los profesionales. IV Jornadas de Intervención Social, 365-386,* Madrid: Ministerio de Asuntos Sociales (1996).

Zissis Papadimitriou is since 1985 teaching General and Political Sociology in the Department of Law at the Aristotle University of Thessaloniki. Between 1974 and 1985 he was research fellow of the Institute of Social Research in Frankfurt am Main. His research work concerns the technological and organisational modernisation in both the German industry as well as the services. He is the author of various publications in German, English and Greek.

Maria Petmisidou is Head of the Department of Sociology of the University of Crete. Her research focusses mainly on social exclusion and poverty in the Mediterranean Area. Recent publications are: (co-author); 'Social Protection in Southern Europe' (*Journal of Area Studies*, 9, 1996); 'Social Protection in Greece: A Brief Glimpse of a Welfare State' (*Social Policy and Administration*, 30, nr. 4, 1996); and *Poverty and Social Exclusion in the Mediterranean Area* (co-editor, forthcoming).

Natalia Rimashevskaya is director of the Institute of Socio-Economic Studies of Population in Moscow, she is also professor at the high school of Economics. In total she has written and co-authored more than 200 publications (several in English). Her current interests include: income distribution, women studies, and social statistics.

Mike Savage is professor of Sociology at the University of Manchester. His interests are in historical sociology, and in social stratification. Among his recent co-authored publications are *Property, Bureaucracy and Culture: middle class formation in contemporary Britain* (1992), *Social Change and the Middle Class* (1995), and *Gender, Careers, and Organizations* (1997).

Amparo Serrano Pascual is doctor of sociology and visiting researcher at the Centre de Sociologie et Economie Regional at the Sociology Unit of the Université Libre de Bruxelles. Her recent publications and researches focused, on the one hand, on the analysis of professional socialisation among youth, the growing uncertainty on the labour market, and the deterioration of the wage earners condition, and, on the other hand, on the evolution of the Welfare State. One of her recent publications related to the topic of this book is: Serrano Pascual, A (1995) Procesos paradójicos de construcción de la juventud en un contexto de crisis del mercado de trabajo *Revista Española de Investigaciones Sociológicas* 71-72, 177-201.

Bram Steijn is assistent professor of sociology at the Erasmus University Rotterdam. He wrote his Ph. D-thesis *De Januskop van de industriële samenleving. Technologie, arbeid en klassen aan het begin van de jaren negentig [The two faces of Industrial Society, Technology, labour and classes in the nineties]* in 1992 together with Marco de Witte. His main research subject deals with the influence of post-industrial society on labour. In this area he focusses on: technology and the quality of working life, flexibilization, and social stratification.

Galina Voitenkova is researcher at the Institute for Social-Economic Studies of Population in Moscow. She is especially interested in the effects of social transformation on social structure, social security, and standards of living. Methodologically she is interested in measurement of poverty.

Introduction

BRAM STEIJN, JAN BERTING
AND MART-JAN DE JONG

This book is the result of a four-day conference held in Rockanje (the Netherlands) in November 1996. The theme of this conference was 'Social exclusion and the growing uncertainty of the middle class'. Of course, the history of this conference goes further back than 1996. Within the Department of Sociology at Erasmus University in Rotterdam, 'the middle class' has always been given special attention.

As early as 1968, Berting wrote *In het brede maatschappelijk midden* ['*Between high and low in society*']. The main thesis of that book was that with the further development of industrial society, the middle class is becoming increasingly larger. In fact, in a mature industrial society, most people will belong to this 'middle class'. However, according to Berting, it would be wrong to view this middle class as a unified homogeneous class. In reality, 'the middle class' consists of a broad variety of heterogeneous categories with very different market and work situations (Berting, 1968: 192 ff). Some will have a good market and work position; other will be less fortunate (in fact, it is probably better to speak of middle class*es*). In the reality of social life, the boundaries between 'the middle class' and the working class are becoming less and less visible. One major conclusion of his study was that lower white-collar workers share the individualistic achievement orientation which is characteristic of the middle class in general. Linked with this orientation is the belief that one should aspire to social mobility. 'Having a career' is extremely important for members of the middle class. At the same time, however, changes in the organisational structure are making it more difficult for lower white-collar workers to develop such a career. In his words: in modern organisations a large number of white-collar workers have become trapped (1968: 194).

Of course, a major assumption of class theory is that the middle class is 'better off' than the working class (compare Goldthorpe, et al. 1969; Goldthorpe, 1980; 1995). Some authors have argued that the difference between these classes will disappear because an embourgeoisement process of the working class is taking place. In the words of Clark Kerr (1969: 96): "*The working class not only tends to disappear as a class conscious and recognizable element in society: it needs to disappear if modern society is to operate with full effectiveness. (...) Workers become citizens.*"

Other authors have argued that the boundaries between the lower middle class and the working class are disappearing because white-collar work is 'proletarianizing' (compare Braverman, 1974; Crompton and Jones, 1984). In the view of authors who

B. Steijn et al. (eds.), Economic Restructuring and the Growing Uncertainty of the Middle Class, 1-5.
© 1998 *Kluwer Academic Publishers.*

hold this view, the work of white-collar workers is becoming increasingly deskilled and will get more and more of the characteristics of the work situation of members of the working class.

We will not discuss these theses in this introduction, as that will be done in several chapters in this volume. However, it is important to state our own view on this matter as this was important when we started planning the conference. This view will be elaborated on in the first chapter by Jan Berting, but essentially our point is that both theses are correct. The embourgeoisement thesis is correct in that, with the development of industrial society, large parts of the middle class have indeed become integrated in the middle class. With the exception of some 'rear' proletarian unskilled manual groups, large parts of the working class have indeed - as stated by Kerr - become citizens.

However, at the same time that manual workers have become integrated in a large, but heterogeneous, middle class, the market and work situation of important categories within this middle class is deteriorating. This process started many years ago (hence, the studies by Braverman, Crompton/Jones, and Berting's statement about lower white-collar workers who have become trapped). However, there are indications that this is affecting more and more groups within the middle class. Berting will discuss this further in his chapter. It should be noted here, however, that the surge in interest in this matter probably started in the US. Rifkin (1995), for instance, has pointed out that increasing automation will eliminate a lot of jobs, which will threaten the economic position of both unskilled and middle-class workers. It is interesting to note that, in Europe, primarily French researchers have taken an interest in this matter (Rosanvallon, 1995; Roustang, 1996). The idea at the start of the conference was that 'social exclusion' is no longer a danger only to the lives of people at the social bottom, but is also increasingly affecting people who belong to the middle class(es). However, the discussion at the conference convinced us that using the term social exclusion can lead to misunderstanding, as this concept is often used with regard to long-term unemployed people, at least in the Northern (or Northwestern) parts of Europe. We decided, therefore, not to use the concept of social exclusion as an overarching one and, hence, not to use it in the title of the book. Nevertheless, the concept of social exclusion will still be used in several chapters of this book with different, though specific meanings.

It is important to note that, 'objectively' speaking, the worsening of the work and market situation of the middle class does not need to be very dramatic. In fact, several chapters in this volume will present mixed empirical results with respect to an 'objective' decline of the work and market position of the middle classes (see especially the chapters by Savage and Steijn/Houtman). However, it will become clear that this deterioration of the work and market position has become a part of the 'collective consciousness' of large parts of this middle class. People are getting the feeling that their economic and social position is threatened and are hence developing feelings of insecurity (see especially the chapters by Berting, Kronauer, and Suarez et al.). This 'subjective' deterioration may be even more important than the strength of the objective process. After all, according to the Thomas theorema, sociologists know that "*if people define a situation as real, it is real in its consequences.*"

The preceding ideas formed the background when we started preparing for the conference. In our view, this deterioration of the market and work situation of (large parts of) the middle class is an important topic. Interestingly, however, there are very few recent European contributions to this research area. Even in the important British study by Butler and Savage (1995), *Social Change and the Middle Classes* it is a minor issue. From the beginning, we wanted to include contributions from both northern and southern European countries. Due to language barriers and certainly also to cultural differences, there is not much debate about class theory going on between researchers from northern and southern European countries. Given the large differences in economic structure between these countries (for instance, their relative economic disadvantage and the existence of a large category of small employers in the southern European countries), we think, nevertheless, that a comparison between these countries is fruitful.

We had no problems in contacting researchers from northern European countries. With two chapters on the British situation, one on Germany, and one on the Netherlands, this volume will give an extensive overview of the situation with respect to our subject area in northern European countries. Unfortunately, we had more problems in contacting researchers in southern European Countries. Fortunately, however, after the conference was held we were able to contact researchers from Spain. With two chapters on Greece (the concepts of these chapters were presented at the conference) and one on Spain, two important southern European countries are included in this volume. It is a pity that we were not able to contact researchers from France. However, partly we are able to make up for this omission as Berting currently lives in France. The reader will notice that he makes use of several French sources in his chapter.

Finally, we decided to include a chapter on the situation in Russia. Of course, the situation of the middle classes in Russia differs fundamentally from the situation in both northern and southern European countries. In fact, there is almost no middle class in Russia. Nevertheless, we believe that this chapter is very relevant as it shows how important the middle class is in stabilising the social structure.

We will now briefly introduce the chapters of this volume. The first chapter by Jan Berting can be seen as the 'real' introduction to this volume. In this chapter, Berting elaborates on the main outline of the changing position of the middle class we have given above. His analysis is placed in a historical perspective. Firstly, he shows how the 'middle classes' expanded in the period after the Second World War. After which he shows how recent economic and organisational changes are affecting these middle classes. As a result, concepts such as uncertainty, vulnerability, and social exclusion are becoming meaningful with respect to the social and economic position of (parts of) the middle class. His chapter also contains an overview of relevant empirical studies in the Netherlands and France.

Chapters two and three are devoted to the situation in Britain. Mike Savage's chapter contains a great deal of empirical information about how economic restructuring has changed the fortunes of the British middle classes since the early 1980s. He focuses on organisational restructuring, state policy, and gender and ethnic divisions. His overall conclusions underline the heterogeneity of the contemporary middle class. Nevertheless, it seems that the middle class, in general, has done quite well since 1980, which appears to contradict the main thesis of this volume. However, he also shows that there are some indications which support our thesis. He argues that this especially holds for the chances of members of the middle class to reproduce their class position in future generations.

Chapter three, by Rosemary Crompton, deals with a different subject area. Her chapter is devoted to the position of middle-class women. Among other things, this chapter gives ample evidence for the existence of heterogeneity within the middle class. This is not only true for gender-specific differences between men and women holding a middle class job, but also for differences that exist between women holding a managerial or a professional middle-class job. Interestingly enough, these last differences seem to exist in several different European countries (both in western as in eastern Europe).

In Chapter four, Martin Kronauer deals with the position of the middle classes in Germany. He focuses on the relationship between unemployment, exclusion, and middle-class uncertainty. Therefore, this chapter can be seen as an elaboration of Berting's chapter for the German case. It becomes clear that - at least in the German case - the sharp rise in unemployment has also affected parts of the middle class. This phenomenon, which is relatively new for this group has clearly lead to feelings of uncertainty within the German middle class.

Chapter five - written by Bram Steijn and Dick Houtman - follows almost the same logic as Mike Savage's chapter. This chapter is structured as an empirical analysis to determine whether or not a process of proletarianization of the Dutch middle-class can be discerned since the beginning of the 1980s. The authors use several indicators of the work and market situation of workers. Like Savage, they got mixed results. Some indicators suggest a process of proletarianization could have been taken place (though probably before the 1980s); on other indicators, members of the middle class(es) are still better off than members of the working class. The young and women are more strongly affected by this proletarianization than other workers. Moreover, the authors stress that they probably underestimated the actual proletarianization as they did not include the unemployed and the existence of feelings of uncertainty in their analysis.

Feelings of uncertainty do, however, play an important role in the chapter on Spain by Eduardo Crespo Suarez, Florentino Moreno, and Amparo Moreno Pascual. Their analysis closely resembles the chapters by Berting and Kronauer. In addition, however, they especially focus on changes in the *middle-class ethos*. In modern capitalism, the ability to deal with uncertainty is an important aspect of this ethos. The authors elaborate on the consequence of this for the position of younger people. Although this chapter is devoted to the Spanish situation, their analysis can probably be generalised to other countries.

The same holds for the chapter by Maria Petmisidou (Chapter seven) that deals with Greece. Even more than in Chapter six, in her analysis, the peculiarities of the socio-economic and occupational structure of southern European countries become clear. These peculiarities (such as a large agricultural sector, a high degree of self-employment, statism, and familialism) make it difficult to compare the class structure of Greece with northern European countries. Nevertheless, her main argument is that becoming socially excluded is not only a risk that is affecting members of the working class, but also members of the middle class in Greece. The peculiarities of the Greece structure, however, have the important consequence that most of this remains hidden.

Chapter eight by Zissis Papadimitriou and George Hadjiconstantinou is also devoted to Greece. In one respect, this chapter can be seen as an addendum to Petmisidou's chapter. It moreover tries to analyse the Greek case in an international (globalisation) perspective. Like Berting and Kronauer, they focus on the relationship between unemployment, social exclusion, and uncertainty.

The chapter devoted to Russia - by Natalia Rimashevskaya and Galina Voitenkova - differs in focus from the other chapters in this volume. This chapter clearly shows that proletarianization of the Russian middle class is not the issue in Russia. The real problem appears to be that there is no middle class at all (at least in our sense)- a fact that greatly destabilises Russian society.

We hope that the above has convinced the reader that 'the growing uncertainty of the middle class' is an important issue. Although the several contributions to this volume each have their own peculiarities, there is also a strong common core. In the final chapter, Mart Jan de Jong elaborates on this common core and peculiarities and will present a sketch for a research programme focused on middle-class uncertainty and vulnerability.

References

Berting, J. (1968) *In het brede maatschappelijke midden*, Meppel.

Braverman, H. (1974) *Labor and Monopoly capital. The Degradation of Work in the Twentieth Century*, New York.

Butler, T., and M. Savage (ed.) *Social Change and the Middle Class*, London.

Crompton, R., and G. Jones (1984) *White-collar Proletariat. Deskilling and Gender in Clerical Work*, London.

Goldthorpe, J.H., D. Lockwood, F. Bechhofer, and J. Platt (1969) *The Affluent Worker in the Class Structure*, Cambridge.

Goldthorpe, J.H. (1980) *Social Mobility and Class Structure in Modern Britain*, Oxford.

Kerr, C. (1969) *Marshall, Marx and Modern Times. The Multi-Dimensional Society*, Cambridge.

Rifkin, J. (1995) *The End of Work. The Decline of the Global Labor Force and the Dawn of the Post-Market Era*, New York.

Rosanvallon, P. (1995) *La Nouvelle Question Sociale, Repenser l'Etat-Providence*, Paris.

Roustang, G., et al. (1996) *Vers un nouveau contrat social*, Paris.

1

Rise and Fall of Middle-Class Society? How the Restructuring of Economic and Social Life Creates Uncertainty, Vulnerability, and Social Exclusion

JAN BERTING

1.1 Post-industrial society and capitalism

The coming of the post-industrial society was accompanied by important changes in the structure of the labour market, most notably the growth of the tertiary or service sector (Bell, 1976). This development was made possible by the increasing automation of industrial production and the rise of modern information systems. The middle classes expanded and many new opportunities for individual professional advancement were created. The debate about the coming of the industrial society and the rise of the *information society* concealed, to a certain degree, that the dominant mode of production was still capitalist. The continued economic growth and the expansion of services in the welfare state contributed to the idea, held by the majority of the population, that in the present stage of capitalist development, the protection of workers against major economic and social contingencies and risks, based on social and economic rights, was assured. Social and economic inequalities decreased while opportunities for higher education and advancement at work increased. The capitalist society became less class-orientated.

In the eighties, however, increasing automation and informatisation reduced the opportunities for employment, which is currently reinforced by a stronger internationalisation and globalisation of the economy. Major private companies are transferring part of the production of commodities, including services, to countries such as India, Indonesia, and Taiwan where labourcosts are considerably lower than in the so-called advanced societies. National governments have no power over these movements. Since international transfer of capital is not controllable on a national level. It is estimated that 1500 billion dollars a day are transferred internationally. Of this huge sum 95% is motivated by pure speculation (Le Monde Diplomatique, 1996: 11). Moreover, intense international competition and the increasing danger of speculative take-overs of companies force management to take drastic measures to reconstruct their organisations. The central concepts are 'reengineering', 'downsizing', and 'lean production'. The OECD continues to emphasise the urgency of reinforcing the market, deregulation, increasing the flexibility of working hours and salary-costs, and revisioning the restrictive labour laws which management considers. The OECD also claims that greater disparity in income is desirable,

B. Steijn et al. (eds.), Economic Restructuring and the Growing Uncertainty of the Middle Class, 7-24.
© 1998 *Kluwer Academic Publishers.*

as it reinforces the relation between individual achievement and rewards: social allowances have to be reduced in order to stimulate the unemployed to accept low-paying jobs. Such a strategy would reduce unemployment and social exclusion in the long run.

During the last fifteen years, the working population has become more vulnerable and feelings of uncertainty have increased. In the European Union, 10% of the male working population and 12% of the female working population are unemployed. The total number of unemployed in the EU is 18 million. Many of them have been unemployed for more than one year (Eurostat Annuaire 1995: 102-103; 116). Trust in the future has decreased, a future that seems more opaque than in the recent past.

There is a growing sense of insecurity and uncertainty not only among workers who have part-time jobs and short-term contracts, but also among those with relatively stable jobs. As Roustang remarks with respect to France: "*There is a general deception. The feeling of insecurity with respect to the job is very widespread and the dissatisfaction pertaining to the working-conditions and the working-relationships is rather general. Everybody feels the duty to give much without receiving a compensation.*"[1]

This feeling of insecurity is heightened by the fact that it is far from clear when this process will end and who will pay for it. For the moment, the results of the restructuration of the economy are rather disappointing and perhaps deceptive. There has been a rather sharp increase in the number of lower incomes in many countries, especially among the young.[2] This uncertainty, especially among the poor and socially excluded, i.e., those without stable social ties, may create a culture of precariousness, an adaptation by informal and often illegal or criminal means to the exigencies of social life.[3]

Although all West European societies are affected by these socio-economic developments, there are nevertheless, important differences between countries. An international comparison of the Dutch Social and Cultural Planning Agency on poverty shows that in the Netherlands, poverty is much lower (6% of the population) than in France and the United Kingdom (both 12%) and in the USA (22%) (Sociale en Culturele Verkenningen, 1996: 91). The high level of poverty in the USA, combined with the relatively low level of unemployment, shows us that poverty is not reduced by a full employment policy. In the USA, the unemployed do not escape poverty by working (Wacquant, 1996: 16). In France, poverty is increasing in young households (under thirty), and unemployment is not yet decreasing.[4] In the Netherlands confidence is growing because of the positive economic development of the last few years and most people are satisfied with the government's policy (Sociale en Culturele Verkenningen, 1996: 7, 8, 15-18). In contrast 84% of the French population was convinced in 1995, that social and economic developments were detoriating, and in 1996, 73% of the French said they were pessimistic about the economic future. 70%, of those with leading positions in economic life said they were pessimistic in this respect (L'Etat de la France 96-97: 465). The percentage of the total population with serious doubts about the French economy rose from 14% in 1982 to 30% in 1995 (L'Etat de la France 96-97: 191). Therefore we have to consider the differences between countries, differences which seem, at least, partly related to political choices. Nevertheless, it is evident that in all advanced societies the recent economic changes and the reduction of the welfare state services have led to an increase in feelings of insecurity, vulnerability, and uncertainty, and a lessening of confidence in positive economic developments. This rather pessimistic view is not only a psychological effect of social and economic exclusion, but is also related to important changes in the labour market which affect the broad middle classes of society. It seems there is no longer a common image of (post-) industrial society and its development. In the next pages, the major social and economic changes that have taken place since 1945, will be outlined in order to arrive at a better understanding of the present situation in which the interaction between *the market* and *society* differs so markedly from the preceding period. We will then return to the debate on the vulnerability, and insecurity of the 'middle classes' and social exclusion.

1.2 Major social and economic transformations: 1945-1996

The present socio-economic situation differs dramatically, as we all know, from the one that prevailed fifty years ago. The *post-war period* (1945-1968) can be characterised, in most western democracies, as a rather optimistic one. Economic growth seemed inevitable as soon as certain conditions were fulfilled. Industrialisation is, from this perspective, the basis of economic growth, propelled by scientific development and technological innovations and not hampered by traditionally, rigid market relations. Class antagonism was diminishing, and society was adapting to the new economic exigencies. This emerging social order was interpreted in terms of social progress, the development of a better society, in which the position of each individual is based on their qualifications and achievements and their position in a new division of labour to which everybody contributes according to his or her talents and skills and is remunerated according to the (market-)value of this contribution. This image or model of the rising society implied increasing individual occupational and social mobility, together with a growing equality of educational opportunities; a levelling of the differences based on class and lifestyles; a concomitant growth of the middle classes as a consequence of the increasing demand for skilled and professional workers; and, consequently, a decrease of collective types of antagonisms, especially of class struggle. Individuals developed an individualistic achievement orientation: they became aware that social advance is increasingly dependent on individual achievements. This consciousness entailed the conviction that in this emerging individualistic achievement-oriented society, persons with 'capacities' and 'talents' had the opportunity to change their social position in a positive way. Those who really made an effort would advance, especially in their professional life.

This concept of individual achievement is the central idea behind the conviction that there is a clear connection in economic life between *investments* in terms of initiative, and risk-taking, based on systematic analyses, education, and experience on the one hand, and *rewards* in terms of income, social prestige, influence and power, on the other. Success in one's working life is predominantly dependent, in this view, on the rational utilisation of opportunities.

The actual development of industrial society reinforced this image. The number of blue-collar workers decreased considerably, while the middle classes expanded rapidly. This was caused by the increase in mechanisation and rationalisation, and by the automation of industrial production. Fewer blue-collar workers were needed to produce more. The administrative, supervisory, managerial, planning, and commercial functions were, for the time being, less affected by this process.

Moreover, a shift took place in the industrial production process in the direction of preparatory and controlling tasks which were, in most cases, defined as nonmanual ones. Technological and organisational developments continuously create new functions and occupations, which generally require advanced professional knowledge. The increasing complexity of socio-economic organisations and the relationships between organisations and the outside world was accompanied by the development of activities requiring a high level of professional knowledge. Finally, the tertiary sector (services regulated by the market) and the quaternary sector (services provided by the state or dependent on state subsidies) also expanded quickly. Society was moving in the direction of a service society dominated by white-collar labour, and in which the number of higher occupational categories increased rapidly. These developments reinforced, as mentioned, the awareness of opportunities for professional advancement. This is, however, not to say that all those who entered the middle classes in this period were motivated by the desire to advance at work. The shrinking of the labour class forced many children of blue-collar workers to accept white-collar work. They were pushed into the (lower) middle classes, rather than attracted by them. However, those who were 'pushed ahead' encountered labour relations, types of work, and labour conditions which influenced their behaviour. They found themselves in this 'broad societal middle class', this heterogeneous collection of occupational categories that is certainly not characterised by a common class consciousness and a collective strategy to defend common interests. The boundaries of the middle class are much too vague and flexible, and the social heterogeneity of the composing elements in terms of power, income, social prestige, lifestyles and opportunities for social advancement is too great for such a development into the direction of a *middle-class consciousness*. We can identify the differences between the self-employed and the dependent categories of workers in terms of their thinking about socio-economic conditions, the nature of their life-chances, and their conception of the achievement principle. But there are also remarkable differences between the civil servants and those who occupy comparable positions in the non-profit sector on the one hand, and those who occupy positions in the private sector, on the other.

Relatively speaking, civil servants have a stronger egalitarian mentality and a stronger orientation towards collective action. They are conscious of the fact that they must compensate for the failures or the lack of private initiatives and for the negative consequences of the marketprinciple, such as income inequality, which are considered inequitable. This militantism of the service class seems to be greater in France than in the Netherlands, but is nevertheless evident there as well (Wijmans, 1982). There are other important distinctions within large organisations, between employees in the lower, middle, and higher ranks which are linked to formal differences in educational capital. Those distinctions are related to different opportunities for advancement in occupational life. Large organisations developed a caste-like structure in which opportunities to rise within the organisation (from lower to middle or from middle to high positions) were almost illusory.

Nevertheless, during the period under investigation, those who were 'middle class' and regarded themselves as such were characterised by a strong individualism, an individualistic achievement orientation, and a strong belief that continued economic growth would create more opportunities for vertical mobility, especially at work. This development was accompanied by the individualisation of society, especially within the middle classes, i.e., a weakening of the traditional bonds and a less important role for traditional institutions.

1.2.1 The disappearance of the traditional labour class

As the middle classes grew, the labour classes shrank, especially in the area of unskilled labour. Sociologists refer to this latter 'class' as *the proletarian rear* and in 1962 the question was raised whether there is still a proletariat in Western Europe (Bahrdt, et al., 1962). The proletarian situation is characterised by a strong uncertainty, by the lack of having a grip on its own fate. The proletarian existence creates, to a limited degree, a certain protection by mutual solidarity - the fraternalistic model - and by collective actions in order to attain certain social goals. The proletariat are prepared to join forces against dangers, which are, according to their convictions, beyond individual's control.

The conclusion was that in this period it was no longer justifiable to speak of the proletarian situation of the (unskilled) workers. Increasing prosperity, the exigencies of the modern industrial production system which are difficult to combine with the idea of class struggle, and the claims of the labour class to an equitable part of the increasing wealth and a higher level of social security, led to the introduction of socio-economic rights. These rights entailed recognizing the state's responsibility to guarantee more than a bare minimum of social and economic needs.

This recognition of the need principle, along with civil and political liberties, had been prepared, technically and philosophically, by the development of the social insurance or risk paradigm: collective insurances are made possible by the solidarity of the members of a society with all those who are the victims of an accident or incident that cannot be foreseen by the individual concerned, but can be calculated on the aggregate level as a probability distribution. The relevant risks must be equally distributed over a population and at the same time, must be precarious (Rosanvallon, 1995: 27). This development had important consequences for social relationships. A decrease in social insecurity meant less dependence on the traditional care systems of the local community, the family, and the charitable institutions. It furthermore enabled long-term planning of one's life. However, dependency on the state welfare agencies increased. On the one hand, the working classes were protected against gross social uncertainties, but on the other hand, they were increasingly integrated within the state's system and the normative framework of society at large (Boli-Bennet, 1981: 175). Socio-economic rights in this new 'administrative society' go together with a sharp increase in state intervention in the life of the citizens (Haarscher 1987: 45; Berting, 1990: 189-307).

Class conflict diminished in this period: collective antagonism no longer divided society. There was full employment and even a shortage of domestic labour that necessitated the import of foreign workers. Employers tried to bind workers and employees to their organisation by offering long-term labour contracts and by involving their employees in decision-making with respect to organisational-technical problems and innovations, and by experimenting with new types of task distributions and work organisation intended to reduce feelings of alienation (e.g., job enrichment, job expansion, delegation of 'power' to autonomous working groups, sociotechnical applications). It is also noteworthy that in both governmental, semigovernmental, and private organisations many physically handicapped people were employed. The low labour supply resulted in many organisations, market-oriented ones included, emphasising not only efficiency, but social functions as well: they offered security and opportunities for advancement within the organisation, and solidarity and togetherness (as in the Human Relations in Industry Movement). However, this absorption of the traditional labour classes by the middle class did not mean an end to social inequality, or social conflict. It only signified the end of 'traditional' class awareness and class consciousness, the end of massive, inclusive social oppositions. 'Middle class society' was a fragmented; or a 'société éclatée' (Bauer and Cohen, 1983: 385).

1.2.2 A malleable society?

The pivotal theme in the preceding discussion is that social life has to adapt itself to the requirements of economic growth, for its own good, at least in the long run. Gradually, however, younger generations started to reject this idea. Economic growth seemed self-evident to them and the role of the economy was to generate wealth, while 'society' would take care of itself. Economic and technological determinism were rejected, society was free, malleable by social actors (social movements, political parties, etc.). As the British social anthropologist Leach put it in 1967 "*All of us need to understand that God, or Nature, of Change, or Evolution, or the Course of History, or whatever you like to call it, cannot be trusted anymore. We simply must take charge of our own fate*" (p. 6). The development of society is dependent upon the struggle between social movements with specific cultural orientations and the established order to design and implement the future (Touraine, 1978: 49). Society is no longer subject to scarcity; there is a wide range of new technologies which can be used by small production units. We now have a multitude of options to shape our social life (Gershuny, 1978: 17 ff).

The generation that rebuilt the post-war economy and reaped some of the benefits of the expanding market opportunities was characterised by a moderate individualism, primarily oriented towards professional advancement, but also by a compliance to authority. This had a seamy side: many people in the middle classes, especially those in the lower ranks, considered the costs of conforming to the individual achievement principle too high. They felt lured into a trap from which it was impossible to escape. Moreover, their strong focus on career and family also carried with it a sense of confinement in a pre-programmed society.

The student revolt of 1968 was clearly connected with an awareness of this seamy side of work and social life. The younger generation that grew up in this climate of highly structured and predictable societal expectations, rejected this work-oriented individualism. Instead, they advocated freedom of lifestyles and any opportunity to change preferences and roles in the 'theatrum mundi' (Maffesoli, 1988: 117). This was, indeed, the decline of the 'old' individualism and the rise of a 'new' individualism, in which self-realisation was a major goal. It had a strong egocentric tinge: hyperindvidualism. Of course, this hyperindividualism was opposed to the 'old' notion of individual achievement - considered selfish - to all types of (formal) authority, including the state, and held entrepreneurial and managerial activities in contempt. Lasch, in his well-known book on the culture of narcissism (1978: 59), speaks in this respect of 'the eclipse of achievement'.

In spite of the ideology of the malleable society and the rapid expansion of the welfare state, no new types of social life were created, either in the professional sphere, or in society at large, although many social experiments took place. Society seemed to fall apart. The state lost its grip on this societal development because the social categories distinguished by public policies became blurred as a consequence of the strong individualisation of society. This process was accompanied by an increasing variety of social relationships which were not anticipated by legislation. However, the extreme contradictions between the major principles on which society is based, such as those between individual achievement principle and the need principle, also engendered much conflict tension in a time of declining economic growth. This societal meltdown was a consequence of modernisation, especially of the emergence of technical and instrumental rationality. This instrumental rationality, indeed, connected the different parts of the society in transition, but was not an integrative principle: it did not create new values, or new societal relationships.[5]

1.2.3 Society as a market place?

The expansion of the middle classes and the breakdown and absorption of the labour class(es), together with the crisis of the welfare state laid the foundation for an ideological and empirical shift towards society as a market place: a strong countermovement against many ideas and policies that were almost taken for granted in the post-war period. At a time of ample labour supply, even of highly skilled professionals, the remaining vestiges of social policy within companies were abandoned in the name of efficiency: the qualifications of the employee must exactly match the task requirements specified by management. Those, who do not have those qualifications are not hired, and those who are employed but do not adapt to the changing standards of their tasks are fired. The number of short-term labour contracts increased, especially among the younger generation (younger than 30 years). The new employee had to be *flexible*, and comply with the ever-changing and stricter requirements of organisational life. In the design of functions and tasks, no account was taken of what the worker could be expected to tolerate in the long run. So, what are the real benefits of this 'flexible' system for the worker?

Furthermore, this is not all. Modern organisations are developing, as a consequence of technological-organisational change, a hierarchical structure that is less vertical steep than in the past. The number of layers is being reduced at the cost of the middle levels, meaning fewer opportunities for advancement (less vertical intragenerational mobility).

Tasks are becoming more complex, but opportunities for the workers to influence the handling of these tasks and task-relations are decreasing, while educational requirements are higher (Steijn and De Witte, 1992). The employee is supposed to adapt to the changing requirements of his organisation, he must be achievement oriented and responsive to rewards, especially in financial terms. This latter requirement is difficult to reconcile with the fact that it is becoming increasingly difficult to ascertain objectively the nature of individual contributions. Moreover, there is no hope of arriving at a consensus about the relationship between achievements and reward (Miller, 1991: 36 ff). Given this emphasis on financial remuneration, it is puzzling, indeed, that management continues to ignore the fact that financial rewards do not produce long lasting motivational effects (Thierry, 1987).

Manpower selection are also changing. It is true that formal educational requirements are still important, but knowledge and accumulated experiences along with socionormative qualifications are also essential, such as communication skills, flexibility, and resistance to stress. In the Netherlands, in 1955, these socio-normative qualifications were mentioned in 17% of all advertisements for personnel; in 1990, the demand for such qualifications had risen to 68% (Moelker, 1992). When an organisation's capacity to commit workers is weak, when the organic solidarity based on mutual dependencies has been eroded, the requirement to conform to the organisation's rules becomes more important in the selection of workers. When workers no longer have a sense of solidarity and loyalty to a system in which position is based on specific abilities and underemployment is the general rule, socionormative requirements are introduced as an alternative to the traditional attachment to the organisation. However, it is evident that such an attachment is weak under the present work conditions.

This weak attachment of personnel to the organisation explains management's need to increase their grip on staff by documenting the private affairs of their (future) employees. This information often has nothing to do with their professional capacities. Moreover, this lack of privacy is not rewarded, as it often was in the past, when loyal workers were offered security against the vicissitudes of economic life (Pennef, 1993: 557 ff).

1.3 Uncertainty and vulnerability

Both the technological and economic processes described in the preceding pages and the expansion of the welfare state led to the grown of the middle classes and to the *integration* of the labour class in the individual achievement society. This is not to say that the labour class became bourgeois as such. In fact, they disintegrated in the process of modernisation. Some segments underwent embourgeoisement so that their value orientation and behaviour pattern converged with the individualistic orientation of the middle classes. Other segments did not.

A result of all this, the labour class is currently absent in the societal conscience (De Witte, 1994). Society can no longer be characterised as classist without causing major methodological problems; Pakulski and Waters even refer to 'The Death of Class'. 'It is simply, for us, an obvious truth that class can no longer give us purchase on the big social political and cultural issues of the age' (Pakulski, 1996). Class is 'passé'. The class paradigm is primarily associated with the position of individuals within the production relations, where people function as producers. A class is relevant as a *social* class with recognisable types of exclusion, struggle, sub- and superordination in relation to other classes. Members of a class have a consciousness of a common position, class implies the recognition of a difference between 'them' and 'us'. This is a necessary condition for collective action (Ibid.). Class is, in this sense, a distinct frame of integration.

The expanded middle class or middle classes, comprising about 80% of the population, is certainly not a class in this sense. This absence of class as an integrative framework was not problematic as long as opportunities for individual advancement increased and the expanding welfare state offered adequate protective services. However the original assets of middle class society, such as highly stable employment and career prospects, partly based on the employee's investment in higher education and training, have been eroded. The precariousness of social life has increased in spite of economic growth. The new, ruthless economy[6] is not a duplicate of the old proletarian situation. Even a diminished welfare state helps prevent most of the extreme types of poverty. But the fact remains that most people in our middle class society are not able to live decently for long periods without being employed. Therefore, the extreme precariousness of the labour market produces uncertainty and anxiety, and prevents many people from engaging in any long-term planning of their social and professional lives. Moreover, this precarious position goes together with weak negotiating potential, both on an individual and collective level, with the demand side of the market. The younger workers in particular are affected by this increasingly unstable labour market (Laval, 1996: 19).

The heterogeneity of the middle classes, the fact that the various segments have quite different perspectives on their life-situation, the fragmentation, the lack of the development of a common consciousness and of real collective strategies to defend their market positions, all make the middle classes easy prey for the market forces even though they are paying the financial and societal costs of the expulsion of labour. As Hutton (1965: 15) remarks: "*The extension of the market principles deep into society has destabilised many areas of social life.*" New types of social inequality have been grafted upon already existing inequalities, aggravating the problems on the level of the nuclear family and society at large. "*Altruism and the civilising values of an inclusive society have been sacrificed on the altar of self-interest, of choice, of opting out and of individualism.*"

It should be noted, that the system of social security has been deeply affected by the processes discussed earlier in this contribution. This system could be developed on the principle of the risk concept in relation to the insurance-system that replaced individual responsibility. The individual is protected against certain risks by applying a political strategy of solidarity. This protection can be seen as a bridge between individual responsibility as participant to market activities (which produce inequalities as witnessed by the recent developments) and the idea of social equality for all citizens (Boudon, et al., 1989: 186). However, the expansion of the social security system in the *third period* (1978-1996) caused various problems. Not only the increasing numbers of those dependent upon the system are important here. It is, in fact, the erosion of the risk concept itself that is pivotal. This concept, on which the insurance system is based, pertains to negative events which are not predictable on the individual level. The massive exclusion now taking place has little to do with chance events, but is a consequence of profound changes in the relationship between the market and society and in the social order.

A second criticism of the risk concept has to do with developments in biochemical research. In the past, most illnesses were generally not predictable, but now it can be ascertained by RNA-tests what illnesses a person will develop during his or her life. However those illnesses for which the organic causes can be determined long before they are realised, are not risks. The risk concept is further undermined by the fact that in many domains these risks are unequally distributed, as demonstrated by statistical evidence. Consequently, some people pay much more than if their premiums were based on their actual chances of incurring a specific negative event. In addition, the debate has been opened on health and individual risks that pertain to the voluntary exposure of some categories of persons to risks, such as certain sports, smoking, and more generally, an unhealthy lifestyle. Should people who try to avoid these risks have to pay for those who take them voluntary? Finally, it should be noted that in some cases, people who earn more have to pay more for certain services (e.g., for medical care). This is a type of income transference that weights more heavily as the balance between 'active' and 'inactive' persons in the population becomes more unfavourable. The majority of the gainfully employed in the middle classes support the system of social security, because increasing vulnerability and uncertainty increase their chances of one day belonging to the category of the social excluded. However the allowances which follow from this right to remuneration according to need do not easily combine with the principle of remuneration according to individual achievement or merit.

Faced with diminishing prospects for advancement and detoriating working conditions, coupled with the threat of unemployment, downward mobility, and less protection from the public sector, many people have become aware of their vulnerability in the labour market and their lack of means to counteract these threats. They have developed a more acute awareness of the fact that, although they, as citizens, have political rights, they have no right to decide on employment issues pertaining to their status as employees.

1.4 Social exclusion

This increasing uncertainty in the middle classes is reflected by an organised exodus of workers from economic life. In the Netherlands, the number of unemployed increased from 238,000 in 1980 to 600,000 in 1995, and the number of those considered not able to work from 349,000 (1975) to 893,000 in 1992 (Statistisch Jaarboek, 1993: 181). This means that the huge *Reengineering* of the production of commodities and services has been paid for by Dutch society. The social security system has been used to exclude many workers who were socially handicapped, that is, they no longer satisfied their job requirements. However, the concept of a social handicap is very vague, considering the growing importance of socionormative requirements to which we referred earlier. The extremely high number of disabled persons is rather absurd, as the Dutch are one of the healthiest peoples in the world (De Jong and Van Schoonhoven, 1992). This figure can only be explained by the fact that the social security laws with respect to the disabled have been generally applied to exclude inefficient workers from the labour market, without considering the consequences of this massive abuse for society as a whole.[7] This large-scale exclusion implies that many people, although they are being cared for, no longer have an obligatory commitment to an important social institution. Gainful employment remains an important source of self-respect and protection against egocentric hyperindividualism that characterises so many people, especially the younger generation, who are dependent upon the social security system without having any of these obligations required in the achievement society. Exclusion based on social welfare ignores the importance of the need for social recognition: being recognised socially in terms of your own specificity and capacities which enable you to participate in the intricate process of social reciprocities. Those dependent on social security are part of a category based on economic exclusion. There are no social institutions which compensate for the loss of social recognition, self-esteem, and solidarity experienced in performing a job. However, most people long for recognition from those they respect and who are able to evaluate their contribution to social and economic life. Therefore, this type of individualism means dependence and reciprocity, certainly not freedom from all commitment.[8]

Since the end of the eighties, these developments have brought the problem of social exclusion into the limelight. Will it create a deep and lasting cleavage within modern society? Some observers even venture to say that these developments may only be the tip of the iceberg.[9]

On the political level, the debate on *social exclusion* has become quite popular, notwithstanding the incredible vagueness of the concept. The concept is not new. It was already in use in the early years of this century. Weber used it to refer to a universal process that it is not specific to a particular historical period. Exclusion is a process in which members of a group restrict competition by limiting the social and economic opportunities of those who are 'different' in one or several respects, such as race, language, religion, local or social origin, and ethnicity.[10] Although it is evident that social exclusion in our society is part of this 'universal' process, the modern interpretation of social exclusion refers to something broader and, at the same time, more specific to the present social and economic developments. It may be, as Paugaum states, "*That exclusion is henceforth the paradigm with which our society becomes aware of itself and its dysfunctioning, and reaches, sometimes urgently and in a state of confusion, for the solutions with respect to problems which are foltering the collectivity.*"[11]

This shift to a 'social exclusion paradigm' may be explained by the fact that the category of excluded individuals is very heterogeneous and unstable: the (long-term) unemployed with very different occupational backgrounds, those who are qualified as unfit to work under the present market conditions, young people who leave the educational system but who fail to find a job in spite of good educational qualifications, unskilled members of various ethnic minorities, those who retire from their professional life at a rather early age etc. However, many do eventually find jobs, while others join the ranks of the socially excluded for good. It is apparent that they are not a class in the sense that they share a common interest and could try, collectively, to improve their situation.

The problem of social exclusion is part of the ongoing individualisation of society which erodes the alternatives for social support for many of those excluded from economic life. The shift to the 'social exclusion paradigm' seems to be related to the fact that the traditional class structure has become very fluid and that class antagonisms, which characterised an earlier period, have vanished. That is not to say that social inequality has disappeared. The technological-organisational changes we are now witnessing are accompanied by the dominant ideology of the market, i.e., that the free market is the only long-term remedy for social exclusion and many other social problems. Social exclusion exists because society is too rigid. More flexibility in workschedules and salary costs, increasing inequality in the remunerationsystem and a reduction in the expenditures of the social welfare system will produce a sound, normal equilibrium; society has to adapt itself to the 'iron laws' of the market.[12] This involves the continued reengineering of enterprises, lean production and McDonaldization; increasing numbers of part-time jobs and intermediate work contracts; underemployment of workers and an increasing emphasis on the 'social' qualifications of employees, i.e., their ability to be 'flexible' and to disregard, when necessary, their social ties.

The shift to the 'social exclusion paradigm' is therefore not only related to the changing character of the class society, but also to this one-sided market-oriented way of observing the world: discussing the position of the socially excluded and making proposals to re-introduce them in economic life and/or reintegrate them into social life, shows your concern about the disadvantaged while, at the same time, you avoid analysing of the processes which create social exclusion. This analysis, however, is urgent because the social position of the socially excluded is quite different from that of the marginal groups during the initial stages of industrial society. These groups had simply not yet been included in modern society. They were the rearguard of traditional society that was gradually absorbed by the industrial system and, later, by the Welfare State. In contrast, the *new* socially excluded, are mostly those who abide by the tenets of modern social and economic life, but who are nevertheless excluded from active participation as a consequence of massive reengineering of economic life in response to globalisation and the rise of the information and service industry.

The emphasis on social exclusion means not only, in many cases, a political disregard for the processes that produce exclusion, but also a disregard of its consequences, such as a growing feeling of insecurity, among those who are still gainfully employed and have indefinite labour contracts, that is, the large majority of all workers, and among students preparing to enter the job market.

Although it is important to know the volume, the social composition and the stability of the socially excluded, we must also analyse how social exclusion is created and how it impacts social life (e.g., sense of uncertainty and vulnerability of the employed, a decreasing commitment to education). Is anxiety about the future increasing?[13] The fact is that the consumption of antidepressants has sharply risen in France. In 1990, the French consumed 138 million boxes of those drugs, six times more than 25 years ago (Roustang, et al., 1996: 8). Although the level of consumption of antidepressants is much lower in the Netherlands, it is steadily increasing.

Social exclusion must be approached as a process and as a relative phenomenon: there are different degrees and types of social exclusion and, related to this, unequal opportunities to combat those types of exclusion. The discussion often refers to: a) the fact that many individuals are excluded from the labourmarket and b) the observation that a number of them lack stable social ties as a consequence of society's lack of integration or cohesiveness. Society is strongly individualised and an individual who loses his job is not sufficiently supported by other social institutional groups or networks. If this statement were true, it would simply mean that anyone who is not gainfully employed is socially excluded, because society is so strongly individualised that it no longer offers an integrated framework. However, this would be too crude a delineation of the category. In fact, between the market and the image of an individualistic society, several elements have to be considered in order to arrive at a clear definition of the phenomenon of social exclusion. We have to consider:

1. the market-economy that produces (long-term) unemployment, stress, and uncertainty;
2. the redistribution of income by the state (social security system) and by private insurance companies;
3. the non-monetary economy, that is, the production of commodities and services without financial inputs, such as direct exchange, self-production, and voluntary activities;
4. the financial reserves acquired by inheritance and/or a person's own activities;
5. the system of family ties, networks of friends, etc. who can, to a certain degree, provide (financial) support and security;
6. the educational system providing qualifications for entry into the labour market.

With this list in mind, we can tackle the problem from different angles; we are now able to distinguish between different types and degrees of social exclusion. We will not present a classification, but restrict ourselves to some examples. One case of extreme social exclusion would be a young person without formal qualifications (6) with only scant opportunities to enter the labour market (1), who has only a minimum of financial support, or none at all, as in the case of an illegal immigrant (3), who has no financial reserves (4), on non-monetary economy (3), and does not have a familynetwork which can provide some security (e.g., a wife who has a full-time job, parents who provide food and shelter). Another case would be a senior manager, 45 years of age, who becomes unemployed (1), but receives substantial financial compensation from his company (1), who is entitled to unemployment allowances for a few years (2), has accumulated considerable financial reserves (4) to which his wife also contributes (4,5) because she has a very well-paid supervisory function (1); both of them are very skilled participants in the non-monetary economy (3) and have good support networks to help him in his quest for a new position in the market economy, as a manager (5) or a consultant (5). If necessary, he can try to acquire new qualifications (6) in order to start a second career in another niche of the economy. The two examples illustrate that the degree of social exclusion is highly dependent on the individual's capacities and resources.

It is likely that feelings of insecurity and anxiety will be high among those employees who have educational qualifications (6) and work experience (1), which are becoming less valuable as a consequence of technological and organisational changes, who are too young to retire as they have not accumulated enough entitlements (2), who have a weak link with the non-monetary economy (e.g., because they have been 'flexible' and moved out of their region of origin) (4 and 5), who did not have a salary or a family background that enabled them to accumulate substantial financial reserves, and who have wives with part-time jobs without career opportunities (5). They know that it will be very difficult, once unemployed, to find a new job on the same level. They may fear, and not without reason, that they will become socially excluded or socially downgraded after accepting a job with a lower salary and few career opportunities.

Statistical data show that working conditions are becoming increasingly less attractive, especially in the lower ranks, and for younger workers (up to 30) and women: short-term labour contracts, part-time jobs, shorter work weeks and consequently less pay, no opportunities for advancement or for learning on-the-job training, jobs with almost no autonomy and which are filled by overqualified workers (Eurostat, Annuaire 1995: 112; Sociaal Culturele Verkenningen, 1996: 46-47). The number of these jobs is absolutely and relatively increasing, creating a category of workers who, although employed, often live at or below the subsistence level. Their life is precarious and all the more so if they lose their uncertain jobs, a precariousness which may be mitigated or disguised by factors 3 and 5 above. It is unlikely that they will be able to accumulate financial reserves.

The risks we are discussing are unequally distributed in our society. Moreover, those who are at the end of the exclusion path clearly feel that the political system does not have a real grip on the processes which lead to exclusion. At the same time, they are not capable of developing a coherent social representation which could transform them into a political force. Some even follow political leaders who advocate a type of protection by social exclusion of immigrants and political refugees and by the closure of the national system. In contrast to the globalization of the market economy, we find a waning of international solidarity among the working classes (Donzelot, 1996: 91).

In the preceding analysis we noted a process of social fragmentation and a growing inequality in the distribution of precarious events. These developments arouse strong feelings of vulnerability, uncertainty, and even anxiety, reinforced by the observation that there is no longer a good correspondence between individual achievement and the distribution of rewards. This stands in sharp contrast to the situation some decades ago, when the growth of the economy and the expansion of education and middle and higher level jobs stimulated optimism. We are now confronted with a high level of unemployment, social exclusion, and the creation of new jobs that offer neither stability nor opportunity for advancement. Moreover, the state machinery reinforces these developments by adopting the same type of market-oriented policies as the private sector or by handing over public services to the market. The social security systems offer less protection than even before. This change hits those individuals at the end of the social exclusion trajectory especially hard.

The important question then, is: How do people cope with these problems? What types of individual and collective reactions and strategies can we distinguish? What social and cultural conditions do are these reactions and strategies depend on? How do they effect social life? (e.g., fanatism, illusion, isolation, revolt, criminality (or 'innovation'), social exclusion of minorities, racism, segregation) (Merton, 1938: 673-682; Todorov, 1995: 109 ff; Jodelet, 1996: 66 ff).

1.5 Towards a revision of the relationship between society and market

As noted earlier, the individualistic achievement principle does not fit the present social conditions of (economic) life. The risk concept seems to be problematic for reasons mentioned above. We now face the social task of reformulating, or perhaps inventing, new principles on which future social institutions and social relationships can be firmly based.

Our society has become more individualised during the last forty years: these days people tend to have very loose ties with the major social institutions. Has society also become more individualistic? This question is not so easy to answer in a society where the individualistic achievement principle is losing its grip and in which so many people subordinate themselves, consciously or not, to new types of social control which standardise the behaviour of large categories of people: new technological control systems, the mass media, and market analyses and surveys. The organisationally vulnerable middle classes are becoming even more vulnerable because the market turns the individual into an immediate object of manipulation.

The relationship between market and society is disturbed, because a strong market-oriented policy does not recognise that the market as a model of society is too shallow. Market processes engender (social) exclusion and a lack of recognition of each person's specific value and need for prestige and esteem. Society must also support institutions which protect individuals against the negative effects of unlimited application of the market principle in all spheres of social life. The middle class society has become very vulnerable and it is the task of the state and the political system to mould, in a democrative process, new societal relations and to 'resocialize' economic life. The market principle is very valuable, but it is not applicable in every domain. It does not always lead to effective production (Lane, 1991) (e.g. not in fundamental research), and has a deleterious effect on the quality of services in other domains while occasionally providing those services at an even higher cost than the non-profit services they replace.

The development of the (post-)industrial society has put us in a situation in which the old principles of the traditional and the industrial society have, at least partly, lost their validity. They have to be reformulated, to be regauged or, perhaps, replaced by new basic principles. There are at least three interdependent basic principles which have to be re-evaluated.

The first principle pertains to *individual achievement*. The ways in which the production of goods and services is currently organised does not offer enough opportunity and space to fill the need for individual specificity and social recognition. It is necessary to broaden the concept of individual achievement by changing the notion of labour and ideas about rewards which, in economic life, are almost exclusively expressed in financial terms. Hopefully, some room can be created to satisfy the need for social recognition for at least some of the socially excluded. The social costs of exclusion are very high for both society at large and the excluded individuals. A reduction of these social and financial costs can be achieved by making the boundaries between society and the market more flexible in order to create new types of "occupations." Work as a *social* activity has to be reinvented.

The second principle involves to *social protection and security*. We noted that the risk concept, which forms the basis of our social insurance system, has worn out. The massive cuts in the system's expenditures cannot solve the problems. In fact, they aggravate them. The new social security paradigm has to prevent inequalities in the exchange processes which are, of course, related to the individualistic achievement principle.

The third principle is that of *social commitment*, the opportunity to belong to and be committed to a (part of a) social order that is considered so worthwhile that one is, in principle, prepared to make a sacrifice.

This need to reformulate the basic principles of social life follows from the observation that the relatively transparent image of the (post-) industrial society as an individualistic achievement society falls to pieces once it is critically contrasted with the social contradictions which social and economic developments entail.

Several of those contradictions and conflicts have been described in the preceding pages. Most people have acquired an acute sense of the vicissitudes of life under the present socio-economic conditions and of the fact that many of the rights they enjoyed as workers have been eroded instead of being reinforced and expanded, as would have been the normal path in a democratic society. As a citizen and at the same time being subject to opaque and uncontrollable decisions in professional life, it is very hard to understand and difficult to accept. This increasing opposition between the citizen and the worker undermines democratic life in a society in which the opportunities for effective collective action in economic life have diminished as a consequence of the rise of a 'middle class' society in which, after an optimistic period, opportunities for individual advancement at work are decreasing.

We will not elaborate upon this contradiction that is linked to the processes of economic and social exclusion, to the increasing tensions between the individualistic achievement principle and the need principle that is based on solidarity, and to the dwindling opportunities to apply the individualistic achievement principle in relation to equitable remunerations. We could respond to this type of analysis by arguing that it is indeed true that we are confronted with many social and economic problems as a consequence of rapid technological developments and the expansion of the international market, but that, ultimately, most people will be better off if politics does not interfere with the mechanisms of the free market. However, international comparative analyses show that the quality of political decisions is important for social life. The consequences of a free market are not there just to be accepted for better or worse. Intelligent social policies can influence the balance between 'better' and 'worse' in a democratically acceptable direction.

Notes

1 "C'est la déception générale. Le sentiment d'insécurité pour son empoi est très étendu et l'insatisfaction à l'égard des onditions et des relations de travail assez générale. Chacun a le sentiment de devoir donner beaucoup sans contrepartie" (Roustang et. al., 1996: 27).

2 Since 1984 the percentage of poor persons under 30 has risen from 9.3% to 18.5% (1994) in France. The povertyline was 36,100F in 1984 and 39,800F in 1995 (l'INSEE, Revenus et patrimoine des ménages, 1996).

3 Referring to Castel's 'culture de l'aléatoire' (1996: 41).

[4] To 12.6% (3,418,100 unemployed) Libération, 1996: 24.

[5] "La rationalité instrumentale est la plaque tournante mais elle n'est pas un principe intégrateur de la modernité" (Touraine 1992: 173).

[6] See Head, 'The New Ruthless Economy' (1996: 47 ff). "In spite of a high level of investments and economic growth, the earnings of the 'production and of non-supervisory workers' (80% of the labour force) fell by 18% between 1973 and 1995, from $ 315 per week to $ 258 per week. By contrast, between 1979 and 1989 the real annual pay of corporate chief executives increased by 19 percent, and by 66 percent after taxes."

[7] Rosanvallon remarks: "Elle est surtout l'aboutissement d'une vision purement financière de l'Etat-providence comme machine à indemnisation, qui doit paradoxalement exclure les individus du marché de travail pour leur apporter une aide" (1995: 120-121).

[8] Juffé (1995: 101): "Une société n'existe que si les gens partagent une valeur, la font connaître aux autres, sont reconnus par elle." The basis of social life is diversity and reciprocity, not the submission of the individual to one truth or one system or one regulating principle (of the market).

[9] Attali (1996): "Enfin, les plus pauvres [...] seront jetés sur les routes de la précarité. Le salariat disparaîtra au profit d'emplois de passage, temporaires, chacun quettant le prochain caprice de l'offre de travail. Là où une surclasse triomphante flottera sur les eaux de la misère, la réussite de quelques-uns se paiera de la marginalisation du plus grand nombre et la violence croissante des déclassés."

[10] "Mit wachsender Zahl der Konkurrenten im Verhältnis zum Erwerbsspielraum wächst hier das Interesse der an der Konkurrenz Beteiligten, diese irgendwie einzuschränken" (Weber, 1968: 63 ff).

[11] Paugam remarks: "L'Exclusion est désormais le paradigme à partir duquel notre société prend conscience d'elle-même et de ses dysfonctionnements, et recherche, parfois dans l'urgence et la confusion, des solutions aux maux qui la tenaillent" (1996: 7).

[12] This is the consistent message of the OECD, that issues continuously 'ultraliberal encyclies' without, however, applying these principles to this organisation itself (See: Le Monde diplomatique, July 1996) inspite of huge increases in the expenditures.

[13] "La crise de confiance qui ébranle le pays n'est pas seulement dans les têtes, elle est aussi dans les faits" "[...] Leur angoisse (des Français) devant un avenir opaque est telle que, comme le navigateur dans la tempête, ils restent à la cape et préfèrent épargner [...] Les Français sont démotivés et abattus" (L'Express, september 1996).

References

Attali, J. (1996) *Chemins de Sagesse, Traité du labyrinthe*, Paris.

Bahrdt, et al.. (1962) *Gibt es noch ein Proletariat?*, Frankfurt am Main.

Bauer, M. and E. Cohen (1983) La fin des nouvelles classes: couches moyennes éclatées et société d'appareils, *Revue Française de Sociologie*, vol. XXV, pp. 385 ff.

Bell, D. (1976) *The Coming of the Post-Industrial Society, A Venture in Social Forecasting*, New York.

Berting, J. (1990) Societal Change, Human Rights and the Welfare State in Europe, in: J. Berting et al. *Human Rights in a Pluralist World, Individuals and Collectivities*, Westport/London, pp. 189-307.

Boli-Bennet, J. (1981) Human Rights or State Expansion, Cross-national Definitions of Constitutional Rights: 1870-1970, in: V.P. Nanda, et al.. (eds), *Global Human Rights*, Boulder, pp. 175 ff.

Boudon, R. et al. (1989) *Dictionnaire de la sociologie*, Paris.

Castel, R. (1996) Les marginaux de l'histoire, in: S. Paugam (ed.) *L'exclusion, l'état des savoirs*, Paris, p. 41 ff.

Donzelot, J. (1996) Les transformations de l'intervention sociale face à l'exclusion, in S. Paugam (ed.) *L'exclusion, l'état des savoirs*, Paris, p. 91 ff.

L'Etat de la France 96-97, Paris.

Eurostat Annuaire '95 *Vue statistique sur l'Europe 1983-1993.*

Gershuny, J. (1978) *After Industrial Society The Emerging Self-Service Economy*, London/Basingstoke.

Haarscher, G. (1987) *Philosophie et droit de l'homme*, Brussels.

Head, S. (1996) The New Ruthless Economy, in: *The New York Review of Books*, vol. XLIII, 4, pp. 47 ff.

Hutton, W. (1965) *The State we're in*, London.

L'INSEE (1996) *Revenus et patrimoine des ménages*, Paris.

Jodelet, D. (1996) Les processus psycho-sociaux de l'exlusion, in: S. Paugam (ed.) *L'exclusion l'état des savoirs*, Paris,

pp. 66 ff
Jong, M.J., and R. van Schoonhoven (1992) *Afscheid van de zorgloze verzorgingsstaat*, Utrecht.
Lane, R.E. (1991) *The Market Experience*, Cambridge.
Lasch, C. (1978) *The Culture of Narcissism American Life in an Age of Diminishing Expectations*, New York.
Laval, G. (1996) Les jeunes, première cible de la pauvreté, *Libération*, 20 september 1996, p. 19.
Leach, E. (1968) *A Runaway World? The Reith Lecture 1967*, London.
Maffesoli, M. (1988) *Le temps des tribus, Le déclin de l'individualisme dans les sociétés de masse*, Klincksieck.
Merton, R.K. (1938) Social Structure and Anomie, in: *American Sociological Review*, vol. III, pp. 673-682.
Miller, D. (1979) *Social Justice*, Oxford.
Moelker, R. (1992) *Zou hij onze werknemer kunnen zijn?* De Lier.
Juffé, M. (1995) *Les fondements du lien social*, Paris.
Juffé, M. (1995) *Les fondement du lien social*, Paris.
Pakulski, J., and M. Waters (1996) *The Death of Class*, London.
Paugam, S. (1996) La constitution d'un paradigme, in: S. Paugam (ed.) *L'exclusion, létat des savoirs*, Paris.
Pennef, J. (1993) Le recrutement et l'observation des ouvriers par le patronat, Etude d'un fichier d'entreprise, *Revue Française de Sociologie*, vol. XXXIV, 4, pp. 557 ff.
Rosanvallon, P. (1995) *La Nouvelle Question Sociale, Repenser l'Etat-Providence*, Paris.
Roustang, G. et al.. (1996) *Vers un nouveau contrat social*, Paris.
Sociale en Culturele Verkenningen (1996), Rijswijk.
Statistisch Jaarboek 1993.
Steijn, A.J., and M.C. de Witte (1992) *De Januskop van de industriële samenleving Technologie, arbeid en klassen aan het begin van de jaren negentig*, Alphen aan den Rijn.
Thierry, H. (1987) Payment by Results Systems, A Review Research 1945-1985, in: *Applied Psychology, An International Review.*
Todorov, T. (1995) *La vie commune, Essai d'anthropologie générale*, Paris.
Touraine, A. (1978) *La voix et le regard*, Paris.
Touraine, A. (1992) *Critique de la modernité*, Paris.
Wacquant, L. (1996) Quand le président Clinton réforme la pauvreté, *Le Monde Diplomatique*, september 1996.
Witte, H., de (ed.) (1994) *Op zoek naar de arbeidersklasse, Een verkenning van de verschillen in opvattingen en leeftijd tussen arbeiders en bedienden in Vlaanderen, Nederland en Europa*, Leuven/Amersfoort.
Wijmans, L.L. (1982) *Beeld en betekenis van het maatschappelijke midden. Oude en nieuwe middengroepen 1850 tot heden*, Amsterdam.

2

Social Exclusion and Inclusion within the British middle classes, 1980-1995

MIKE SAVAGE

2.1 Introduction

This chapter explores some of the ways in which economic restructuring has changed the fortunes of the British middle classes since the early 1980s. For, whilst the period since at least 1945 till the middle 1980s, was one of growing prosperity for the middle classes, there have, in the past decade, been arguments that the middle classes are now facing growing problems. I particularly want to focus on the three issues of *organisational restructuring, state policy*, and *gender and ethnic divisions*.

In order to place my discussion in context I begin with a short analysis of how to conceptualise the middle classes. Section 2.3 examines general issues concerning economic polarisation in Britain and shows that there is a little evidence of polarisation within the middle class. Section 2.4 then looks at more specific debates about the decline of the 'organisational career' and examines the extent to which the middle class career is undergoing fundamental change. I argue that there is some evidence that the middle class career is indeed fragmenting in important ways and that this is breaking down the relationship between age, security and income. Section 2.5 takes this analysis a stage further by looking at the social mobility of young adults in Britain, in order to show how the careers of new entrants to middle class jobs are changing in the 1980s. Finally, a speculative conclusion brings the threads of the chapter together and explains how the restructuring of the middle class career may have significant implications for the well being of the middle classes as a whole.

2.2 British debates about the middle classes

Sociological debates about the fortunes of the middle classes have traditionally been organised around disagreements between Marxist and Weberian writers, though there are recent signs that this tension is becoming more confused. Theories of middle class *proletarianisation*, dating back to Klingender (1935) were revived by Braverman's classic book *Labour and Monopoly Capital* (1974), and were widely debated during

B. Steijn et al. (eds.), Economic Restructuring and the Growing Uncertainty of the Middle Class, 25-43.
© 1998 *Kluwer Academic Publishers.*

the later 1970s and early 1980s (Abercrombie and Urry, 1983; Crompton and Jones, 1984). Nonetheless, the Weberian emphasis on the distinctively advantaged work and market position of the white-collar middle classes began to gain greater assent during the 1970s especially as the expansion of non-manual employment continued apace (Lockwood, 1958; Giddens, 1973).

In Britain, the early 1980s were a particularly important period in crystallising the growing consensus that proletarianisation theories were mistaken, especially as the theory of the *service class* (originally developed by the Austro-Marxist Karl Renner, and developed subsequently by Ralph Dahrendorf) began to command widespread attention. There were two main writers who championed the idea of the service class. John Goldthorpe used the idea in the context of his studies of social mobility (Goldthorpe, 1980; Erikson and Goldthorpe, 1992), whilst John Urry, with various collaborators, used the idea within a neo-Marxist framework to show how the middle classes were active forces in the contemporary transformation of capitalist societies, especially as they became 'disorganised' (Abercrombie and Urry, 1983; Lash and Urry, 1987). The theory of the service class subsequently became a main debating point in British sociology during the later 1980s and early 1990s (Savage et al., 1988; Crompton, 1992; Savage et al., 1992), with debate centring on the question of whether the service class, which included professional, managerial and administrative employees, was too inclusive to recognise the variety and complexity of middle class formation (see most recently Butler and Savage, 1995 for a comprehensive discussion).

Although Urry and Goldthorpe worked within rather different theoretical and research traditions their formulation of the service class concept nevertheless had much in common. The crucial innovation of the service class idea was to suggest that conventional views of the middle class as composed of all non-manual (or 'white-collar') workers were mistaken. They claimed that the non-manual middle classes were fractured into two main groups: a relatively de-skilled and proletarianised group of junior clerical workers, shop assistants, and personal service workers on the one hand, and a generally privileged group of professionals, managers and administrators on the other (i.e. the 'service class'). Both writers saw this service class as having distinctively superior work and market situations to other occupational groups. It is important to note that Goldthorpe in particular made it a central part of his definition of the 'service class' that is was secure and not subject to instability or the prospects of downward mobility (see Goldthorpe, 1982). Further, although these writers accepted that deskilled white-collar workers were in much inferior positions to the service class itself, they also noted that - at least for men - there were very good prospects of promotion from lower middle class to service class employment (see also Stewart et al., 1980).

Until the middle and even later 1980s, British sociologists focused more on the distinctively advantaged and secure position of the 'service class', vis-a-vis the social classes. At the same period the Conservative Government indeed championed a 'two-nation' politics (see Jessop et al., 1988) which seemed to enhance the position of the middle classes. In particular it shifted the tax base from progressive to regressive means, and presided over an economic policy which led to a marked accentuation of economic polarisation (e.g. Pond, 1987). In the context of these changes, it seemed quite appropriate to focus attention not on the insecurity of the middle classes, but on their ever accumulating advantages and privileges vis-a-vis the manual working classes and to some extent junior white-collar workers.

Nonetheless, by the later 1980s it is possible to detect a new 'worries' about the middle classes. Certainly, the media have been full of stories about the 'white-collar recession' and the declining security of the middle classes. Three particular developments have attracted interest. The first concerns economic restructuring and in particular the changing nature of organisational hierarchies which, it has been claimed, is making the positions of many managers redundant and reducing the security of middle class careers. The second concerns the changing politics of the welfare state and the way that government reform affects middle class interests. Finally, there are also important questions related to the changing politics of gender, (as well as race and ethnicity) in Britain, as older forms of gender exclusion within the middle classes have changed to more complex forms of gender division and demarcation.

2.2.1 Organisational Restructuring

Goldthorpe's and Urry's theories of the service class depended on a neo-Weberian theory of bureaucracy in which the large, bureaucratic organisation acted as a 'shelter' for its senior managerial employees. Both writers emphasised how the structural advantages of 'service class' employees - whether they be managers exercising authority or professionals who generally employed in large organisations (frequently in the public sector) - were underscored by the development of internal labour markets. It is precisely this bureaucratic base which has been seen by some writers as being called into question by current forms of economic restructuring. Rationalisation, downsizing, the externalisation of management functions, contracting out, etc all seem to have marked a shift from co-ordination by the 'visible hand' of the organisational hierarchy to the 'invisible hand' of the market.

Currently, there are two rather different perspectives on such changes. Savage et al. (1992) have argued that organisational restructuring has increasingly exposed managerial groups to high degrees of insecurity, although the professional middle classes have largely managed to avoid this because their base in the public sector has allowed them to remain relatively insulated from significant change, at least until the 1980s. Savage et al. saw such changes as linked to major shifts in the nature of organisational practices, as the decline of 'Fordist' economies entail the failing ability of organisational hierarchies to co-ordinate economic activities, and drew upon the now extensive literature documenting the 'squeeze' on middle managers in many firms. On the other hand, Goldthorpe (1995: 325) has recently insisted that the extent of change should not be exaggerated and continues to emphasise the resilience of the service class. *"I would urge, it is important here not to be misled into constructing long-term trends out of the expedients of recession or the passing fads of management consultants.[...] Furthermore, it would in any event be unfortunate if speculation on possible threats to the stability of the service class in the future were to distract attention from the rather remarkable degree of stability that has in fact characterised this class during the recent past."* In the second section of this chapter I examine in some detail whether economic restructuring has adversely affected the position of groups within the middle classes. In particular I shall focus on debates concerning the viability of the *organisational career* in order to assess whether there has been any serious decline in the security of middle class careers. I will also look more generally at trends concerned with social mobility in order to see whether Goldthorpe's stress on service class reproduction is overplayed.

2.2.2 The politics of the welfare state

A second way in which the middle classes have been seen as under threat concerns the implications of state restructuring and welfare reform. Here, the starting point is the argument developed by LeGrand (1975) and adopted by Savage et al. (1992) which claims that the middle classes have been important beneficiaries of welfare provision, and that restructuring the state may undermine middle class interests. LeGrand's argument is based on the fact that the welfare state provided occupational positions for many professional employees, especially in the health, education and social work services. He also argues that many of the beneficiaries of state welfare services tend to be the middle classes. For reasons which have been much debated by sociologists, middle class children tend to stay on at school longer than working class children, tend to obtain better qualifications, and are more likely to go on to higher education (Halsey, Heath and Ridge, 1980). They therefore tend to benefit more than the working classes from a system in which education is paid for as a public good. Similarly, numerous studies have shown that despite a health service which is (generally) free to its users, class gradients in mortality have, if anything, increased since the Second World War (Townsend et al., 1986). Free universal health care has not levelled away class gradients in health in the way that might be anticipated.

There is also consensus that the early reforms of the Thatcher government did not seriously challenge this situation. The most dramatic cut back of the early years was the almost complete cessation of constructing council (i.e. public) housing. Council house building was unusual amongst state welfare services in being provided largely by manual workers and being directed at those in working class positions. It was therefore highly unusual, and it is therefore instructive that it was the first major service to be cut. Elsewhere, the government actually presided over a period of general expansion of public spending (despite its own rhetoric which claimed to be 'rolling back the state'), which perpetuated middle class privileges underwritten by the state. Thus Savage et al. (1992), drawing on evidence up to the later 1980s, emphasise the way that Conservative reforms had done little to shift the middle class interests entrenched in the state

However, there is some more recent evidence which suggests that this may be changing. In recent years the Government has mounted a serious attack on some professional privileges, especially in the health service and in the education system which at least appear to threaten middle class power. In the Health Service the introduction of general management has called into question the professional 'autonomy' of clinical professionals (Flynn, 1992), whilst in the education system there have been attempts to monitor professional performance more stringently, through introducing league tables of schools and Universities, and increasing the inspections of staff Pay increases have also tended to be restricted in the public sector, and job security has also been threatened. In the third section of this chapter I consider more directly how state reform and restructuring appears to be affecting the middle classes.

2.2.3 Gender, race and ethnicity

One of the striking changes taking place within the British middle classes is the marked movement of women into some 'middle-class' occupations. The traditional middle class career rested upon gendered forms of exclusion (Crompton and Jones, 1984; Crompton, 1986). It was possible for middle class men to enjoy secure jobs with good promotion prospects in part at least because women (in particular) were employed as a disposable workforce at the bottom of organisational hierarchies and were not offered any serious prospects of career development. In Britain, it was common to employ women on 'female-only' grades which offered lower salaries to men with fewer increments, and denied them significant promotion prospects. These were not outlawed until the early 1970s.

The chapter by Crompton provides a full analysis of how gender relations within the middle classes are changing and I do not propose to discuss this topic in specific terms in this chapter, though I will refer to gender issues where appropriate. It is, however, worth adding that there is growing discussion concerning the extent to which black people are moving into the middle classes. Evidence here suggests considerable variation according to the specific ethnic minority concerned. Although black Afro-Caribbeans tend to be disproportionately located in occupations outside the middle classes, some Asian group (though not Bangladeshis) are actually somewhat over-represented in professional jobs. From being an almost entirely 'white' class in the 1960s, there are now complex processes of ethnic division within the middle classes.

2.3 Economic Polarisation in Britain

In Britain there has been a marked accentuation of income inequality in the past fifteen years. In fact income inequality has grown unusually fast in Britain compared to other developed countries. To give a few illustrative figures. The real incomes of the richest 20% of households rose from £275 per week (1994 prices) in 1977 to £500 per week in 1990 (an increase of 81%, or 6% per year). Excluding housing costs, the real incomes of the poorest 20% of households fell from £70 per week to £60 per week in the same period (Rowntree, 1995: figure 2.5). This is a stark reflection of a society in which rewards have increasingly been directed at those who are already well off However, analyses based on polarisation by income levels do not indicate whether some types of 'middle class' occupations may not share in the general trends described above. By 1991 something in excess of 30% of the workforce was in the 'service class' of professionals and managers, whilst the white-collar middle class comprised of more than 50% of the workforce. It is however by no means easy to assess long term occupational trends in income over time, since the official occupational classification was fundamentally revised in 1990, so making it difficult to compare across these dates. I have therefore had to resort to producing two tables, one examining change between 1982 and 1990 (table 2.1), and the other between 1991 and 1994 (table 2.2).

Table 2.1
Gross weekly income, levels and change by selected occupational group 1982-1990

Occupational Group		Men			Women	
	1982	1990	% change	1982	1990.	% change
Profs supporting mgt and admin	210.2	442.7	+110.6	147.4	333.0	+125.9
Profs in health, ed, welfare	184.7	340.1	+84.7	127.3	255.4	+100.7
Literary, artistic, sports	184.9	362.3	+95.9	131.4	266.4	+102.7
Profs in science, engineering, tech	183.8	353.8	+92.5	120.2	248.0	+106.3
Managerial	176.6	343.9	+94.7	109.2	235.6	+115.8
Clerical	129.6	230.4	+77.8	92.9	180.0	+93.8
Selling	136.7	257.2	+88.1	73.3	150.8	+105.7
Security	169.2	290.6	+71.7	140.5	263.7	+87.7
All non manual groups	177.9	352.9	+98.3	104.3	213.0	+104.2
All groups	151.5	290.2	+91.6	97.5	197.0	+102.0

Notes: Incomes are gross weekly incomes for full time adults, including those whose pay is affected by absence. Figures are *not* adjusted for inflation.
Source: New Earnings Survey.

Table 2.1 breaks down 'middle class' employees into three main occupational groupings, and examines the trends in their levels of remuneration between 1982 and 1990. Not all non-manual groups saw increases in their level of incomes above the national average. In general, those in professional and managerial occupations saw their income levels rise faster than those in lower white-collar employment. It can indeed readily be seen that 'professionals in management and administration roles', who even in 1982 were clearly the best paid of the selected occupational groups, had by 1990 seen their relative advantages increasing still further. 'Professionals in management and administration roles' is composed of a hybrid range of occupations, some of which would be regarded as 'pure professionals' (for instance accountants), but others, such as computer programmers, systems analysts, personnel managers or company secretaries are less likely to be seen in these terms. One thing they do have in common is that they nearly all are employed in the private sector and have therefore been able to benefit from the marketisation of economic relations in the years since 1979.

There is a major contrast here with the fortunes of professionals working in 'health, education and welfare'. Incomes amongst these workers rose less than most other occupational groups, and certainly less than the overall national average. For men in this category, their levels of income fell relative to the average for all groups. In 1982 they tied with literary, artistic and sports workers as being in second place in the income league table behind the 'professionals supporting management and administration', but by 1990 they had clearly been outpaced by a number of other middle class occupational groups. Although women in this group fared better than their male counterparts, their changing position relative to other women was rather similar. Another professional group distinguished is that working in science, engineering and technology, whose performance was slightly better than those in health, education and welfare, and was in fact closely in line with the national averages.

Extrapolating from table 2.1, it appears that there are reasonable grounds for arguing that the state employed professionals in health, education and welfare did witness a marked set back in their economic fortunes and this does suggest that state reform was a significant factor affecting this group within the middle class.

Table 2.2
Changes in Income, by OPCS occupational classification, 1991-1994

Occupational Group	Men			Women		
	1991	1994	% change	1991	1994	% change
Managers + Admin	446.1	507.7	+13.8	290.4	344.9	+18.8
Professionals	426.6	485.5	+13.9	333.7	396.8	+18.9
Associate Prof + tech	373.6	428.7	+14.7	274.3	320.7	+16.9
Clerical and secretarial	234.0	265.5	+13.5	194.2	221.7	+14.2
Personal and Protective	267.4	293.8	+9.9	168.2	190.5	+13.3
Sales	271.4	300.1	+10.6	166.0	195.3	+17.7
Craft	268.2	299.7	+11.7	148.4	168.8	+13.7
Plant and Machine Op	248.9	279.7	+12.4	157.7	184.7	+17.1
Others	215.6	235.4	+9.2	144.7	162.1	+12.0
All non-manual	372.8	424.8	+13.9	233.8	274.6	+17.5
All occupations	312.9	355.6	+13.6	217.2	255.8	+17.8

Notes: All figures are gross weekly earnings, for full time adults, including those whose earnings were affected by absence. Figures are *not* adjusted for inflation.
Source: New Earnings Survey, 1991; 1994.

After 1990 a different set of occupational categories have been used to examine earnings changes, and the trends evident in the short period between 1991 and 1994 are set out above (see table 2.2). In these new occupational categories professionals are split into only two categories. Here, a rather different pattern is revealed than in table

2.1 for the two professional groups outperform all other groups, albeit not by a marked amount. For male employees 'associate professionals and technical workers' see the fastest rate of increase, followed by professional themselves, whilst for women workers it is the category of professionals which do best. In some respects these figures are less sociologically useful than those used in table 2.1 since they do not distinguish between state and privately employed individuals, but they certainly indicate that professionals as an aggregate group, far from suffering, have actually out-performed (albeit marginally) other groups.

There would appear, prima facie, to be some evidence that some of the 'core' professions may have suffered from slightly lower than average rates of pay increase, but they have been more compensated for by increases to professionals elsewhere. It is possible, however, to be somewhat more precise. Although the changing occupational classification makes it difficult to report longer term trends accurately, evidence for some smaller 'professional' groups where consistency of reporting is maintained is available, and table 2.3 includes evidence from some of the specific professional groups. It should be noted that (with the exception of nursing) figures for women are not available because of their small sample size.

Table 2.3
Earnings change of selected 'professional' groups, 1982-1994.

Occupational Group	1982	1994	% change
Accountants	229.1	500.7	+118.7
Architects and town planners	208.8	474.7	+127.4
University lecturers	255.4	563.7	+120.7
Medical practitioners	319.8	779.8	+143.8
Mechanical engineers	207.2	510.8	+146.5
Civil engineers	193.6	485.4	+150.7
Social Workers	159.5	349.2	+118.9
Nurses (male)	120.1	340.4	+183.4
Nurses (female)	101.0	307.8	+204.2
All Occupations	151.5	340.4	+134.7

Figures are gross weekly earnings, for full time employees, including those whose earnings are affected by absence.
These figures do *not* take inflation into account.
Source: New Earnings Survey 1982, 1994.

Table 2.3 reveals remarkably divergent fortunes amongst different types of professional groups. One interesting indication concerns whether the rate of increase is greater or less then that of the workforce as a whole (where earnings rose by 134.7% between 1982 and 1994). Here it can be seen that five groups saw rates of increase above this, and five saw rates of increase below. It is however striking that the medical professionals of medical practitioners and nurses, where theories of deprofessionalisation have been pioneered and championed both emerged strongly as gainers in a relative as well as an absolute sense. The weak showing of accountants is also interesting.

In general terms, then the service class as a whole appears to have enjoyed a considerable improvement in its levels of income over the past fifteen years. There are some exceptions, and some public sector professionals in particular have seen their income increase less than the national average (though they have still increased in real terms). However, in order to take this discussion further we need to relate this question to job security and promotion prospects, for these have usually been seen as areas in which the middle classes, especially in the public sector, are strong.

2.4 The Organisational Career, Prospects, and Job Security

It is generally accepted that traditionally, the middle class career was based in large bureaucratic organisations, and that it was based on career ladders in which employees could expect promotion as their working lives developed, and that it was rare for these middle class employees to experience downward mobility. The worst fate which such employees could anticipate was being sidelined so that although they might have little chance of upward promotion they still had high levels of job security. The risk of redundancy was minimal (see generally Goldthorpe, 1982). During the middle and later 1980s a number of writers began to suggest that the organisational career was no longer as secure had previously been envisaged. The portents of change were especially clear in the financial services industry. This sector had traditionally been marked by very rigid internal labour markets, where men could enter as junior clerks and where most men could earn promotion to management positions (women being confined to clerical employment). One study of Lloyds Bank (Stovel et al., 1996) indicates that virtually all male entrants who entered during the 1930s were promoted to managerial positions if they stayed with the bank for thirty years or so. During the 1980s the financial services adopted more flexible labour market practices as financial markets were themselves de-regulated, and in the 'Lawson boom' of the mid 1980s, employment in smaller banks, and in specialist financial services meant that increasing numbers of workers were not employed by the leading banks. The recession of the later 1980s saw many of the large banks begin to embark on a major restructuring operation. For the first time ever large numbers of managerial workers were made redundant, nearly all workers aged over fifty being given early retirement, and the traditional managerial job of being a branch manager was affected by the creation of specialist managers (see Halford et al., 1995; 1997).

There is no doubt that there was a very marked attack on middle class workers in these sectors and that the growth of unemployment in this sector led to much talk of a 'white-collar recession' in the early 1990s. What is less clear, however, is whether the financial services sector is typical or unusual of the white-collar workforce as a whole. Table 2.4 provides some evidence on this point. It compares the chances of redundancy for different middle class group during various periods in the early 1990s when the supposed 'white-collar' recession was at its height. It calculates redundancy rates as a proportion of every 1000 workers in these given categories. The three 'service class' groups are contained in the first three rows. Here it is clear that managers have a chance of redundancy slightly below the average for all employees; professional employees have a rate considerably less than half the national average, and 'associate professionals' lie between these two groups. Table 2.4 makes it clear that it continues to the be manual workers who have faced the worst prospects in the recent recession.

Table 2.4
Redundancy Rates by Occupational Group (% of national average in brackets)

Group	Spring 1991	Spring 1992	Spring 1993	Spring 1994
Managers	12.8 (71.9)	12.4 (82.1)	8.6 (69.4)	9.9 (102.0)
Professionals	7.6 (42.7)	6.2 (41.0)	6.1 (49.2)	4.5 (46.4)
Associate profs	13.1 (73.6)	10.9 (72.2)	9.0 (72.6)	5.7 (58.8)
Clerical workers	14.2 (79.8)	14.5 (96.0)	10.1 (86.5)	7.7 (79.4)
Craft workers	33.1 (186.0)	27.7 (183.4)	20.7 (167.0)	18.1 (186.0)
Personal service	9.8 (55.1)	6.9 (45.7)	6.6 (53.2)	5.7 (58.8)
Sales assistants	16.6 (93.3)	14.9 (98.7)	15.3 (123.4)	10.2 (105.2)
Plant operatives	30.1 (169.0)	22.6 (149.7)	23.2 (187.1)	16.2 (167.0)
Others	19.8 (111.2)	16.8 (111.1)	14.8 (119.4)	9.2 (94.8)
All Occupations	17.8	15.1	12.4	9.7

Source: New Earnings Surveys, various years

These figures indicate that although managerial workers are not especially likely to lose their jobs, they are not particularly 'sheltered' either. Their situation is in marked contrast with that for professional workers, whose continued relative job security over all other occupational groups is quite clear from table 2.4. It is likely that the main reason for the advantages of professional workers is due to their location in the public sector, which has, by and large, avoided carrying out large scale redundancy programmes. However, it might be pointed out that bodies in the public sector has other ways of attempting to secure job reductions, for instance by not renewing temporary contracts, by introducing schemes of early retirement, or by encouraging workers to leave voluntarily. We therefore need to be cautious in assuming that the redundancy rates reported in table 2.4 accurately reflect the prospects of workers in various middle class groups.

The possibility raised is that although actual redundancy may still be relatively unusual, there has been considerable disruption to the very nature of the middle class 'career' in recent years, and that this disruption may well have significant implications for the outlooks, attitudes and politics of middle class groups. Traditionally, the middle class career was a device by which professional and managerial workers could anticipate increased incomes, conditions of work, and security over the course of their life. The classic middle class 'career' (enshrined most famously in Whyte's vision of the 'organisation man') was thereby a device for conveying security over time to those fortunate enough to be on such career tracks. This was in marked contrast to those in the working class, whose income tended to reach a peak early in their lives, when they were most physically fit and able, and who could look forward to a middle and old age of steadily declining income and job security.

It can however, be argued that it is precisely this secure, predictable 'career' which is currently under threat. There is some evidence which suggests that the relationship between age, security, and income is becoming eroded. Table 2.5 examines the relationship between income and age for four selected occupational groups, and for men and women. The four occupational groups are selected to pick out two 'service class' groups and two manual working class groups, so that their profiles can be compared.

Looking first at table 2.5 for men, it is clear that there continue to be significant differences between the age-income gradients of the two 'middle class' groups and the two manual working class groups. For professionals and managers, median income levels are higher for men in their fifties than in their thirties. Nonetheless, it is also noteworthy that incomes peak for managers in their forties, and that although professionals earn slightly more in their fifties than earlier in their lives, this increase is limited. Table 2.3 indicates that the figures for women are different again. Women managers reach an earnings peak as early as their thirties, and subsequently see an even more marked falling off in income levels than do female manual workers. Professional women, however, see a slight increase in their income levels into their fifties.

Table 2.5 suggests that the relationship between age and income for 'middle class' groups is not particularly marked and this may be indicative of the erosion of the middle class career itself. Detailed case study research I have carried out in the banking industry (Halford and Savage, 1995; Halford, Savage and Witz, 1997) does indeed suggest that there are important shifts taking place in the meaning of the career. Traditionally career advancement involved both an increase in job security, in income levels, and in non-monetary benefits (support for housing costs, pension contributions etc.). Today grading systems have been changed so that job security *falls* as workers become promoted. When a bank worker moves into a management position, he or she moves into a payment system where they accept that some of their pay is dependent on meeting targets, where they accept that they are not paid overtime (but that they are expected to do overtime to meet their job commitments). I have argued that changes of this type reconstruct the internal labour market as one based around a 'Faustian gamble'. Ambitious workers who want to become managers run the risk of losing a degree of job security.

Table 2.5
Median full time male weekly earnings, by age group, 1995

Group	25-29	30-39	40-49	50-59	All Ages
Managers	354.4	452.6	504.7	482.0	456.4
Professionals	368.5	460.7	490.9	503.3	460.7
Craft workers	281.3	311.6	318.4	298.0	292.5
Plant ops	260.2	286.2	297.1	284.9	274.8

Median full time male weekly earnings of age groups, as % of the median for all ages

Group	25-29	30-39	40-49	50-59	50s - 30s
Managers	77.7	99.1	110.6	105.6	+ 6.5
Professionals	80.0	100.0	106.6	109.2	+ 9.2
Craft workers	96.2	106.5	108.9	101.9	- 4.6
Plant ops	94.8	104.3	108.2	103.9	- 0.4

Median full time female weekly earnings, by age group, 1995

Group	25-29	30-39	40-49	50-59	All Ages
Managers	323.3	361.2	336.7	311.6	329.9
Professionals	342.6	409.0	410.6	419.7	396.2
Craft workers	224.3	238.0	221.3	215.5	215.3
Plant ops	191.6	202.8	190.9	184.7	186.6

Median full time female weekly earnings of age groups, as % of the median for all ages

Group	25-29	30-39	40-49	50-59	50s-30s
Managers	98.0	109.5	102.1	94.5	- 15.0
Professionals	86.5	103.5	103.6	105.9	+ 2.4
Craft workers	104.1	110.5	102.8	100.0	- 10.5
Plant ops	102.7	108.7	102.3	98.9	- 9.8

2.5 Middle class career mobility in contemporary Britain

Let me now turn to consider in more detail some broad evidence on the nature of career patterns in Britain today so that I can investigate further the analysis of the degree of insecurity in middle class jobs. Here I will draw upon survey data from the National Child Development Study which records the changing occupations of a sample of around 10,000 individuals, all born in 1958, between 1981 and 1991. As it turns out, these dates are extremely useful for allowing us to examine the nature of individual transitions in the 1980s. In 1981 the individuals in the study were aged 23. Nearly all had finished education, but most had only entered the labour market relatively recently and were therefore still 'finding their way'. By 1991 these same individuals were 33 and had been exposed to the labour market for well over a decade. They were approaching the age which Goldthorpe has claimed to be that of 'occupational maturity' - that is to say, the age at which people tend to have moved into the highest social class position which they are destined to reach. This ten year period therefore allows us to consider the nature of early adult careers in the 'turbulent times' of the 1980s to consider the job prospects of a representative sample of young people , and to begin to consider whether the sorts of structural changes detected at a macro level can be seen to operate in the context of individual people's lives.

The NCDS represents an excellent source for the consideration of these issues. It contains very full information on the employment situation of respondents in 1981 and 1991, as well as evidence derived from earlier waves of the survey which can be used to explore whether familiar social background has any bearing on the fates of individuals. There is also a further advantage in using the NCDS. The dates of study co-incide almost exactly with the OPCS Censuses, allowing information from the NCDS to be referenced to official data. A particularly important source here is the Longitudinal Study, which links together 1% of individuals from the Census between 1981 and 1991. This is very similar in some ways to the NCDS, except that all age groups are represented in the LS, rather than the specific cohort born in 1958 which is examined by the NCDS. Nonetheless, comparison of the LS and NCDS can allow us to consider the extent to which there are cohort specific shifts occurring during the 1980s.

In what follows I provide evidence from the NCDS which examines different aspects of work-life mobility in Britain in order to consider patterns of exclusion within the middle classes.

2.5.1 Closure and demarcation within the 'service class'

Table 2.6 examines mobility patterns within the salariat between 1981 and 1991, and includes also an indication of whether these young adults experienced downward mobility during this ten year period. One of the striking features of table 2.6 is the considerable amount of movement within the middle classes. This is, to some extent, unsurprising, given that these young adults will be developing their careers at this period, but it nonetheless does emphasise the degree of lateral mobility within the middle classes which occurred during the 1980s. Turning first to table 2.6, which examines male mobility, it is noteworthy that all four groups see large proportions of their numbers move into management positions in large organisations. These management positions are clearly a common destination for middle class men whose entry into the salariat is nonetheless rather different. The fact that professional men tend to move into managerial positions during their working lives is well known (Goldthorpe, 1982; Savage et al., 1992), and if anything appears even more marked for these early adults.

Table 2.6
Male Management - Professional Transitions, 1981-91

From 1981 to 1991	Large mgr	Small mgr	Prof employee	Ancillary
Large mgr	42.6	42.3	28.0	27.3
Small mgr	8.5	10.6	2.5	2.5
Prof self-employed	-	.7	5.7	.7
Prof employee	6.4	2.8	36.9	11.2
Ancillary worker	12.8	9.9	8.9	29.0
into self-employment	-	6.0	1.9	2.0
other downward move	19.7	27.7	16.1	27.3
N	47	49	157	403

Source: NCDS
Notes: Origins groups of large employers (SEG 1.1) and professional self employed (SEG 3) excluded because of low numbers (2 and 3 respectively)

It is equally clear, however, that few men move into managerial positions in small enterprises. The highest proportion, 8.5% is found for men who had previously worked in large management, and this does indicate some level of downward mobility, but in general it would appear that there are marked boundaries between managerial positions in smaller and larger units.

Whilst there is considerable work life mobility into management positions in larger units it is notable that few managers move into professional employment. This is interesting in view of the arguments of Mills (1995) who claims, using data from the Social Change and Economic Life Initiative that there is now considerable mobility from management into the professions, and indeed such mobility now outstrips that from the professions to management. The evidence from Table 2.6 suggests that for younger adults at least, there is no evidence of a growing openness of professional positions to those who have worked as managers. There continue to be very clear boundaries around professional work which make it difficult for those outside its ranks to enter it.

Finally, another transition which is notable by its absence is that into self employment. During the 1980s there was a marked rise in self employment in Britain, reversing a long term trend towards its decline. There was also some evidence that an increasing number of employees from the 'service class' were choosing to move into self-employment (Savage et al., 1992). However, this evidence from the NCDS shows that this increase in self employment is geared very much among older workers (which is not a very surprising finding), and that most young workers continue to rely overwhelmingly on advancing their career through the labour market. Indeed, one of the striking findings from the NCDS is that despite the concerns about the erosion of organisational positions as firms restructure, nonetheless, most young men appear to be most attracted to moving into senior management positions. Positions of clear authority remain the major destination of middle class young men.

Table 2.7
Female Management - Professional Transitions, 1981-91.

	Large mgr	Small mgr	Prof employee	Ancillary
Large mgr	30.4	20.8	25.0	9.3
Small mgr	-	5.7	3.6	3.0
Prof self	-	-	17.9	.5
Prof employee	4.3	1.9	21.4	2.4
Ancillary	26.1	9.4	17.9	44.5
Downward	39.2	63.2	14.2	40.3
N	23	53	28	656

The flows evident for women (table 2.7) have several similarities to those for men, but some notable differences. Rates of downward mobility are high for all 1981 groups with the striking exception of professionals. Even those women who remain in the service class seem to be highly mobile within it - the main exception being women employed as 'ancillary workers' (mainly nurses and teachers) who have good prospects of being in the same occupation ten years later.

2.5.2 Upward Mobility into the Salariat, 1981-91

It is well known that the majority of people who are employed in the middle classes move into such positions during their working lives, though there are also arguments which emphasise that this process may be changing. Both Mills (1995) and Gershuny (1995) use work history data derived from the SCELI project to argue that entry into the middle classes now tends to occur earlier in people's working lives than has traditionally been the case and therefore that there is a growing process of closure between the middle classes as a whole and other social groups. Whereas traditionally many (male) white-collar workers and some blue-collar workers could hope for promotion to junior management positions later on in their careers, they argue that such promotion routes are declining as management positions are filled earlier, on the basis of credentials and or performance on 'fast track' trainee schemes.

Table 2.8
Male upward mobility into the salariat 1981-1991

	Large mgr	Small mgr	Prof	Ancillary	upwardly mobile	N
Junior white-collar	26.6	3.0	5.3	12.4	46.3	394
personal service	8.5	10.6	4.3	6.4	28.8	47
manual foremen	13.8	1.1	3.4	4.9	23.2	268
skilled manual	6.9	1.2	2.7	4.0	14.8	821
semi-skilled manual	4.9	.6	2.8	3.7	12.0	326
unskilled manual	10.3	1.0	2.1	4.1	17.5	97
own account	9.3	4.1	1.8	5.2	17.4	172

Source: NCDS

Table 2.8 indicates that many men continued to see good prospects of upward mobility in the 1980s. This is especially true for those young men employed in clerical or junior white-collar work, nearly half of whom had entered the salariat by 1991. It is difficult to know how this proportion compares with earlier periods. It is well known that this group has historically had very good prospects of moving into the middle classes (Stewart et al., 1980), though it is interesting to point out that some scepticism has recently been cast on the extent to which such mobility is the norm (Mills, 1995). It is again interesting to note that managerial positions in large enterprises are by far the most common destination position for these white-collar workers. Perhaps more surprising is the fact that the second highest rate of upward mobility is found amongst the personal service workers. Such workers have been seen some writers as part of the new 'post-industrial' proletariat (see the discussion in Esping-Anderson, 1995).

Table 2.8 shows clearly that they actually have relatively good prospects of upward promotion, albeit into management positions in small enterprises - possibly the same sorts of retail units as they were previously employed in. Table 2.9 provides comparative data for women.

Table 2.9
Female Upward Mobility into the salariat 1981-1991

	Large mgr	Small mgr	Professional	Ancillary	upwardly mobile	N
junior white-collar	8.1	2.6	0.9	10.1	21.7	780
personal service	7.5	2.2	0.7	9.0	19.4	134
semi-skilled	2.5	1.7	-	9.2	14.3	119
unskilled	4.2	-	-	8.3	12.5	24
own account	8.8	5.9	-	11.8	26.5	34

Source: NCDS
skilled manual and manual foremen omitted due to lack of numbers.

It is extremely interesting to compare this table with table 2.8 since these cohorts of women entered the labour market in the late 1970s and early 1980s after the legal outlawing of discrimination against women.

Prospects of upward mobility for women continue to be generally less good than do those of their male counterparts, especially from the category of junior white-collar workers. It is however notable that rates of upward mobility from the semi and unskilled manual working class are now rather similar for men and women, and that the rate of upward mobility is actually greater for female own account workers than for their male equivalents.

2.6 Conclusion

The most important point arising from this chapter is that in general terms the middle classes have done exceptionally well since 1980. Of course some middle class groups have done better than others. Professionals working in the private sector seem to have enjoyed the best prospects, whilst professionals in the public sector have experienced a certain degree of relative decline in their income levels (though they have continued to enjoy good levels of job security). Managers in the private sector have experienced a certain degree of uncertainty as firms restructure. Even here, however, it should be pointed out that managers tend to have fared much better than manual workers!

Nonetheless, some important changes are occurring to the middle classes which may indicate that patterns of division will increase in the next few years. The most significant of these may well be concerned with the life course. Traditionally, one of the main distinctions between the middle classes and the working classes lay in the fact that the former could anticipate looking forward to a more prosperous and secure future as their lives advanced - or at least could be confident that they would be protected from significant downward mobility. This set of expectations was based on the nature of the bureaucratic internal labour market. Today, we have seen that young people continue to enjoy good career prospects in their early working lives, until the age of 33. From this point onwards, however, greater uncertainty occurs. Median incomes appear to level off from their thirties, whilst job security also declines as redundancy is directed principally at older workers (frequently through early retirement programmes). Much further work is needed to examine these issues in more detail, but there are interesting indications here that the middle classes may be adopting more of the traditional working class model where income peaks relatively early in the working life.

One way of reflecting on the significance of these changes is to consider how they relate to traditional axes of exclusion within the middle class. In the past the middle classes rested fundamentally on a gendered base. The exclusion of women from the service class underwrote male prospects, job security and privilege. However, as women have been successful in moving into parts of the middle class, and hence provided more competition for men, so age has possibly emerged as a more important axis of demarcation and division. Younger people with the right qualifications have excellent short term prospects, but there may be greater difficulties for older members of the middle classes.

In order to bring my (admittedly, highly speculative) remarks to a close, let me finish by considering the question of class reproduction. Goldthorpe (1995) emphasises that the 'service class' has been remarkably successful in reproducing its class advantages inter-generationally. The majority of the children of the service class themselves enter its ranks. Erikson and Goldthorpe's (1992) research suggests that this fact holds true cross-nationally. Yet, it can be suggested that there are concerns today that this process of class reproduction is under threat, and that it is these worries that account for the considerable malaise evident amongst the middle classes themselves.

The argument is schematic but would take the following form. The middle classes have relied strongly on the welfare state to allow them to shore up and transmit their advantages to their children. Following the introduction of comprehensive education from the early 1970s, entry to state schools is determined primarily by residential location. As state funded schools become increasingly short of resources, middle class parents worry more about the quality of these schools. Some parents opt out of the state system and send their children to private fee paying schools, which have become the most successful in enabling their children to gain qualifications. Other parents move to residential locations which are known to be close to 'good' state schools, but this entails moving to expensive areas where their finances may be stretched. If their children do well enough to go to University, they will also have to pay an increasing amount towards their children's education, since the grant system (whereby local authorities paid University fees as well as a small financial grant to students) has been cut back to be replaced by a loan system, and where parents are encouraged to offer more financial support.

At the same time that the educational system makes the problem of pushing one's children through the school system more difficult, the labour market is changing so that the middle class career becomes somewhat more fraught and difficult as individuals reach their later thirties and forties. This was traditionally the time when successful individuals could 'relax' knowing that they had achieved a measure of security, and whereby they could devote more of their financial resources to their children's education, but today this may be overshadowed by labour market worries. It is important to note that these worries may not be 'realistic' - in the sense that I have shown that in reality the job security and level of remuneration remains far better than for other social groups. But this does not mean that there are not grounds for concern at the level of the individual.

A further 'worry' about class reproduction develops also as the population ages and as the parents of the middle classes in their forties thinks about the economic position of their parents, now likely to be in their sixties and seventies. During the 1980s a number of commentators in Britain argued that as a growing number of households owned their houses outright, so more wealth would be inherited inter-generationally (see especially Saunders, 1990; and see the critical discussion in Savage et al., 1992, and Hamnett, 1995). It would indeed appear that around one-quarter of service class households have received an inheritance during their lives. Nonetheless, in many cases, where elderly relatives need care, their houses frequently need to be sold either to pay for it directly, or to meet criteria for eligibility for state support. Just as the middle aged middle class household worries about their children's prospects, so they see their parents fortunes 'disappear' to pay for caring services.

References

Abercrombie, N., and J. Urry (1983) *Capital, Labour and the Middle Classes*, London.
Braverman, H. (1974) *Labor and Monopoly Capital*, New York.
Butler, T., and M. Savage (1995) *Social Change and the Middle Classes*, London.
Crompton, R. (1986) Women and the Service Class, in: M. Mann and R. Crompton (eds.), *Gender and Stratification*, Cambridge.
Crompton, R. (1992) Patterns of social consciousness amongst the middle classes, in: R. Burrows and C. Marsh (eds.), *Consumption and Class*, Basingstoke, pp. 140-165.
Crompton, N., and G. Jones (1984) *White-collar proletariat, deskilling and gender in clerical work*, London.
Erikson, R., and J.H. Goldthorpe (1992) *The constant flux*, Oxford.
Esping-Andersen, G. (ed.) (1993) *Changing Classes*, London.
Giddens, A. (1973) *The class structure of the advanced societies*, London.
Goldthorpe, J.H. (1980) *Social Mobility and the Class Structure in Modern Britain*, Oxford.
Goldthorpe, J.H. (1982) On the service class: its formation and future, in: A. Giddens and G. McKenzie (eds.), *Classes and the Division of Labour: essays in honour of Ilya Neustadt*, Cambridge, pp. 162-185.
Goldthorpe, J.H. (1995) The service class revisited, in Butler and Savage (eds), *Social Change and the Middle Classes*, London.
Halford, S., and M. Savage (1995) Restructuring organisations, changing people, gender and careers in banking and local government, *Work, Employment and Society*, vol. 9, 1, pp. 97-122.
Halsey, A., A. Heath, and J. Ridge (1980) *Origins and Destinations*, Oxford.
Hamnett, C. (1995) Home ownership and the middle classes, in: Butler and Savage (eds.), *Social Change and the Middle Classes* London.
Jessop. B., K. Bonnett, S. Bromley, and T. Ling (1988) *Thatcherism, a tale of two nations*, Cambridge.
Klingender, F.D. (1935) *The Condition of Clerical Labour in Britain*, London.
Lash, S. and J. Urry (1987) *The End of Organised Capitalism*, Oxford.
Le Grand, J., and R.E. Goodwin (1987) *Not only the poor, the middle class and the welfare state*, London.
Lockwood, D. (1958) *The blackcoated worker*, London.
Mills, C. (1995) Managerial and Professional Work Histories, in Butler and Savage (eds.) *Social Change and the Middle Class*, London.
Pond, C. (1987) The changing distribution of income, wealth and poverty, in C. Hamnett, L. McDowell, and P. Sarre (eds.), *The Changing Social Structure*, London.
Rowntree J. (1995) *Report on Income and Wealth*, London.
Saunders, P. (1990) *A Nation of Homeowners*, London.
Savage, M., J. Barlow, P. Dickens, and A.J. Fielding (1992) *Property, Bureaucracy and Culture: middle class formation in contemporary Britain*, London.
Savage, M., P. Dickens, and A.J. Fielding (1988) Some social and political implications of the contemporary fragmentation of the "service class", *International Journal of Urban and Regional Research*, vol. 12, pp. 455-476.
Stewart. A., K. Prandy, and R.Blackburn (1980) *Social Stratification and Occupations*, London.
Stovel, K., M. Savage, and P. Bearman, (1996) Ascription into achievement, models of career systems at Lloyds Bank 1890-1970, *American Journal of Sociology*, vol. 102, 2, pp. 358-399.
Townsend, P. (1986) *Inequalities in Health*, Harmondsworth.

3
Women's employment, the household and middle class heterogeneity

ROSEMARY CROMPTON

3.1 Introduction

A number of different threads have run through feminist commentaries on the 'middle classes'. First, the middle class/occupational structure has been seen to be 'gendered' in that it has reflected the division of labour between men and women in both the 'public' and the 'private' spheres. Thus historically, masculine exclusionary practices have formally excluded women from professions such as medicine and law, and kept them out of managerial positions. At the same time, women's employment in the 'lower professions' and subordinate occupations such as clerical work has supported that of men. Furthermore, women's work in the domestic sphere has also maintained men's superior occupational status, by liberating them from domestic responsibilities (particularly amongst the 'middle classes') (Crompton, 1986). This approach emphasises the intertwining of class and gender, that is, the difficulty of separating 'class' from 'gender' processes in giving an account of the occupational structure (Scott, 1986). A further strand of feminist critique has emphasised the way in which particular occupations have been psychologically and culturally 'gendered', that is, rendered 'masculine' or 'feminine'. Bureaucratic structures (through which senior managers progress) have been described as reflecting masculine qualities such as emotional distance, reason, and an emphasis upon abstract thinking, and parallel arguments have also been developed in respect of high-ranking professionals (Witz, 1992; Massey, 1995; Davies 1996).[1]

As we shall see, women are increasingly moving into higher-level occupations in management and the professions. In the light of the arguments sketched out above, what are the likely consequences of these developments? With the erosion of the barriers against women's entry into higher-level positions, are we moving towards a gender-neutral (i.e. androgynous) occupational structure in which increasingly, women occupy the same occupational slots as men? Or will there be a gendered restructuring of the middle class occupational structure? If the wives of middle class men are increasingly in employment, then they will not be available to carry out domestic work. Will there, therefore, be transformations in the interpersonal sphere and in the domestic division of labour? Such possibilities are discussed by authors such as Beck (1992) and Giddens (1992), for example. Finally, as the middle classes 'feminise', are

B. Steijn et al. (eds.), Economic Restructuring and the Growing Uncertainty of the Middle Class, 45-59.
© 1998 *Kluwer Academic Publishers.*

there possibilities of occupational transformation from within, as women increasingly find themselves in occupations supposedly requiring 'masculine' characteristics? In this chapter, we will focus on the consequences of the intertwining of class and gender in the division of labour between men and women in both employment and the domestic sphere. Thus we will discuss not only the increasing entry of women into middle class occupations, but more particularly, the reciprocal effect of this change in the gender composition of the middle classes for the domestic division of labour. The analysis of women's labour force participation is a major research area (Hakim, 1992; Rubery and Fagan, 1993; Scott ed., 1994). One feature of recent research on women and employment is that it has been focused largely *within* the field of paid work itself. That is, the employment/family interface has not been investigated in respect of particular occupations or employment situations. This is paradoxical given that a major criticism developed by feminist researchers of the 70s and 80s emphasised the essential *interdependence* of paid and unpaid work.[2]

3.2 Women's entry into 'middle class' employment and its consequences

Although occupational parity has by no means been achieved, the proportion of women in middle class employment is rising steadily. For example, in Britain, men were 80% of higher-level employers and managers in 1981, but only 71% by 1991. Men were 90% of professionals in 1981, but 87% of self-employed, and 82% of employed professionals by 1991 (Crompton, 1995). In particular occupations, the recorded rate of increase in female participation is even more dramatic. For example, women were only 4% of judges, advocates, barristers and solicitors in 1971 but 27% by 1990; 20% of administrative and executive local government officers in 1971 but 51% by 1990, 18% of doctors and dentists in 1971 but 30% by 1990, and 25% of teachers in higher education in 1971 but 30% by 1990 (Hakim, 1992). However, although women are moving into middle class occupations, they are often to be found in gendered occupational spaces which happen to be 'family-friendly' (Savage, 1992). It has also been argued that key middle class occupations are more fundamentally 'gendered' in that they draw upon an essential masculinity dominated by reason and abstract thought, as well as demanding the kinds of hours and work flexibility which are just not compatible with the work of caring for other people (e.g. the IT experts studied by Massey, 1995; and Davies, 1996 on the professions).

Classification difficulties make cross-national comparisons problematic, but a similar pattern of female entry into higher-level occupations seems to be taking place all over Europe. For example, in Spain and Italy, women have made rapid inroads into jobs in higher education, and in Spain and France, women are an increasing share of computer professionals. Women have increased their share of higher grade jobs in public administration in Belgium, Germany, Spain, Italy, the Netherlands, and the UK, and they have also improved their relative levels of employment in Banking. Rubery and Fagan (1993) argue that underlying this general tendency for women to improve their occupational positions are changes in recruitment policies supporting the direct entry to higher-level positions of the well-qualified, and women are everywhere improving their formal educational qualifications. Indeed, Savage et al. (1992, see also Savage, 1996) have argued that middle-class women are more likely to rely upon their educational /cultural assets in order to achieve occupational success, rather than occupational or property assets, which are found to a greater extent amongst men. This would suggest that women are more likely to become concentrated in professional, rather than managerial, occupations. As we shall see, this gendered occupational restructuring has implications for the domestic division of labour, as well as the resegregation of middle class employment itself.

Thus the changing gender composition of the middle classes raises a number of broader questions. One development which has been widely recognised is the contribution, albeit indirect, which the improved employment prospects for some women have made to the increasing material polarisation of households. Women with good jobs and good job opportunities tend to marry and/or enter into partnerships with similar men, and fewer of them are leaving the labour force when they have children (Harrop and Moss, 1994). With rising unemployment and growing insecurity at the other end of the spectrum, these processes contribute to growing social polarisation (Gorz, 1989). This is an important topic, but not one that will be developed at any length here.

One of the most striking consequences of the increase in women's employment is the declining birth rate. Although rising levels of women's employment are obviously not the only cause of declining fertility, it is clearly a contributory factor to the decline in the birth rate, which is taking place all over Europe. The EU as a whole has seen a decline in fertility from a rate of 2.61 in 1960 to 1.48 in 1992, and in all European countries (with the exception of Ireland) fertility is now below replacement level. Indeed, it has been suggested that 'Below-replacement fertility has emerged as a characteristic feature of post-industrial society' (Sporton, 1993). In Belgium, Denmark, Germany, France, Luxembourg Netherlands and the UK the decline in fertility rates began in the 1960s and slowed after the mid 70s (although still remaining below replacement level). In Greece, Spain, Italy and Portugal, there was no corresponding decline in fertility from the 1960s, but an even more rapid decrease from the mid 70s. In 1991, fertility rates in these Southern countries had reached their lowest ever: 1.30 in Spain, and 1.28 in Italy (Social Portrait of Europe, Luxembourg 1996). As we have seen in our discussion above, these are also the countries in which women's entry into higher-level positions appears to have improved very recently

Recent commentaries suggest that there will be no significant reversal in fertility trends in the future. Demographers attribute these trends to greater opportunities for female labour force participation, and the fertility-reducing practice of cohabitation (Sporton, 1993: 61). he latter is an indication of how changes in fertility have also been associated with among the motivations of changes in traditional mores. Thus Brunetta concludes that: "*[...] the causes of fertility decline in the second demographic revolution should be sought post-industrial society, in particular the increasing advance of individualism, with its destructive effects on traditional values such as marriage and parenthood*" (1993: 168-169).

Some women in middle class employment, therefore, may 'solve' the difficulties (for women) associated with the combination of employment and family life by having only one child, or none at all (as we shall see in our later discussions, these women are likely to be managers, rather than professionals). In other households, the caring and domestic work once carried out by the middle class wife may be substituted by hiring paid domestic labour. In many countries (e.g. the Scandinavian welfare states, and France), some caring work has, to varying degrees, been transferred to the public sector. However, in countries with 'marketised' welfare and service provision, such as Britain, such labour must be privately hired, or informally arranged through friends and family.

In fact, studies of childcare arrangements in Britain suggest that most parents rely on informal care, and in any case, a high proportion of British women work part-time (Finlayson et al., 1996). The direct hiring of domestic help is a feature of only a minority of households - although precise figures are very difficult to establish given that much of this employment will be highly informal. Gregson and Lowe (1996) have studied the increase in paid domestic labour (i.e. nannies and cleaners) brought about by the increase in paid employment amongst middle class women. They found that although some households had no difficulties in the handling of this market solution to their domestic labour problems, others were uncomfortable of entering the unregulated, personally stressful and potentially exploitative world of domestic labour employment relations (the wages of paid domestic workers are low). However, "*[...] they found themselves compelled to employ waged domestic labour in order to reproduce the dual-career pattern of employment*" (p. 163). Gregson and Lowe continue: "*[...] to explain the resurgence of waged domestic labour entirely in terms of the nature of service-class employment would be misplaced [...] the resurgence of waged domestic labour in middle class Britain also reflects middle-class men's unwillingness to perform a sizeable share of domestic labour.*"

Whether taken on willingly or forced by circumstances, the hiring of paid domestic labour by households represents an individualistic solution to the problem at hand. Jordan et al.'s (1994) qualitative research was centred on a rather different set of household arrangements, but these authors, too, have stressed the individualism of the middle classes. In the 35 households studied by Jordan et al., the female partner, although equally as well qualified as the male partner, had usually chosen to give her employment career a lower priority. These wives, therefore, were available for domestic labour given their lesser involvement in paid work, in Chafetz and Hagan's (1996) terms, they were 'satisficers', seeking to reconcile employment and family goals rather than maximise either of them. The women's long-term strategy, Jordan et al. argue, was rational in that their investments in their men's long-term careers gave them access to the incomes, fringe benefits and pensions associated with the key asset of the (relatively scarce) secure, well paid, job. A number of criticisms might be made of this argument, not least that women's access to men's employment benefits cannot be guaranteed in the case of divorce or separation. Nevertheless, as a mode of adaptation it is one which is likely to perpetuate relatively traditional gender relations[3], although Jordan et al. demonstrate that changing attitudes to gender relations are nevertheless reflected in a partnership code which allows women enough autonomy to pursue their own purposes and interests within the relationship (p. 174). Jordan et al. however argue that the individually rational strategies of 'putting the family first' may be collectively irrational. The anticipated competition for the scarce 'positional good' of a secure job forces parents to invest heavily in education etc. for their children. Paradoxically, however, such jobs become even more difficult to get as an increasing number of other parents make similar investments, thus the pursuit of positional advantage is ultimately self-defeating.

The practical strategies developed by middle-class households, therefore, are likely to reinforce individualism rather than collectivism. Paid domestic labour generates a new category of domestic servants, who are relatively unprotected in employment terms, and dependent upon very individualised employment relations. Individualistic family strategies lead to the declining value of educational credentials etc., and increasing uncertainty that the children so expensively invested in will repay their parents human capital outlay.

In respect of the middle-class employment/family interface, therefore, households may (a) decide to have only one or no children; (b) hire domestic labour, and (c) give priority to the man's employment leaving the wife 'free' to carry out domestic work. A further strategy, however, might be to re-negotiate the domestic division of labour within the household, in that the man takes on more domestic responsibility. Hoschild's study, *The Second Shift* (1990) showed that working wives were, indeed, anxious to re-negotiate the domestic division of labour, but that their efforts had not, on the whole met with much success. Hochschild describes the *stalled revolution*, in which women have taken an increasingly full part in the world of paid work, but this has not been matched by a corresponding increase in the amount of domestic work carried out by men. Rather 'family myths' have developed which effectively legitimate the man's unequal share, as well as constrained 'emotional economies' stretching over the cracks in deteriorating relationships. It may be noted that women's 'second shift' described in this US research bears many resemblances to the 'double burden' of working women in the state socialist countries. Rather more optimistically, Gershuny et al. (1994) have recently argued that a process of 'lagged adaptation', reflecting both the extent of the women's paid work as well as the domestic division of labour characteristic of their families of origin, is in train (p. 183). In the following sections of this chapter, we will examine some recent evidence relating to occupational differences in characteristic patterns of the domestic division of labour.

3.3 Methodology

The following section reports on a cross-national study of two specific (feminising) occupations: medicine and retail banking. These occupations were chosen as reflecting a number of contrasts: professional vs. managerial; public sector vs. private sector; and rates and trajectories of occupational feminisation. Case studies of these occupations have been carried out in each of the participating countries (Britain, Norway, Russia, and the Czech Republic). In addition, fifteen (minimum) biographical interviews have been carried out with women in each occupation in each country (120 interviews in all). The women were aged between 30 and 55. All doctors had completed their post-registration qualification, and all bankers held managerial positions. All were currently employed. Interviews were semi-structured and tape recorded, and a common recording document was used to transcribe (translated) interviews. The interviews were coded from the recording document.[4]

Clearly, these interviews do not represent a 'sample' in the usually accepted sense of the term (although in our discussions, some statistical tests have been used to highlight the differences between the two occupational groups). However, the very tightly focused selection of interviewees, together with the cross-national research design, make us confident of making generalisations on the basis of these small numbers. We would argue that a kind of 'repeat saturation' of data and evidence has been achieved in this method.[5]

3.4 Occupational Comparisons: the evidence

In the case of women managers, research in Britain has demonstrated that, whereas male managers are highly dependent upon the domestic input of their wives, female managers in partner and/or child households are disproportionately responsible for domestic work, and are far less likely than male managers to have children in any case (Wajcman, 1996). Aggregate level British data confirms this suggestion, and, furthermore, indicates that the household and family formation patterns of women managers are rather different from those in professional occupations. Data from the Sample of Anonymised Records of the Census (1991) (SARs) shows that whereas 63% of self-employed, and 44% of employed, women professionals aged between 30-50 lived in households with children, only 41% of women higher-level managers of the same age did so. In contrast, 71% of managerial, 65% of employed and 75% of self-employed professional *men* in the same age group were lived in households with children (Crompton, 1995).

For one country, therefore, we have clear evidence that women managers are likely to 'economise' on the domestic demands made on them by having few or no children, and that there is here a contrast with women in professional occupations. The findings we report in this chapter suggest that this phenomenon may be a general one.

The characteristics of the women interviewed in the four countries reflected anticipated occupational differences, for example, 47% of the bankers, but only 3% of the doctors, had changed their occupations over their working lives, and whereas all of the doctors had been educated beyond graduate level, a minority of the bankers had only modest levels of educational achievement. In other respects, however, the women were very similar: 44% of the doctors, and 47% of the bankers, had fathers in professional or managerial occupations, 73% of the doctors, and 76% of the bankers, were married or living in a partnership, and the mean age of the doctors was 42, bankers 40. In analysing the interviews, however, it became apparent that there were quite marked differences between the women in the two occupations in their attitudes to family building and the eventual numbers of children in their families, as well as in their domestic division of labour. Table 3.1 summarises some of the findings:

Table 3.1
Career intentions, children, and the domestic division of labour[6]

	Doctors (%)	Bankers (%)
Early career/family intentions: **		
Put career first, or 'just drifted'	54	78
Career decision shaped by anticipated family responsibilities/intentions	46	22
Children: *		
No, or only one child	46	68
More than one child	54	32
Own domestic division of labour: *		
Traditional (respondent does most)	79	55
Other+	21	45
Childcare		
Respondent main responsibility	58	38
Other +	42	62

** $\chi2$ significant @ 99% level
* $\chi2$ significant @ 95% level
+ includes shared with partner, partner does most, help from others (paid/relative)

How do we account for these systematic variations in the family/employment biographies of women in these two occupations? It may be suggested that the answer lies in the nature of the occupations themselves. Despite considerable variations in national contexts (see Crompton and Harris, 1997), the experiences of women in medicine and banking are also characterised by important cross-national continuities. These derive from the contrast between 'professional' and 'managerial' occupations.

3.5 The Professional/Managerial contrast and its implications for women's work and family lives

Within the sociology of occupations, the distinction, initially made by Parsons (1954), between 'professionals' and 'bureaucrats' (managers) has generated a virtual sub-area of research and debate (e.g. Burrage and Torstendahl, 1990). However, it is not the intention to examine this debate in any depth here. Rather, in using this distinction, it is intended only to explore its consequences for women's work-life and family patterns.

The classic *profession* is characterised by a formal and extensive body of knowledge and expertise which is acquired through a long period of training. Professional standards are nationally (and usually internationally) recognised. Once the training and registration period has been completed, the professional is in possession of a 'licence to practice'. Professionals may sell their skills directly to the consumer (for example, as doctors in private practice).[7] Or they may be employed by organisations such as hospitals and clinics. During their careers, professionals may move into work situations in which there are extensive 'managerial' elements. For example, the Conservative Government's policy of the marketisation of the National Health Service has increased the 'managerial' content of a whole range of NHS positions. For the purposes of this argument, however, the point being emphasised is that 'professional' work such as medicine is largely concerned with the application of a recognised body of skills and expertise. As such, it may be purchased in flexible tranches as and when required.

Whether or not *management* is characterised by an explicit and recognised body of expertise is a hotly contested issue. There has been a massive expansion of management training, but managers, unlike professionals, do not require a 'licence to practice'. Managerial careers are forged in an organisational context. In the classic bureaucratic model of organisations, the bureaucratic hierarchy provides a series of graded occupational slots to which managers can aspire. Recent trends, including 'delayering' and organisational 'downsizing' have, supposedly, had a considerable impact on the traditional bureaucratic career (Kanter, 1986). However, this has not transformed the fundamental difference between classic professional and managerial occupations which is being emphasised: that is, that professional knowledge and expertise is regulated by an external standard, whereas managerial expertise is directly evaluated by the employing organisation.

It may be suggested that these differences in the nature of 'professional' and 'managerial' occupations have been systematically reflected in the employment and family patterns of the bankers and doctors interviewed as follows:

- The long period of training required of doctors has had a tendency to be associated with the 'forward planning' of the domestic career as well, which is reflected in the choice of 'family friendly' medical specialties by many women doctors. Although there have been many upheavals in the way in which medical services are supplied (indeed, the doctors interviewed were much more likely than the bankers to say that the changes they had undergone were for the worse), there is nevertheless an underlying continuity in the content of medical training and specialisation (Crompton and Le Feuvre, 1997).
- The planning of medical and family careers is associated with 'satisficing' behaviour on the part of women doctors, through which conventional assumptions

about domestic work (i.e. that it will be organised by the woman) tend to be reproduced.

- The 'satisficing' strategy is reinforced by the wide availability of flexible and part-time work in medicine.[8]

In contrast, in banking:

- There is no long period of formal training before taking up employment: expertise is acquired whilst in employment. Changes in the organisation of banking services have (unlike medicine) changed the *content* of managerial jobs.[9]
- The rapidity of organisational change means that women in bank management have not, historically, been able to contemplate the long-term forward planning of their employment and family careers to the same extent as doctors. Rather, their employment situation has tended to encourage 'reflexive' behaviour.
- In the employment context of banking, a 'satisficing' strategy for women would normally be associated with a move to part-time working, found only amongst non-managerial staff Employment flexibility, therefore, is problematic for women managers. Thus rather than merely 'satisfice', women managers with enhanced domestic responsibilities will seek to make changes in the organisation of domestic work in their households.

It is being argued, therefore, that these occupational and employment-related differences explain the systematic variations in family building, and in the domestic division of labour, between the doctors and bankers interviewed. The next section presents a series of individual biographies which illustrate the processes summarised above.

3.6 Work-life Occupational Biographies[10]

Banking

(i) England

2/25: Tania (42): left school at eighteen after A levels to work in the bank. She found bank work boring, but noticed that managers had better jobs and decided that this was what she wanted. Took (and passed) the banking exams but, still frustrated by her 'mundane level' of work, applied for a job elsewhere in the bank. She made two further geographical moves (with promotion), and married in her thirties with the intention of having children. At this point she turned down a move which would have meant promotion, but in fact restructuring generated more opportunities in her local area which she seized with both hands. She m(.Uis now pregnant for the first time. Her husband does most of the domestic work (she works longer hours). He will take his share of childcare (his hours are more convenient).

On occupational mobility: "*I looked around and saw a load of plonkers getting on...There were some guys of very average ability being promoted, because they're guys, and it used to really annoy me tremendously[...] I'd just come back from my holidays (to a new job) I had long hair and I was quite tanned, and (I thought) they're never going to take me seriously[...]so I went and had all me hair cut off'*

(ii) Norway
3/27 Kari (38): Auditor. Went to business college and stayed with accounting 'by accident', because she enjoyed it more than she anticipated. She had three different jobs before she joined the bank in the 80s, around the time she married. She wanted to continue with her studies but her husband was unsympathetic. She continued nevertheless, but she divorced from her first husband in her early 30s. She has two children by her second partner, who works flexible hours. He finishes work earlier than she does so he takes care of the children and always makes dinner.

On her work: "*I do not have any desire to change jobs right now but [...] I'm prepared to grab the opportunities that arise [...] I would love a managerial position, but right now I am more interested in the professional side of my job - and I'm responsible for seven staff I like to feel that I can make a difference.*"

(iii) Czech Republic
1/21 Olga (45): As a young woman, she wanted to make a career in sport but was prevented from this by illness. Went to business college, then entered a state-owned engineering works as a clerk and rose to department manager. Left after the 'velvet revolution' (1989) because the director (a Party member) thought (mistakenly) that she was after his job. Got a job in the newly-privatised banking sector (Investment and Post Bank), changed to the Komercni bank in 1991. She is now in charge of a division which employs 150 people. She has one daughter, and is divorced from her first husband who did not know if he wanted a competent woman or a 'hen'. Her current partner is very co-operative, is happy to do everything in the household and is a good cook.

On her work and career: "*[...] even the most stupid man has bigger chances than the most intelligent woman [...]the job distribution of men and women in banking shows that women are discriminated against [...] men cover up for one another, and some men hate women at work.*"

(iv) Russia
4/28 Nahezda (44): The daughter of workers, she was active in the Party and went to university to study Political Economy, where she met her husband, an engineer. He was sent to the North where jobs were difficult to find, but she found employment (in an administrative position) with the local Komsomol Committee. She then got a job with a Trade Union. In 1991, through Party connections, she got a job at Sberebank (the state savings bank). She is now the main breadwinner, and has re-negotiated the

domestic division of labour with her husband (who has a poorly paid job in a defence enterprise). He now takes the major responsibility for household tasks and the care of their son.

On employment in the 'New Russia': "*Men have a more conservative way of thinking than women. Women have to think how to survive and feed their children, therefore they need to adjust quicker[...]I am not afraid of any kind of work. It is very fortunate that I work in the bank, but if the situation changes for the worse, well, I will have to find my way.*"

Doctors

(i) England

2/02 Carol (46): She wanted to be a doctor from a very young age (about twelve). "*I just had the idea and it stuck there.*" She did well at her all-girls school, and went to medical school in Scotland, where she met her future husband (who is now a consultant). As she had always wanted to have a family, she decided to become a GP so she could work part-time. Her first child was born during her first year as a GP, and she has always worked for 20 hours a week, continuously through the birth of her three children. She has always taken the major responsibility for childcare and domestic work, and her husband is a 'breadwinner' who doesn't notice things that need to be done in the household.

On medicine and family life: "*[...] there always has to be a senior surgeon there (at the hospital), its very difficult to fit in with family life. Most surgeons are married to women who stay at home and look after the children.*"

(ii) Norway

3/06 Anne (55): Becoming a doctor was something she wanted to do from being a small child, her parents warned her about the many years of study involved. Initially, she intended to specialise in paediatrics but by the time the moment came to specialise, she was already married with two children (she has four adult/teen children and is now widowed). She realised that paediatrics would mean weekend and evening work and long hours, so changed her specialty to radiology, where the hours were shorter and there was no weekend work. She has worked continuously, bringing up her children with the help of nannies. She took the main responsibility (more than her fair share) for the household tasks and planning, but she never really thought about it.

On employment: "*I once got a job and the boss said that if I had not been the best qualified, he would have chosen one of the two male applicants, but there would have been an uproar. He didn't have anything against me personally but he thought that a woman would not sacrifice more than necessary for the job and he was probably right. I didn't commit myself 100% to the job.*"

(iii) Czech Republic
1/05 Jarka (43): Both her parents were doctors, and she always wanted to study medicine, although her parents advised against it. She always wanted a family as well, and from her childhood experiences, she knew what would be involved. She has known her husband since childhood, and when she was deciding on her specialty (radiology, specialising in neurological examination) she took his career as a surgeon into consideration. Her husbands work requires his full involvement, and he is at work practically all the time. She has two children, the second is disabled. She does all the housework herself but her major problem is caring for her handicapped daughter (at a special school).

On her past decisions: "*My husband is cleverer than myself - I knew this when I married him, that he would be professionally dominating in the relationship. My husband's work and career is at the centre of family life, and I try to keep problems away from him.*"

(iv) Russia
4/04 Irina (39): Her mother was a doctor, and she thinks that the decision that she would be a doctor was taken for granted, from an early age she knew about it. She and her husband have two children (their grandparents helped with childcare). She specialises in paediatrics, and has been in continuous employment although she would work part-time, ideally three days a week, if she could. She thinks that women are responsible for housework and does her own, although her husband will help if he is asked.

On women's role: "*I think that women can be happy only within the family, any kind of family, otherwise why is it that only women have children? It is her predestination, to live for her family and her husband [...] I do not believe in happiness for a woman without a family, it means she has got no past. Career is just for a while. But then, what has she lived for?*"

3.7 Conclusion

Here we will return, in the light of the evidence reviewed in this chapter, to the questions raised in the introduction. First, the possibility of occupational androgyny: there has always been occupational segregation within the middle classes, as well as at the lower levels of the occupational structure. Educated women have, historically, been concentrated in occupations such as teaching, nursing, and social work, occupations which require professional qualifications but which by convention have not been regarded as having the same status as professions such as law and medicine. There seem to be clear indications that this gender segregation will persist, and the increase of women in 'middle class' occupations will not be evenly distributed. A process of gendered restructuring is taking place even as women move into higher level occupations within the middle classes. More women are going into medicine, but the extent of internal segregation within the medical profession is extensive, and women tend to cluster in 'female' or 'family friendly' specialties (Crompton and Le Feuvre, 1997). More women are moving into management, and male-dominated occupations such as engineering, but again, they tend to cluster in niches which require professional and technical expertise, rather than the wielding of organisational power (Devine 1992; Savage, 1992; Evetts, 1994). Because expertise can be delivered in flexible tranches, such jobs often prove to have 'family-friendly' hours as well.

These trends, it should be emphasised again, are not new. As has been noted above, Savage et al. (1992) have already argued that in contrast to men, women tend to draw upon cultural/educational assets in gaining middle class positions, rather than property or oganisational assets. However, our in-depth analysis of the linkages between particular occupations and characteristic domestic divisions of labour suggests that women who take the cultural assets route may also be characterised by relatively stereotypical work-life biographies as far as the domestic division of labour is concerned. Although the women doctors may be pioneers in that they are moving into previously male dominated occupations, requiring long and arduous training, the particular accommodation of work and family life they achieve may not give rise to substantial amendments to the gendered *status quo*. In contrast, women using their strategic and political resources in order to enter managerial positions within retail banking have been more likely to have had less gender stereotypical biographies.

Finally: women are moving into male-dominated middle-class occupations which have been held to embody 'masculine' characteristics. It has been suggested that a 'transformation from within' of these occupations might be possible in consequence (Davies, 1996). However, our examination of the interaction between men's and women's market and domestic work, an approach which has been emphasised in earlier debates within second-wave feminism (Stacey, 1981) suggests that the pace of any change will only be gradual.

Notes

1 A further debate which is not relevant to this chapter is the 'unit of analysis' problem: that is, whether the woman's 'class' should be measured by her family or occupation, see Crompton, 1993.

2 One exception to this generalisation would be empirical research on the domestic division of labour, see Gershuny et al., 1995. For a recent statement of the interdependence of paid and unpaid work, see Glucksmann, 1995.

3 In terms of Crompton, 1996, this strategy combines options i and ii. (p. 73). A criticism of Jordan et al..'s study would be that their selection of respondents did not tap in to the heterogeneity of middle class family strategies.

4 The research (Gender Relations and Employment: a Cross-National study) is funded by the ESRC (R000235617), the British Council, and the University of Bergen. Interviews have been carried out by Elena Mezentseva, Irina Aristakheva, Prof Marie Cermakova, Dr Irena Hradecka, Dr Jaroslava Stastna, Dr Gunn Birkelund, Merete Helle, Rosemary Crompton and Fiona Harris.

5 Besides comparability and cost, another methodological consideration informing the research design derived from the nature of the phenomenon under investigation. Gender relations are structured at all levels of society, thus their investigation requires research at the macro (national) meso (occupational) and micro (individual) levels. Besides the occupational and interview material which is discussed in this chapter, aggregate national information has been compiled from census data etc., and we also have access to the International Social Survey gender and family relations module for Britain, Norway and the Czech Republic.

6 As we have stressed in our methodology section, the emphasis of the data collection was qualitative, rather than quantitative. We have adopted the strategy of coding of results and associated statistical tests as an economical way of presenting our research findings.

7 In Britain, General Practice Principals are in fact self employed, although their income largely derives from the NHS.

8 The point may be made that this generalisation is valid only for the West, as part-time work was/is virtually unknown in Eastern Europe. However, our interviews suggest that considerable latitude was given to the mothers of small children - taking time off when they were sick, leaving early to collect them from school. Indeed, it was suggested that 'marketisation' was going to make the combination of work and childcare more difficult, as these practices were likely to disappear.

9 For example, there is now much more of an emphasis upon the selling of financial services in the West. Changes in the East have been even greater with the coming of marketisation.

10 These biographies have, of course, been selected in order to illustrate the contrast between the two occupations. However, although many bankers were without children this is not reflected in our selection. This is because amongst the bankers, the presence of children in the household best illustrates moves beyond 'satisficing', i.e. the re-negotiation of the domestic division of labour, and/or the change to another partner.

References

Beck, U. (1992) *Risk Society: Towards a New Modernity,* London.

Brunetta, G. (1993) The role of women in the post-industrial economy, in: D. Noin and R. Woods (eds) *The Changing Population of Europe,* Oxford.

Burrage, M., and R.Torstendahl (1990) *Professions in theory and History,* London.

Chafetz, J. S., and J. Hagan (1966) The Gender Division of Labor and Family Change in Industrial Societies: A Theoretical Accounting, *Journal of Contemporary Family Studies,* vol. 27, 2, pp. 187-219.

Craib, I. (1987) Masculinity and male dominance, in: *Sociological Review,* pp. 721-743.

Crompton, R. (1993) *Class and Stratification,* Cambridge.

Crompton, R. (1995) Women's employment and the 'middle classes', in: M. Savage and T. Butler (eds) *Social Change and the Middle Classes,* London.

Crompton, R., and M. Mann (eds) (1986) *Gender and Stratification,* Cambridge, 2nd edition.

Crompton, R., and N. LeFeuvre (1997) *The feminisation of the professions liberales, theoretical and empirical implications,* Seminar, The restructuring of gender relations and employment, University of Bergen.

Davies, C. (1996) The sociology of the professions and the profession of gender, *Sociology* vol. 30, 4, pp. 661-678.

Devine, F. (1992) Gender segregation in the engineering and science professions, *Work Employment and Society,* vol. 6, pp. 557-75.

Evetts, J. (1994) Women and career in engineering, *Work Employment and Society,* vol. 8, pp. 101-112.

Finlayson, L., R. Ford, and A. Marsh (1996) Paying more for child care, *Employment Gazette,* July, pp. 295-303.

Gershuny, J., M. Godwin, and S. Jones (1994) The Domestic Labour Revolution: a Process of Lagged Adaptation, in: M. Anderson, F. Bechhofer and J. Gershuny (eds) *The Social and Political Economy of the Household,* Oxford.

Giddens, A. (1992) *The transformation of intimacy,* Cambridge.

Glucksmann, M. (1995) Why "work"? Gender and the Total Social Organisation of Labour, *Gender Work and Organisation,* vol. 2, 2, pp. 63-75.

Gorz, A. (1989) *Critique of economic reason,* London.

Gregson, N., and M.Lowe (1995) Too much work? Class, gender and the reconstitution of middle-class domestic

labour, in: Savage and Butler (eds), *Social Change and the Middle Class*, London.
Hakim, C. (1992) Explaining Trends in Occupational Segregation: The Measurement, Causes, and Consequences of the Sexual Division of Labour, *European Sociological Review*, vol. 8, 2, pp. 127-152.
Harrop, A., and P. Moss (1994) Working parents: trends in the 1980s, *Employment Gazette*, pp. 343-351.
Hochschild, A. (1990) *The second shift*, London.
Jordan, B., M. Redley, and S. James (1994) *Putting the family first*, London.
Kanter, R (1986) The reshaping of middle management, *Management Review*, January, pp. 19-20.
Massey, D. (1995) Reflections on gender and geography, in: Savage and Butler (eds) *Social Change and the Middle Class*, London.
Molyneux, M. (1979) Beyond the domestic labour debate, *New Left Review*, vol. 116, pp. 3-27.
Pahl, R. (1995) *After Success*, Cambridge.
Parsons, T. (1954) The Professions and Social Structure, in: *Essays in Sociological Theory*, New York.
Rubery, J. and C. Fagan (1993) *Occupational Segregation of Women and Men in the European Community*, Social Europe supplement 3/93, Luxembourg.
Savage, M. (1992) Women's Expertise, Men's Authority, in: M. Savage and A. Witz (eds) *Gender and Bureaucracy*, Oxford.
Savage. M. (1995) Class analysis and social research, in: Savage and Butler (eds) *Social Change and the Middle Class*, London.
Savage, M., A. Dickens, and T. Fielding, (1992) *Property, Bureaucracy and Culture, Middle Class Formation in Contemporary Britain*, London.
Scott, A. McEwen (ed) (1994) *Gender segregation and social change*, Oxford.
Sporton, D. (1993) Fertility: the lowest level in the world, in: D. Noin and R. Woods (eds), op cit.
Stacey, M. (1981) The Division of Labour Revisited, in: P Abrams (ed) *Practice and Progress, British Sociology 1950-1980*, London.
Wajcman, J. (1996) The domestic basis for the managerial career, *Sociological Review*, vol. 44, 4, pp. 609-629.
Witz, A. (1992) *Professions and Patriarchy*, London.

4
Social Exclusion and Increasing Uncertainty of the Middle Classes: The West German Case

MARTIN KRONAUER

4.1 Introduction

Is there a connection between high unemployment, social exclusion, and the growing uncertainty of the middle classes in Germany? There is no easy answer to this question. First of all, while unemployment has been on the rise in Germany since the seventies, there was little middle-class concern about it until very recently. Something seems to have changed in the relation between unemployment and the middle classes, but what is it? Secondly, the concept of 'social exclusion' is not widely used in Germany (unlike in France), either in public or in the social sciences. It has become more prominent in the discussion only in the last two years, and there is still much confusion about its meaning. In what sense, if at all, does unemployment in Germany lead to social exclusion? And even if an agreement is reached upon what 'social exclusion' as a result of unemployment in Germany means, there still remains the question of whether social exclusion and middle-class uncertainty are linked.

In the following, I propose some answers to these questions by first approaching them separately and then trying to link them together. I will begin with middle-class uncertainty in Germany today and discuss why unemployment did not raise much middle-class concern before the 1990s. I will then turn to social exclusion resulting from unemployment, make some conceptual suggestions, and present empirical evidence. Finally, I will argue that in the mid-nineties a new nexus between unemployment, exclusion and middle-class uncertainty emerged which will have far-reaching consequences for German society. For pragmatic reasons, I will concentrate on the case of West Germany since there are still enormous differences between the East and the West in the quantity and quality of unemployment as well as in the social character and self-perception of the middle classes.

4.2 Middle-Class Uncertainty

On September 13, 1996, the German weekly 'Die Zeit' came out with the frontpage headline 'Die Angst vor dem Abstieg' (The fear of decline). The subtitle read: 'When

B. Steijn et al. (eds.), Economic Restructuring and the Growing Uncertainty of the Middle Class, 61-71.
© 1998 *Kluwer Academic Publishers.*

profits grow and jobs disappear'. With the same issue, the chapter started a series of chapters called 'The meager years: Decline in Germany', and the weekly publication of results of a representative survey on the effects of unemployment on the daily lives and expectations of Germans.

This media event is in itself a significant indicator of a *growing uncertainty of the middle class.* The prestigious 'Zeit' addresses mainly an academic and professional readership, and some of the chapters in the series articulated the particular fears of this audience. In reporting, for instance, about downsizing at the largest German bank or the problems of young academics trying to establish their careers, they picked upon experiences which are ever more common in Germany today. 'Die Zeit' did not remain alone in its coverage of the topic. The more popular magazine 'Der Stern' followed suit with even stronger words: 'Angst vor dem Absturz' (Fear of crashing down); "One quarter of the population will no longer be able to maintain its standard of living." And the frontpage announced 'Angriff auf die Mittelschicht' (Attack against the middle class) (Der Stern, febr.13, 1997).

So far, however, the evidence of insecurity among the German population is still quite inconclusive. According to a 1996 'Zeit' survey, the vast majority considered the economic situation in general to be not so good or even bad. At the same time, however, about three quarters viewed their own financial situation as positive. In this respect more people (38 %) saw improvement over the last years than a deterioration (25 %). Nevertheless, the vast majority also reported having to cut down at least to some extent on expenditures. And looking into the future, most people were worried about their financial situation at retirement age (Die Zeit, Sept. 27, 1996: 33-38).

What these survey findings indicate is a critical point in the development of people's sense of security. There is a gap between a sense of individual well being and the perception of overall economic development, as well as between the perception of one's own present financial situation and one's expectations for the future. This suggests that it is not so much an *actual* social decline that worries most Germans, but the *potentiality* of social decline in the future.

To acquire a more differentiated picture of how worries grow and are distributed among different employment-status groups we can draw upon longitudinal survey data on the development of welfare in Germany published by the Wissenschaftszentrum Berlin (Berlin Science Center). According to those data, the overall number of West Germans stating 'profound worries' about their economic situation had increased from 1990 to 1994 by 5% to 18%. However, the survey shows a considerable class divide. Among the employed, anxiety was most widespread and expressed to an average degree among the working-class population, particularly the un- and semiskilled. In the various categories of the middle class (managers, skilled and higher skilled white-collar workers and professionals, and lower-skilled white-collar workers), on the other hand, they were far less pronounced in their worries, except for the quite heterogeneous category of the 'self employed' which includes the small scale shop keeper as well as the dentist and the large-scale entrepreneur. Economic fears had grown markedly in the higher ranks of the white-collar middle class, but were still below average (see Bulmahn, 1996: p. 34, 46).

No doubt, there is a growing sense of insecurity in the German population in the mid-nineties, but judging from the surveys it is, in most cases, still more prospective in character than nourished by an already experienced social decline, and it is, likewise, still more strongly represented in the working class than in the middle classes. It is no surprise that one group sharply deviates from the average: Almost half of the unemployed, according to Bulmahn, stated that they had substantial economic worries.

Turning from perceptions to living conditions of the middle classes, there are actually not many signs of decline up to the early nineties. Between 1970 and 1989, real household income per capita increased for all the main employment-status groups in West Germany, although not uniformly across groups. Income inequality as measured by household quintiles remained fairly stable with the 'bottom' sixty percent even making some gains in that period (see Geißler, 1996: p. 47, 61). Using the ratio of real household income per capita to the average income, as another measure of income distribution, it can be seen that the quintessential middle-class category, the self-employed ('Selbständige'), were actually the big winners of the eighties, their success story being only briefly interrupted by the recession of the early nineties. This category benefited most from the considerable redistribution of incomes by means of taxation in tge last decade. White-collar workers and civil servants maintained their relative income positions, and so did blue-collar workers until the early nineties when they began to suffer a drop in relative income as well as in real wages. Hardest hit in terms of their relative income position were the unemployed with a steady decline since the mid-seventies, the time when mass unemployment again became a problem in West Germany (see Schäfer, 1995: 620 ff).

I am aware that these are only very rough indicators. They are strong enough, however, to contrast starkly with data from the country in which the crisis of the middle classes has for many years been source of growing public and political concern and a hotly debated issue, the USA. Here the income inequality of households as measured by quintiles has markedly increased since the early seventies. While the top 20% were able to enlarge their share of the total household income considerably, the great majority either stagnated or (as happened to the bottom 60%) actually lost ground (see Danziger and Gottschalk, 1995: 42). But even more significant in terms of middle-class decline is the drop in real income of 80% of the full-time working males in the same period. An increase in working hours and real wages of women partially offset the income loss on the household level. But it could not fend off the decline in real household income for the majority of the population (see Thurow, 1996: 23).

It is reasonable to conclude, as was underlined by the comparison to the US, that up to the early nineties the vast majority of West Germans enjoyed a considerable prosperity even though unemployment increased sharply in the first half of the eighties and since has established itself at a much higher level than it ever was in the seventies. Pointedly speaking, one could say that a *double reality* has emerged in West Germany in the eighties. For the seventy percent of the West German working population who were more or less firmly entrenched in the employment system and did not experience any unemployment, the rules of class compromise ('social partnership') inside the firms, of collective bargaining on the regional level, and of welfare state protection, for which Germany has internationally been acclaimed as a 'model', worked fairly well. Uncertainty was more or less confined to those exposed to the threat and reality of unemployment, and here again the hardest hit were not the members of the middle classes but the most vulnerable segments of the working class. Cynically speaking, one could even say that high unemployment was a means of protecting those inside the employment system from giving up too much of their own security. West Germany in the eighties did not follow the neo-liberal path, as the UK did, of creating jobs by smashing the unions, lowering wages, and eroding the financial basis of the lower middle classes. But it also did not pursue a public employment policy by raising taxes to create more well paying jobs. The principle of monetary conservatism, a hallmark of German policy, guided the actions, again primarily to the benefit of the higher income strata. In short, exclusion on the labour market in Germany was much less a threat to the middle classes than a way of handling the employment crisis by protecting them. Things changed, however, in the nineties. Before discussing these changes, I will briefly consider the notions and realities of exclusion on the labour market and social exclusion in West Germany.

4.3 Exclusion on the Labour Market

In 1982, unemployment in West Germany crossed the 2 million mark, for the first time in more than thirty years. Except for the three years after unification when West Germany benefited from the opening up of the market in the East, it has not fallen below that line since. Meanwhile unemployment has reached post-war record hights. In April 1997, more than 3 million men and women in West Germany and more than 1.3 million in East Germany were registered as out of work. This amounts to unemployment rates of 11% in the West, 19% in the East, and 13% for the nation (the unemployment rates measured against the civil workforce without the self-employed).

Rising unemployment indicates that the West German 'model' of post-war capitalism has been subjected to increasing pressure. It was based on export-oriented quality production in industry, and its success was generated by a comparatively well paid and highly qualified workforce, an educational system that provided the necessary qualifications, and a considerable degree of social stability secured by intermediary, legally protected institutions of collective bargaining, and the employment-related provisions of a highly developed welfare state. But speaking about the German 'model' of capitalism also requires keeping in mind that it has always been characterised by policies of reducing the workforce participation of particular social groups. The era of relative full employment was, in fact, based on a low participation rate of women; compare Germany for example to the Scandinavian countries with their high rate of women in public employment on the one hand, and the US with a high participation rate of women in full-time private employment on the other. According to OECD statistics, the employment rate of women (as measured against the female population age 15 to 64, and including the unemployed) increased in West Germany from 48% in 1970 to only 58% in 1989, compared to an increase from 59% to 81% in Sweden and from 49% to 68% in the US (Häußermann and Siebel, 1995: 55). More forcefully than in other highly developed industrial societies, women in West Germany are relegated to work in and for the family, and this tenet of political conservatism is positively supported by taxation laws favouring the male-breadwinner household, and negatively influenced by a lack of institutions which could enable women to combine child rearing and employment. Since the seventies, generous early-retirement schemes also induced older workers to leave employment and make room for the young. This policy of restricting the supply of labour rather than creating work by public initiative is very much in tune with the overarching interest of all German governments in monetary stability, an interest which has also been enforced by the strong position of the Federal Bank (see Esping-Andersen 1990: 169 ff, 185 ff).

Pressure on the 'model' has been building since the eighties and different sources contribute to it. International competitors (e.g., in the automobile and machine-tool industries, two strongholds of German export) improved the quality of their products while still producing at lower costs. Volatile and unfavourable exchange rates further impede exports and stimulate firms to relocate their plants abroad. At the same time, West German industry has encountered considerable difficulties in establishing itself with innovative products in expanding markets such as the semiconductor, computer market, and telecommunications. In short, while incentives to increase labour productivity are present and growing, there are few promising new fields of private or public employment opening up together. Both tendencies result in high unemployment.

Unemployment in West Germany is at the same time a highly dynamic and a ominously constant affair Since the mid-eighties, a high turnover in the unemployed population has been accompanied by a hardening of long-term and extreme long-term unemployment. As a short-term experience, unemployment reaches into ever larger segments of the population, including segments of the middle class. As a long-term or even permanent experience, it strikes primarily the most vulnerable individuals on the West German labour market, i.e., workers older than 45, un- and semiskilled workers, and women.

To speak of 'exclusion' in the context of unemployment requires some clarifications, since the notion is so contentious. I suggest that a distinction has to be made between (1) the statistical category of long-term unemployment; (2) the concept of exclusion on the labour market; and (3) the concept of social exclusion.

The statistical category *long-term unemployment*, i.e., unemployment which lasts longer than one year, is a first, important indicator of the problems people face re-entering employment. It is also an important indicator of financial hardships, since in Germany most unemployed people lose their eligibility for unemployment insurance benefits after one year, and their income declines to the even lower level of unemployment aid, given they do not lose their unemployment support altogether because of shared income with a spouse. However, this indicator does not make it clear how long unemployment actually lasts, and what happens afterwards, whether people are able to find gainful employment again or not. Long-term unemployment does not necessarily mean definite exclusion from employment.

Looking at this first indicator, a sharp rise in long-term unemployment can be seen in the first half of the eighties, followed by a small decrease in the early nineties, and a subsequent climb up to an even higher plateau than had been reached in the eighties. One significant reaction on the part of the federal bureaucracy was to change the criteria for measuring the duration of unemployment in 1985. As a result, the official figures are grossly misleading from that point on. Serious estimates suggest that those figures have to be increased by about 40% to provide an approximately realistic picture (see Wagner, 1995: 753). In September 1996, the last date for which official figures exist, this would amount to more than 1.26 million long-term unemployed out of a 2.7 million in West Germany alltogether.

The concept of *exclusion on the labour market* will be reserved for those social constellations in and by which people are definitely locked out of employment, or have only slight a chance of ever (re)gaining it. In this respect, a particularly important change took place in West Germany during the eighties. As I pointed out, exclusion from the labour market is nothing new in post-war Germany and has in fact always been a characteristic feature of the West German welfare state. The new quality in the eighties consists of a change in its social form. For the first time, exclusion on the labour market does not merely happen in the socially protected forms of early retirement or of women kept in their families, but to a large and increasing extent in the form of unemployment.

Exclusion on the labour market by unemployment is not quite as easy to measure as long-term unemployment. We have to rely on predictions based on probability. One fairly strong, but also conservative indicator is extreme long-term unemployment, i.e., unemployment lasting longer than two years. In a study which we conducted in the late eighties in a region with high unemployment in Lower Saxony, only 10% of all unemployed men who had been out of work for more than two years on the first date of inquiry had found employment eighteen months later, two thirds were still unemployed (see Kronauer et al., 1993: 68-76). Other studies in West Germany as well as in France confirmed the sharp decrease in chances on the labour market after two years of unemployment. It is, of course, a conservative indicator, because the factors which determine a high risk of labour-market exclusion are at work from the very beginning of unemployment, and only became clearly apparent after a longer period of time.

Exclusion on the labour market by unemployment turns from a mere probability to a definite social reality for the individuals themselves when they decide to give up their own efforts to find regular employment. Here again, the two years of unemployment proved to be an important turning point. Most unemployed men at that point ceased their own search for a job, and only went to the employment agency because they had to do so in order to keep their benefits. Women tended to retreat even earlier.

In looking only at this conservative indicator (extreme long-term unemployment), it is observed that labour-market exclusion as a result of unemployment first appeared in West Germany to a relevant degree in the mid-eighties. It is also grossly underestimated in the official statistics, this time by at least 50% (see Kronauer, 1995: 203 ff). Increasing the official figures by this margin indicates that in September 1996 more than half of the long-term unemployed, and a quarter of all unemployed in West Germany (in absolute numbers about 680.000 people) had been out of work for such a long time that they barely had any chance to reenter employment again.

One important question remains to be answered: Where do people go, sociologically speaking, when they are forced to retreat from the labour market? Here, the important distinction between 'exclusion on the labour market' and 'social exclusion' becomes relevant. Exclusion on the labour market, even as a result of unemployment, does not necessarily also lead into social isolation. For some people, society still provides a status alternative to employment which at least protects them from stigmatisation. Women can still take on the role of a housewife, even if they do not like it but are forced to do so, while their husbands earn enough money. And some older unemployed individuals manage to organise their circumstances as a kind of transitional stage into retirement, particularly when they have the material means. To be sure, whenever people are forced to retreat from employment against their will, they are victims of social inequality. But this does not in every case imply being and feeling excluded from society at large. Social exclusion is a particular, extreme, form of social inequality, but not every kind of social decline and social inequality can be meaningfully termed social exclusion.

With, however, the extremely long-term unemployed becoming ever younger and the period of unemployment longer, and with an increasing number of unemployed single women and single mothers, ever more people are lacking any protection by a socially accepted status alternative. Since those status alternatives, as a rule, are also at least to some extent financially rewarded (the married woman in Germany, for instance, benefits from taxation rules that support married couples, and retires with early retirement provisions receive pensions which are at least higher and less stigmatised than unemployment benefits), the people who are bereft of status protection are also confronted with particularly strong financial stress. For them, *exclusion on the labour market and social exclusion coincide* (for a more detailed discussion of the category 'social exclusion', see Kronauer, 1997).

Of course the distinctions suggested here have implications for sociological inquiry. Social exclusion by unemployment can no longer be detected by looking at statistics alone. It is equally important to get in touch with the people themselves and to listen to them. This has actually been the basis of our study on unemployment in two small West German towns (see Kronauer et al., 1993). In a combined quantitative and qualitative approach, the new reality of permanent unemployment became visible.

After two years of unemployment and many fruitless efforts to find employment again, most of the men (the majority is the ages of 45-55) had retreated from the search for a regular job. This step signalled both realism and a need to protect themselves from further painful disappointment. But it also implied that unemployment had become a definite and permanent reality in their lives. For all of them, it had far-reaching consequences: firstly, it meant living in severely restricted financial and material circumstances. Secondly, it meant being dependent one way or another on unemployment benefits or public assistance, without any hope of changing this situation in the foreseeable future by one's own action. Thirdly, it implied a more or less pronounced awareness of no longer being a part of a society which was centered on employment and money. The traditional workers' perception of society, us on the bottom and, them on the top, had been replaced by an inside-outside perspective.

In trying to deal with these circumstances, some of the unemployed avoided social contact as much as possible, and retreated inwards within their restricted confines in resigned submission. Primarily this was the last resort of single men. Or they created their own 'milieus', backed by their spouses and in close contact with other unemployed, in order to more actively adapt to those conditions. In the first case social isolation takes on the form of an encapsulation of the individual, in the second, the encapsulation of the group. Whatever coping mechanism was which they attempted, all of the unemployed experienced exclusion on the labour market as social exclusion (see Kronauer et al., 1993: 172-208).

In summary, two social implications of the labour-market development in the eighties have to be stressed in looking at the three indicators together:

- Unemployment in West Germany has not only taken on a new quantitative dimension, but equally important a new social quality as well. For the first time, unemployment is deeply affecting the structure of West German society, both by increasing inequality through labour market exclusion, and by the resultant creation of a new social stratum of permanently unemployed through social exclusion.

- Even though only a small minority of the West German population is affected by long-term unemployment, exclusion on the labour market due to unemployment, and social exclusion, this has much wider implications. It drastically demonstrates that the traditional labour-market policy of keeping people out of employment by subsidizing them, no longer works; The 'surplus' population has grown too large, and the costs have become too high.

4.4 The New Link between 'Exclusion' and 'Middle-Class Uncertainty' in the Nineties

I had argued that mass unemployment in the eighties was the price paid for protecting the middle class, and also large segments of the working class, from losses in income and security. The middle class, if not outrightly benefiting from exclusion on the labour market, at least did not have to worry about it all that much. This no longer holds true in the nineties. Three important changes occurred:

- While employment in West Germany still increased during the eighties - it did not increase strongly enough to prevent rising unemployment -, in the nineties it decreased for the first time. Between 1992 and 1995, more than one million jobs were lost (see ANBA, 1996: 73). Unemployment rose sharply. The past 1989 unification process had provided West Germany with an economic boom, while other European countries were already in the downswing. As it turned out, however, West Germany was only able to postpone the recession but not avoid it.

- In an answer to recession and growing international competition, corporations not only cut production jobs but also became serious about 'lean management'. In 1990, not only workers but also managers reported to an above average degree to have 'great worries' about their employment security. However, class differences still clearly showed. While four years later the managers' worries had subsided, insecurity had spread futher among the workers, most markedly among the un- and semiskilled workers (see Bulmahn, 1996: 35, 47).

- The welfare state was beset by a deep financial crisis. The political decision by the Kohl government to cover most of the unification costs (expenses for large-scale early-retirement schemes, requalification, and unemployment benefits) using West German social insurance funds in order to avoid tax increases was, together with the rising costs of unemployment in the West, too much of a burden for the German welfare state. The greater majority of the population is now concerned about the stability of pensions. Rising contributions to the social security system no longer seem to guarantee adequate security in the future. Employers, who cover half of the social insurance charges, are complaining about rising non-wage labour costs. Increasing public debt and reductions in public employment have become another source of middle-class insecurity. It makes it harder not only for workers but ratio for college graduates to find employment which fits their qualifications (see Büchel, 1996). Hardest hit, however, are the unemployed and the poor who have suffered cuts in unemployment and welfare benefits.

In this critical situation of a deepening crisis in employment, growing financial strains on the welfare state, and increasing uncertainty in the German population, even among the middle classes, a fierce political struggle involving the basic institutions of post-war social integration has begun. Mass unemployment and exclusion on the labour market are now no longer a 'second reality', largely kept out of public attention, but have become a crucial element, if not a weapon, in this struggle. The two 'pillars' of the West German 'model' are embattled, the institutionalised rules of 'social partnership' between capital and labour on the one hand, and the provisions of the compensating welfare state on the other. Strong factions of the economically and politically dominant classes, represented by the employers' associations, but also inside the governing coalition, are pushing for deregulation and a widening of income inequality within the employment system, as well as for lowering the standards of welfare state support for the unemployed and the poor. They legitimise their offensive not only by claiming this will improve economic competitiveness, but equally by promising it will reduce unemployment and welfare-state expenditures. They present the 'American job machine' as the model to emulate. A new, double nexus threatens to emerge between mass unemployment and exclusion, on the one hand, and middle-class insecurity on the other. Exclusion on the labour market becomes an argument and lever for promoting inequality among the employed, thereby fostering an already growing uncertainty. Fear of social decline among the employed, in turn, can easily lead to increased social competition and redistributive struggles against those who are already in the weakest position on the labour market, thereby strengthening social exclusion. It is the US that currently provides the most worrisome example of a declining middle class fighting a war against the poor (see Wacquant, 1996).

Germany is now at a cross-roads. The old policies and institutional arrangements already produced new inequalities and social divisions in the eighties. For reasons given, they no longer work. But the alternative of an 'American' answer to the employment crisis, even when adapted to German circumstances, would predictably lead to even more social inequality, and increase the risk of social exclusion for the most vulnerable segments of the population. It is ironic that praise for the 'American way' is becoming ever louder while highly acclaimed economists in the US are pointing out the devastating social and economic effects of income polarisation and middle-class decline (see Reich, 1993; Thurow, 1996; Freeman, 1997). The crucial question is, therefore, whether Germany will be able to invent new policies, changing from a primarily restrictive and compensatory employment policy to a more innovative and activating one, and creating new industrial relations which bridge the growing gap between those inside and outside the employment system. Which way Germany goes will be affected strongly by the reactions of the middle classes; will they abandon the welfare-state tradition or be ready to enter new welfare-state alignments?

References

ANBA (1996) *Amtliche Nachrichten der Bundesanstalt für Arbeit. Arbeitsmarkt 1995,* Nürnberg.

Büchel, F. (1996) Der hohe Anteil an unterwertig Beschäftigten bei jüngeren Akademikern, Karrierezeitpunkt- oder Strukturwandel-Effekt?, in: *Mitteilungen aus der Arbeitsmarkt- und Berufsforschung No. 2.,* pp. 289-294.

Bulmahn, Th. (1996) Sozialstruktureller Wandel: Soziale Lagen, Erwerbsstatus, Ungleichheit und Mobilität, in: Zapf, W. and Habich, R. (eds.): *Wohlfahrtsentwicklung im vereinten Deutschland,* Berlin, pp. 25-50.

Danziger, S., and Gottschalk, P. (1995) *America Unequal,* Cambridge, MA/London.

Der Stern (1997) *Angst vor dem Absturz,* 13. Februar.

Die Zeit (1996) *Die Angst vor dem Abstieg,* September 13; *Die mageren Jahre,* September 13 and September 27.

Esping-Andersen, G. (1990) *The Three Worlds of Welfare Capitalism.*Cambridge.

Freeman, R. (1997) Immer mehr Armut - die USA auf dem Weg in eine Apartheid-Wirtschaft?, *Harvard Business Manager,* No.1, pp. 69-78.

Geißler, R. (1996) *Die Sozialstruktur Deutschlands,* Opladen.

Häußermann, H., and Siebel, W. (1995) *Dienstleistungsgesellschaften,* Frankfurt am Main.

Kronauer, M. (1995) Massenarbeitslosigkeit in Westeuropa: Die Entstehung einer neuen 'Underclass'?, in: *Soziologisches Forschungsinstitut Göttingen (ed.): Im Zeichen des Umbruchs.* Opladen, pp. 197-214.

Kronauer, M. (1997) 'Soziale Ausgrenzung' und 'Underclass' Über neue Formen der gesellschaftlichen Spaltung, *Leviathan*, Vol. 25, No.1, pp. 28-49.

Kronauer, M., Vogel, B., and Gerlach, F. (1993) *Im Schatten der Arbeitsgesellschaft*, Frankfurt am Main/New York.

Reich, R. (1993) *Die neue Weltwirtschaft, das Ende der nationalen Ökonomie*, Frankfurt am Main/Berlin.

Schäfer, C. (1995) Soziale Polarisierung bei Einkommen und Vermögen,.zur Entwicklung der Verteilung 1994, in: *WSI-Mitteilungen, No. 10*, pp. 605-633.

Thurow, L. (1996) *The Future of Capitalism*, New York/London.

Wacquant, L.D. (1996) Clinton reformiert Armut zu Elend, in: *Le monde diplomatique/die tageszeitung*, 13 september.

Wagner, A. (1995) Langzeitarbeitslosigkeit: Vielfalt der Formen und differenzierte soziale Lage, *WSI-Mitteilungen No. 12*, Düsseldorf, pp. 749-760.

5
Proletarianization of the Dutch Middle Class: Fact or Fiction?

BRAM STEIJN AND DICK HOUTMAN

5.1 Introduction

A major theme in Berting's chapter in this book is that the advent of 'middle class society', a fulfillment of the optimism of the postwar period, is accompanied by a deterioration of the socioeconomic situation of large segments of the same middle class. This means that the class position of the contemporary middle class is relatively worse than the class position of the same middle class a few decades ago. One can, therefore, say that Berting's analysis supports the concept of the proletarianization of the middle class.

The chapter by Savage shows that this argument has some validity with respect to the British middle class. Nevertheless, his analysis also shows that large parts of the British middle class did quite well in the 1980-1995 period; usually they were still doing better than members of the working class. In this chapter therefore, we will look for empirical evidence whether the class position of the Dutch middle class has worsened in recent years. By doing so, the goal is to supplement Berting's analysis and make comparisons with other countries possible.

In Section 5.2, some theoretical problems relating to the conceptualisation of 'proletarianization' in general and 'middle-class proletarianization' in particular will be discussed, which in turn will lead to the formulation of our research questions. Subsequently, in Section 5.3 the data and measurement procedures are discussed, followed by the presentation of the findings in Section 5.4. Finally, in Section 5.5, the main findings are summarized and their theoretical and social significance elaborated on.

5.2 What is 'middle class proletarianization'?

Of course, emphasizing what we mean by 'middle class proletarianization' is important at the outset of the analysis. The concept is used to refer to a process of structural economic change, which affects the economic position of the middle class, more specifically, a process that causes the economic or class position of those who are

B. Steijn et al. (eds.), Economic Restructuring and the Growing Uncertainty of the Middle Class, 73-92.
© 1998 *Kluwer Academic Publishers.*

members of the middle class to become increasingly similar to that of those who are members of the working class (Braverman, 1974; Crompton and Jones 1984; Glenn and Fieldberg, 1977; Roberts et al., 1977).

Thus, the problem of (middle class) proletarianization as studied in this chapter has nothing to do with the debate about whether or not we are witnessing a process of 'working class embourgeoisement' (e.g., Goldthorpe et al., 1969; Roberts, et al., 1977; Steijn and De Witte, 1992; De Witte, 1994). Whereas the latter process refers to a gradual erosion of traditional working class value-patterns and lifestyles, the former refers to changes within society's economic structure. To frame the distinction in well-known Marxist terminology: while 'proletarianization' refers to changes in society's *Unterbau*, 'embourgeoisement' refers to a changing relationship between this *Unterbau* and society's *Ueberbau*. In this respect, our assessment of the empirical validity of the thesis of middle class proletarianization has no implications for the thesis of working class embourgeoisement. Both can in principle be valid (or invalid) at the same time and the empirical confirmation of one implies in no way the rejection of the other. This having been said, the crucial theoretical problem to be dealt with at this point is how to indicate validly the degree to which someone's economic position is proletarianized?

We follow Roberts et al., who have suggested three relevant indicators (1977: 124-125). In their opinion, all of these have deteriorated in case of the middle-class. They regard this as empirical evidence of the existence of a process of 'middle-class proletarianization'. First, they point at the erosion of the market advantages of some sections of the white-collar workforce. More specifically; the increasing job insecurity of members of the middle class and the decreasing differences with respect to income and fringe benefits between manual and non-manual workers. Second; they point out that middle class opportunities for career and promotion are deteriorating. Whereas in the past the market position of members of the middle class used to be characterized by good career prospects, this advantage may be withering away (compare also Berting, 1968; Steijn and de Witte, 1992). Third; and finally, they argue that the working conditions of the middle class are becoming increasingly similar to those of the working class. In our analysis the proletarianization thesis will be tested with respect to these three indicators against empirical data from the Netherlands stretching back to 1985.

Finally, another theoretical clarification is necessary: what exactly do we mean by a 'deterioration' of the economic position of the middle class? For purposes of analytical clarity, distinction is made between a 'strong' and a 'weak' version of the thesis of middle class proletarianization. The *strong version* refers to a process of *absolute proletarianization*. For this version to be empirically confirmed, a process needs to be found in which the economic position of the middle class becomes more similar to that of the working class as conceived of as an *Ideal type* in a Weberian sense. This 'ideal' working class is characterized by a weak and vulnerable labour-market position, a lack of chances to escape from this situation and adverse working conditions (compare Berting, 1995). An absolute proletarianization process implies that the position of large parts of the middle class have actually worsened on these aspects.

Despite the answer to the question whether or not such a process of absolute middle class proletarianization is actually taking place, however, the middle class might (or might not) nevertheless become more similar to the *really existing* working class, conventionally understood as the aggregate of those who are in manual jobs, in those three respects. As an absence of absolute proletarianization of the middle class leaves open the possibility that such a process of *relative proletarianization* is taking place, we wish to test this 'weak' version of the thesis of middle class proletarianization as well.

The 'weak' version of the thesis of middle class proletarianization makes its occurrence deliberately dependent upon developments within the working class. After all, when the economic position of the working class improves while that of the middle class remains basically unchanged, we are nevertheless witnessing a *relative* decline of traditional middle-class advantages. Hence, we will use the concept of relative proletarianization for these cases.

It must be stressed that in this conceptualization proletarianization explicitly refers to structural processes. Limitations of the data (see below) prevent looking at the *subjective* proletarianization, i.e., the perception by members of the middle class of (negative) changes in their position. According to Berting, an important aspect of the contemporary position of the middle class is that feelings of insecurity among members are growing. Although this subjective side of proletarianization is an important aspect, we are unfortunately not able to address it in this chapter.

As Berting also points out, there is no such thing as 'one' homogeneous middle class. This circumstance is taken into account by means of two strategies. First, by compressing the well-known EGP class scheme, a distinction is made between a 'higher' and a 'lower' middle class, both of which are compared with the working class. Second, heterogeneity prevails; even within those three relatively crude classes in particular with respect to non-class cleavages such as age and gender, but also with respect to economic sector (either government or private sector). Obviously, these distinctions within classes also have to be taken into account, if we want to find out whether certain categories on the labour market are more susceptible to proletarianization than others. Crompton, for instance, points out that proletarianization is a highly 'gendered' process: it strikes women far more often than men (Crompton and Jones, 1984; Crompton, this volume). A similar line of reasoning applies to age. As labour laws and institutional arrangements within companies and industries tend to offer the most protection to those employees who have been working for a longer period, relative newcomers are more likely to fall victim to processes of economic restructuration. For an extensive discussion of this vulnerable position of the young the reader is referred to the chapter by Suarez, Moreno, and Serrano Pascual in this volume. Finally, it is necessary to take the economic sector into account. Savage (this volume) points out that governmental budget cuts have particularly hit those professional groups that are strongly dependent upon the state.

It has already been mentioned briefly that we want to study changes on the Dutch labour market since 1985. It is, therefore, time to pose the exact research questions which are to be dealt with explicitly in this chapter. There are three of them. First, are there any indications of a process of middle class proletarianization, in either an absolute or a relative sense? Second, are there any indications that women, the young, and/or civil servants take up more proletarianized positions than men, the elderly, and/or those employed within the private sector? Third, and to the extent the second question is answered affirmatively, are there any indications that the economic position of these categories has deteriorated since 1985?

5.3 Data and measurement

5.3.1 Data

To test our hypotheses data were used which were provided by the *Organisatie voor Strategisch Arbeidsmarktonderzoek (OSA)* (Organization for Strategic Labour Market Research), a publicly sponsored organization.[1] Every two years about 4000 people are interviewed. This survey is designed as a panelstudy, with the basic objective of maintaining a panel that is representative of the Dutch labour force. Consequently, those who are unable to participate in a new round of the survey (e.g., because of retirement) are replaced by people with (almost) the same characteristics.[2]

Part of the survey is standardized, which means that some questions (especially those about the current job) are asked in every survey. Another part contains questions that vary from survey to survey. With respect to our research questions, the survey contains a substantial amount of relevant material. Moreover, the fact that these surveys have been held since 1985 makes it possible to look for trends. Unfortunately, however, we cannot go back further than 1985.

In this chapter, three OSA-surveys were used: those of 1985, 1990 and 1994.[3] In principle, the analysis was limited to respondents with a paid job, which means that we will not include the self-employed, students, people who are involuntarily unemployed, etc. The last two categories have been skipped because we cannot determine whether or not they occupy a middle class position. The first category (the self employed) has been left out, because it cannot be compared with the other categories with respect to the three main dependent variables (labour market position, career opportunities, and working conditions). For comparison with the chapters on Spain and Greece, however, it is important to note that in each year only about 7% of the employed population in the Netherlands is self-employed. In the Netherlands, like in Germany or Britain, the composition of the middle class is totally different from southern European countries like Spain or Greece.

Students and self-employed were also excluded in the analysis of the survey data from 1990 and 1994. Those who were involuntary unemployed in 1994, however, were included in one of our analysis, because unemployed people in 1994 could have had a job in 1985 or 1990 (see below).

5.3.2 Measurement

Class position

In this section we will discuss the measurement of the concepts that are relevant for our analysis. Class positions of individuals were determined by means of the widely-used EGP class scheme (Goldthorpe, 1980; Erikson and Goldthorpe, 1992). There are several versions of this class scheme. Our starting point was the version that distinguishes between eight classes: the higher (I) and lower controllers (II), both composed of managers, professionals, and administrators; routine non-manual labour (III); the self-employed (IV); manual supervisors (V); skilled manual workers (VI); semi/unskilled workers (VIIa); and agricultural workers (VIIb). Although one can question the exact conceptualization and measurement of class in this scheme (Crompton, 1993; Steijn and De Witte, 1994), its wide use makes comparison with other research possible.

The full scheme was not used in our analyses. As mentioned above, the self-employed (class IV) were left out. Moreover, we also excluded farm workers (class VIIb), because these workers have a very particular (non-industrial) class position. The analyses were therefore limited to workers in paid employment, and working in the secondary, tertiary or quartiairy sector of the economy. Consequently, the analysis for 1985 contained 2277 respondents, for 1990 2660 respondents, and for 1994 2749 respondents.[4]

Table 5.1 gives information about the distribution of our respondents in paid employment among these classes.

Table 5.1
Distribution of respondents among classes in 1985, 1990, and 1994 (in %)

	1985	1990	1994
higher controllers (EGP I)	8.8	7.2	9.2
lower controllers (EGP II)	22.9	23.9	26.8
routine non-manual workers (EGP III)	29.3	29.9	27.7
manual supervisors (EGP V)	2.3	2.2	3.0
skilled manual workers (EGP VI)	15.3	15.8	14.1
semi/unskilled manual workers (EGP VIIa)	22.4	21.1	19.2

In most of the analyses presented in this chapter, further restrictions were made by compressing the class positions distinguished in Table 5.1 into a threefold version of the EGP class scheme (Erikson and Goldthorpe, 1992: 45-46). In this version, the higher and lower controllers together form the 'service class', the routine non-manual workers and the foremen/supervisors form the 'intermediate class', and the skilled manual workers and semi/unskilled workers are grouped together as the 'working class'. Goldthorpe introduced the concept of the 'service class' to define 'higher' occupational groupings such as professional, administrative and managerial employees, who share a common 'service relationship' with their employer. Members of the service class render services to their organization in return for such compensation as career prospects, employment security, etc. (Goldthorpe, 1995: 315). This is a debatable issue (Savage, 1995: De Graaf and Steijn, 1996), but it suffices here to say that this service class can be seen as a 'higher' middle class. At the same time, the intermediate class can be seen as a 'lower' middle class.

Of course, this collapsing of the EGP class scheme into a threefold scheme is only relevant for our 'weak' test of the proletarianization thesis. In the 'absolute' version of the thesis (which in fact involves a stronger test of the thesis), a non-existing 'ideal-typical' working class is used for comparison. One can discuss whether this collapsed threefold class scheme is the best instrument with respect to the degree of relative proletarianization of the middle class. Of course, one can also choose to use a twofold (middle class vs, working class) or a fourfold (with a higher and lower working class) scheme. It is clear that, in the end, the exact choice is always somewhat arbitrary. Our main reasons for our choice for a threefold version is that this fits theoretically with the way the EGP scheme is used in the literature. It is more or less a normal procedure to use this version.

This said, it must be stressed that conclusions about relative proletarianization will always be arbitrary. It is probably true that (relative) proletarianization of (a part of) the middle class can more easily be determined if more classes are discerned. A twofold version, in our view, does not sufficiently take into account the existing heterogeneity of the middle class. When using a more elaborate scheme, with more working classes, the chances are greatly increased that some parts of the middle class will be seen to be worse off than parts of the working class (and hence be judged to be proletarianized). Recognizing the arbitrariness of our decision, the threefold version was used as a strong test of the proletarianization thesis was intended.

Defined in this way, Table 5.1 underscores Berting's remark that the majority of the (working) population belongs to the middle class. It also shows that even in the short period from 1985 to 1994, the number of the working class in the panel declined (excluding the self-employed, from 37.7% in 1985 to 33.3% in 1994).

Labour market position

The labour market position is one of the three aspects of the economic position of the middle class considered in this chapter. Three separate indicators were used: income, type of labour contract, and the risk of becoming unemployed.

Income is measured by means of the net yearly personal income of the respondents. The mean income and standard deviation for each of the three years under consideration were fl. 22,177 and fl. 10,465 (1985), fl. 25.065 and fl. 12.452 (1990), and fl 28.901 and fl. 15.245 (1994). Of course, in our analysis we controlled for the weekly number of working hours.

With respect to the *type of labour contract* a distinction was made between those with a permanent and those with a flexible contract (i.e., a temporary contract, employment through a temping agency or as a standby worker). The percentage of flexible workers in each year was: 10.4 (1985), 12.2 (1990), and 11.4 (1994).

The *risk of becoming unemployed* provides a more direct indication of one's job security. To determine this risk, we combined the samples of 1990 and 1994, which yielded a matched sample containing 1312 respondents. Next, we determined whether respondents who held a paid job in 1990 had become unemployed in the period between September 1992 and September 1994.[5] The crucial empirical question with respect to middle class proletarianization in this case was whether or not a relationship existed between class position in 1990 and having been hit by unemployment during the aforementioned period of two years.

Career opportunities

Career opportunities were measured by means of a similar logic as the risk of becoming unemployed. In 1990 and 1994, respondents were asked whether or not their job was the same as two years before. If not, they were asked why they had moved to another job.[6] 'Because this new job implies promotion', was one possible answer to this question. Obviously, this particular answer indicates upward mobility. Once again, the 1990 and 1994 samples were matched. The matched sample was used to assess the relationship between class position in 1990 and upward mobility in the 1990-1994 period.

Working conditions

The working conditions of our respondents constitute the third indicator for the degree to which one's job has a 'proletarian' character. In each of the three years under consideration, the respondents were asked about different aspects of their working conditions. Unfortunately, however, only two useful indicators for the working conditions remain, because most (wordings of) questions differ among the three samples. They are, the degree of autonomy and the degree of monotony. Each of those indicators has been dichotomized.

Age, gender, and economic sector

The operationalisation of *age and gender* is, of course, quite straightforward. We dichotomized age in such a way as to create a distinction between those 30 years of age or younger on the one hand and those older than 30 on the other. The percentages of 'young' respondents in each of the three years under consideration were 37.1% (1985), 43.1% (1990), and 29.2% (1994).[7] The percentages of male respondents in each year were 65.4% (1985), 63.3% (1990), and 59.5% (1994).[8]

Finally, how was the *economic sector* measured? The questionnaire contained a question in which respondents could indicate whether they worked in the public or in the private sector. In the three years under consideration, the percentages of those working in the public sector were 38.7% (1985), 30.2% (1990), and 20.2% (1994).[9]

5.4 Results

In this section, the results of the analyses are reported. In subsequent sections, the findings are discussed with respect to the labour market position (5.4.1), career opportunities (5.4.2), and working conditions (5.4.3).

5.4.1 Labour market position

As mentioned previously, we focused on three indicators of the labour market position: income, type of labour contract and unemployment. For each of these indicators, we first report our bivariate findings concerning the (changing) relationship between class and those indicators. If necessary, these findings are elaborated with respect to differences between age groups, men and women, and economic sectors.

Income

Table 5.2 contains the (changes in the) relationship between class and income.

Table 5.2

Analysis of (co)variance: net yearly income by class in 1985, 1990, and 1994 (controlled for number of hours worked; in Dutch fl.)

Class	1985	1990	1994	% increase 1985-1994
Higher Middle Class	26.937	31.801	36.491	35.5
Lower Middle Class	20.671	23.242	26.707	29.2
Working Class	19.314	21.288	23.571	22.0
Total	22.134	25.250	29.178	31.8
eta	0.31*	0.35*	0.37*	

* = $p < 0.001$

Table 5.2 demonstrates that with respect to income the middle class has done quite well in recent years. Its average net income has increased more strongly than that of the working class. Although this is particularly true of the higher middle class, it applies to the lower middle class as well. Consequently, the association between class and income has actually increased since 1985. Those results are similar to those found for Great Britain by Savage (this volume). Obviously, those findings contradict the thesis of middle class proletarianization, both in its absolute and its relative variety.

Table 5.3 offers a multivariate elaboration of those findings. In this multivariate analysis of variance (ANOVA), the income effects of age, gender and economic sector were included as well. Although only main effects are presented in the table, we will also discuss several interaction effects, which shed light on the question whether or not some groups are more susceptible to proletarianization than others.[10]

Table 5.3
Results of multivariate analysis with income as dependent variable

	1985	1990	1994
Independent variables	**beta**	**beta**	**beta**
<u>Covariate</u>			
Number of working hours	**B = 632**	**B = 728**	**B = 304**
<u>Main effects</u>			
Class	**0.30****	**0.32****	**0.37****
Age (0 = under 31)	**0.25****	**0.26****	**0.15****
Sector (0 = public)	**-0.05****	**ns**	**ns**
Gender (0 = woman)	**0.24****	**0.24****	**0.48****
Variance explained	**59%**	**55%**	**49%**
N	**2042**	**2168**	**2459**

** $p < 0.01$

The first thing that can be observed in looking at Table 5.3, is that the beta of class in the ANOVA-analysis is similar to the eta in the bivariate analysis. Thus, age, economic sector, and gender have effects that are independent of class. Economic sector only affected income in 1985, but younger and female workers received lower incomes than older and male workers in all of the three years under consideration. The economic position of women and younger workers is thus more proletarianized than that of men and older workers. The effect of gender strongly increased during the 1990-1994 period, while that of age decreased. This means that the proletarianization of women with respect to income has increased during that period, while at the same time that of the young decreased.

Although the finding that young and female workers received lower incomes applies to all three classes, two significant interaction effects necessitate qualifications of this general finding. First, in each of the three years the interaction effects of age and class are statistically significant. The income gap among the three classes in each of the three years is less wide for the younger workers. In 1994 for instance, younger members of the higher middle class earned fl. 26,912 and younger members of the working class fl. 21,343. At the same time, in the case of the older workers, those amounts were no less than fl. 39,652 and fl. 24,577, respectively. This means that younger workers in the middle class were relatively more proletarianized than older workers. Though this gap is comparable in each of the three survey years however, this does not denote an increasing relative proletarianization of young members of the middle class.

The same holds for women. The income differences between men and women in the higher middle class are relatively smaller than in the working class. Although middle class women clearly take up a more proletarianized position than middle class

men, compared with men they are nevertheless less proletarianized than working class women. In this case this difference between working and middle class women also did not change much over the years although, as mentioned previously, the position of women in general has deteriorated since 1990.

We have already pointed out that income differences between the private and the public sector are almost non-existent. The same applies to the interaction effect of economic sector and class: in neither of the three years under consideration was it statistically significant. It can be concluded that workers in the public sector are not more proletarianized than workers in the private sector, or are they in the process of becoming so.

In summary there are no indications of a proletarianization of the middle class with respect to income - either in its absolute or its relative variety. Women and the young are the most proletarianized categories within the middle class. However, this finding equally applies to the working class. We are not dealing with a 'middle class phenomenon' here. On the contrary, it applies to the working class to an even greater extent. Those interesting differences between the middle class and the working class might be attributable to a wider institutionalization of relatively universally applied systems of job evaluation and remuneration in the former case, which tend to dampen the differences between age and gender categories. Of course, this is merely a speculative interpretation. Importantly, the proletarianized position of women with respect to income even deteriorated during the period 1990-1994, whereas it has become somewhat less pronounced in the case of the young.

Type of labour contract

With respect to the type of labour contract, the results are slightly different, as Table 5.4 shows. As it happens, differences between classes proved extremely small, and not significant at the .01 significance level.

The figures do not indicate a clear process of absolute or relative proletarianization of the middle class since 1985. Nevertheless, it is remarkable that on this indicator members of the higher and lower middle classes proved to be almost as proletarianized as members of the working class. Although we did not use data on the 1950s, 60s and 70s ourselves, the literature on class and stratification clearly shows that this has been different in the past (Lockwood, 1989 [1958]; Berting, 1968; Goldthorpe, 1995).

Table 5.4
Percentage of workers with a flexible contract by class in 1985, 1990, and 1994

Class	1985	1990	1994
Higher middle class	10.9	9.2	9.2
Lower middle class	8.8	14.0	11.6
Working class	10.7	11.7	13.1
Total	10.2	11.6	11.2
Cramer's V	0.03	0.06	0.05
N	2159	2275	2642

The multivariate analysis (not presented here) gives additional support to the finding above. In this analysis, the significant effects of class that existed in 1990 and 1994 disappeared, which underlines the conclusion that nowadays members of both middle classes have an almost equally insecure labour market position as members of the working class.

Overall the most proletarianized categories proved to be the younger and the female workers. However, this applies equally to all three classes distinguished here, which means that the proletarianized position of women and the young is not a typical middle class phenomenon.

Risk of becoming unemployed

Table 5.5 deals with the relationship between class position in 1990 on the one hand, and unemployment during the period 1992-1994 for those respondents who were interviewed in 1990 as well as in 1994.

Table 5.5
Unemployment during 1992-1994 period by class position in 1990 (in %)

	% unemployed during 1992-1994 period
Higher middle class	2.0
Lower middle class	3.8
Working class	4.5
Total	

N = 1312 Eta = 0.06 $p > 0.05$

As these data are static, we cannot determine whether there is an absolute or relative proletarianization process going on since 1985 with respect to this indicator. However, as it is known from the existing literature, in the past members of the middle class (contrary to members of the working class hardly suffered from unemployment), it makes sense to compare both middle classes with the working class (Lockwood, 1989: 55; Berting, 1968).

It can be concluded that although members of the higher and, to a lesser degree, the lower middle class do have a lower risk of becoming unemployed than members of the working class, the association between class and unemployment is extremely weak. Our multivariate (ANOVA) analysis, which adds age, gender and economic sector gives additional support to this conclusion. In this analysis (not included here), the already small differences almost disappear. Only economic sector and age proved to affect the risk of becoming unemployed. Workers in the public sector, whatever their class position, have a much lower risk of becoming unemployed than workers in the private sector. Moreover, older workers are less susceptible to unemployment than younger workers.[11] The relatively proletarianized position of those two categories on the labour market has not changed over the years; it has neither deteriorated, nor improved since 1985. The circumstance that women do not take up a more proletarianized position than men (with the risk of becoming unemployed) is the most remarkable finding. As has been seen previously after all, they are much more proletarianized with respect to income and type of labour contract.

Summing up our findings with respect to the three indicators for the labour market position, it is necessary to distinguish between income on the one hand and type of labour contract and risk of unemployment on the other. With respect to income, the middle class has evidently done quite well since 1985: there is no evidence whatsoever of a process of middle class proletarianization. As far as the other two indicators are concerned, the situation is more complex. On the one hand, there are no indications in the 1985-1994 period that the middle class became increasingly characterized by less secure and more flexible labour contracts or by an increasing risk of unemployment. This is neither the case in an absolute, nor in a relative sense (i.e., as compared with the working class). On the other hand, however, the middle class, remarkably, did not enjoy a privileged position in those respects as compared with the working class in 1985, 1990 or 1994 either. To the extent that the traditional idea about middle class advantages with respect to job security is empirically adequate, we must conclude that prior to 1985 a process of middle class proletarianization took place, which yielded a situation in which the previously advantageous position of the middle class (even of the higher middle class) had disappeared. Of course, we cannot determine whether this pre-1985 proletarianization process was absolute or relative. To establish that, more empirical research is needed.

5.4.2 Career opportunities

Table 5.6 is based on a matched sample derived from the 1990 and 1994 samples. It presents the relationships between class position in 1990 and upward mobility.

Table 5.6
Upward mobility during 1992-1994 period by class position in 1990 (in %)

	respondents who got promoted in 1992-1994 period
Higher middle class	5.6
Lower middle class	4.3
Working class	3.2
Total	4.3

N = 1312 Eta = 0.05 $p > 0.05$

There is no association between class and the likelihood of promotion. In the beginning of the 1990's therefore, the career opportunities for members of the middle class were no better than those of the working class. This finding is consistent with the aforementioned results with respect to the risk of becoming unemployed and the type of labour contract. As the existence of good career prospects has been an important characteristic of the position of the middle class in the past (Lockwood, 1958 [1989: 57]), this also indicates the existence of a relative proletarianization process in the period before 1985.

A multivariate analysis (ANOVA; table not included here) yields some interesting additional results in this respect. While the class effect remains insignificant, women (2.8%) were promoted less often than men (5.0%), and younger workers (6.6%) had better opportunities for upward mobility than older workers (3.2%). This last conclusion was true of men only, however. Finally, a significant interaction effect of age and gender was found: while younger males were promoted more often than older males (9% versus 4%), there was no such difference between younger and older women (both 3%). Again, those findings provide evidence that women take up more proletarianized positions than men.

Finally, there is a significant effect of class and economic sector. In the private sector, the likelihood of promotion is highest for members of the higher middle class (i.e., 8%, versus 4% for the lower middle class and 3% for the working class). In the public sector, however, their opportunities for upward mobility are lower (a mere 3%) than in both other classes (6% for the lower middle class and 4% for the working class). This finding supports the idea that governmental cuts are negatively affecting the career chances of middle class employees in the public sector as compared with others.

Apart from the last mentioned finding, these results are consistent with the findings with respect to the risk of unemployment and the type of labour contract: there are no indications that the middle class has an advantaged position in either of these respects. Again, the question whether or not things were different during the 1960's and 1970's remains to be studied in future research. What was found, however, is a more proletarianized position in the case of women as compared to men and, perhaps somewhat surprisingly, a less proletarianized position in the case of the young as compared to the old.

5.4.3 Working conditions

The next factor which can be discussed is working conditions. To be able to place our findings in perspective two claims about job autonomy need to be underscored. In his well-known *Labour and Monopoly Capital*, Braverman (1974) defends the thesis that the advance of capitalism will proletarianize the working conditions of large parts of the white-collar workers. Secondly, according to Crompton and Jones, this is particularly true in the case of women (whom they refer to as a 'white-collar proletariat').Table 5.7 reports on the autonomy of the respondents.

Table 5.7
Percentage of workers with autonomy by class in 1985, 1990, and 1994

Class	1985	1990	1994
Higher middle class	85	89	80
Lower middle class	77	79	65
Working class	67	70	56
Total	76	79	68
Eta	0.18*	0.20*	0.22*
N	2232	2336	2742

*$p < 0.01$

For all three classes, the autonomy has increased in the 1985-1990 period, but decreased in the 1990-1994 period. This shows an absolute proletarianization process for both the higher and the lower middle class. Relatively, however, the higher middle class has not proletarianized in this period, because the autonomy of respondents in this class has detoriated less than that of members of the lower middle class and the working class. Comparing 1985 with 1994, we can determine a small relative proletarianization of the lower middle class.

The multivariate analysis, which includes age, gender, and economic sector, does not yield a substantively different pattern with respect to the relationship between class and autonomy. In 1994 for example the (multivariate) beta of class equals the (bivariate) eta in Table 5.7; 0.22. In 1994, gender (0.14), age (0.06), and economic sector (0.06) all have significant independent effects on the autonomy of the respondents. Compared with those three effects therefore, the class effect is considerably stronger. Simular results can be found for 1985 and 1990 (although in those years the economic sector had no significant effect). This means that independent of class membership, which is itself strongly related to job autonomy, the women's work situation is significantly more proletarianized than that of the men.

We also find in 1985 and 1994 An interaction effect between class and gender can also be found in 1985 and 1994. Interestingly, the autonomy of male members of the lower middle class (77%) is close to that of males in the higher middle class, whereas the autonomy of female workers in the lower middle class (57%) is closer to females in the working class (51%). This effect gives some support to the contention held by Crompton and Jones.

In summary, it is evident that Braverman's prediction has not been fulfilled, but it appears that Crompton and Jones are correct in underscoring the proletarianized status of middle class women.

Finally, we turn to our last indicator for the degree to which one's work has a proletarianized status: the degree of monotony (Table 5.8).

Table 5.8
Percentage of workers with monotonous work by class in 1985, 1990, and 1994

Class	1985	1990	1994
Higher middle class	17	18	13
Lower middle class	39	39	32
Working class	49	54	50
Total	35	38	31
Eta	0.28*	0.31*	0.33*
N	2232	2336	2742

* $p < 0.01$

The relationship between class and monotony in the work situation is quite strong: members of the working class experience monotony far more often than those of the higher and lower middle class. There is no trend towards proletarianization for the two latter two classes. Absolutely, members of these classes experienced less monotony in 1994 than in 1985. Relatively, the gap between these classes and the working class has increased. With respect to this indicator, there is no trend towards proletarianization detectable.

The multivariate analysis (again not presented here) yields similar results: controlling for age, gender, and economic sector does not affect the class effect. The effects of age, gender, and economic sector are smaller (though in 1990 and 1994 the age-effect is not significant).

Summing up our findings regarding these two indicators of the work situation, no clear indications of middle class proletarianization in either sense exist. On both indicators, the scores of members of the higher middle class are much better than those of the other two classes. Only with respect to autonomy can one detect a small absolute proletarianization effect; this, however, counteracted by the fact that, relatively speaking, the autonomy of the working class has detoriated faster than that of the higher middle class.

Furthermore, there are indications that women in particular (in both the higher and lower middle class) have more proletarianized working conditions than men. Although younger workers also have fewer favourable working conditions, this holds for all classes. Younger middle class workers are, therefore, not more proletarianized than members of the working class. With respect to the economic sector, detecting anything at all is very hard. Overall, it seems that the working conditions between the private and public sector are very similar.

5.5 Conclusions

In this chapter, a distinction was made between a 'strong' and a 'weak' version of the thesis of middle class proletarianization. Whereas the *strong version* refers to a process of *absolute proletarianization* (i.e., an increasing similarity between the 'existing' middle class and an 'ideal-typical' working class), the weak version refers to a process of *relative proletarianization* (i.e., an increasing similarity between the 'existing' middle class and the 'existing' working class, which implies a relative erosion of traditional middle class advantages). We not only assessed the (changing) economic positions of the working class and the middle class, however, but also studied the degree to which age and gender, as well as economic sector (private or public) were related to proletarianization.

What are our findings? First, and foremost, we have certainly not witnessed a marked process of middle class proletarianization since 1985, either in an absolute, or in a relative sense. However, there are important differences with respect to the indicators of proletarianization investigated.

Overall, the data do not indicate a clearly visible strong process of absolute or relative proletarianization with respect to the work situation (autonomy and monotony) of our respondents. More interesting are the results with respect to what Lockwood (1989) has called the 'market situation'. This situation includes income, job security (type of labour contract and risk of unemployment), and career chances. Income yields a pattern that is consistent with the traditional idea of an economically privileged middle class. The income gap between the middle class and the working class has in no way whatsoever narrowed. On the contrary: it has only widened since 1985. Obviously, with respect to income there is no such thing as a 'process of middle class proletarianization' discernible. However, this conclusion certainly does not apply to the remaining indicators for the market situation of the middle class (job security and career chances). Since 1985, surprisingly, the middle class has hardly ever taken up a stronger position than the working class. Traditionally, sociologists have assumed that a relatively strong market position is a key characteristic of a thriving middle class and this remarkable finding leaves open two possible interpretations.

Of course, a first possibility is that sociologists have always been mistaken: although the middle class has always enjoyed (and continues to do so) a high income its job security and mobility chances have, contrary to sociological conventional wisdom, never really differed from that of the working class. Although this interpretation might, at least to some extent, be plausible, we do not believe that it offers a satisfactory explanation. After all, empirical studies from the 1950s, 1960s and 1970s demonstrate that the difference between both classes definitely used to be there. So it makes more sense to opt for a second interpretation: a process of middle class proletarianization might have been in progress before 1985, which has yielded a situation from 1985 onwards in which the previously advantageous position of the middle class (even of the higher middle class) has disappeared. As this means that the middle class and the working class have grown more alike, it also means that a process of relative proletarianization has developed. Future research with data that go back further into the past will have to show whether absolute proletarianization has also taken place.

Notwithstanding these qualifications, we feel safe to conclude that there are no clear indications of a process of middle class proletarianization since 1985. This is true for both the higher and the lower middle class. On almost every indicator the lower middle class is positioned between the higher middle class and the working class. Overall, this suggests that, at least since 1985, the lower middle class has not been harder hit by a proletarianization process than the higher middle class, if at all.

What then can be said about gender, age, and economic sector? Although it seems plausible to assume that economic restructuring and government budget cuts during the 1980s particularly affected public employees, this idea is clearly not confirmed by our analysis. With the exception of mobility opportunities, there are very few differences between the economic positions of those working for the government and those working for private companies. With respect to age and gender however, there are differences. It is evident that the position of women and the young is far more 'proletarianized' than that of men and older workers. It is equally evident, however, that we are not dealing with a typical 'middle class phenomenon' here. By and large, a similar difference between age categories and the sexes exists within the working class. Notable exception to this is, however, that the autonomy of female lower middle class workers is lower than their male counterparts.

In summary; there are no clear indications of a process of middle class proletarianization, although such a process might have been in progress before 1985 with respect to job security and mobility potential; although women and the young take up relatively proletarianized positions, they do so largely independently of their membership of the middle class. Nevertheless, this last finding is important in itself. As more and more women enter the labour process and assume relatively proletarianized positions, it means that in absolute numbers more (female) members of the middle class are experiencing proletarianization.

The relatively limited indications of the existence of a process of middle class proletarianization may come as a surprise to some readers. However, it must be stressed that we have excluded two elements of a possible proletarianization process which are dealt with in other chapters. In the first place, subjective side of proletarianization was not discussed. An important element in the chapter by Berting is the existence of a growing insecurity within the middle class. The chapter by Suarez et al., deals with the same insecurity, especially among the young. Although their actual proletarianization may be limited in this scope, people can nevertheless become insecure because they feel threatened.

In the second place, we limited our analysis to people who had a paid job. In several chapters it is stressed that people who are potentially members of the middle class (i.e., higher-educated younger people) have difficulties in even finding a job, or have to satisfy themselves with a job at a lower level than desired. It is this insecurity in economic position of people who are potentially members of the middle class but have not reached that state, that can greatly stimulate feelings of insecurity. If we take these developments into account, the actual proletarianization of the middle class in Dutch society may be greater than accounted for in our analysis.

Notes

1 The authors are grateful to the OSA for providing the data.

2 Unfortunately it appears that the OSA has not proven completely able to fullfill its objective of being a representative panel of the Dutch labour force in all the years under study. In some years the panel has some rather eccentric characteristics (i.e., with respect to age). These are sometimes due to changes in the wording of questions but, as we believe, they are also caused by the difficulties in maintaining a panel that is both a panel and representative of the Dutch labour force in general. From several OSA-publications it becomes clear that with respect to most variables the sample is a good representation of the Dutch labour force. However, especially in 1985 and 1990 younger respondents are underrepresentated (compare note 6). Fortunately this is unimportant, with respect to our main research goal, that the surveys are representative on each characteristic of the labour force, as we are primarily interested in differences between different classes (compare Zetterberg, 1965).

3 As stated above, the survey is a two yearly panel study. However, the second survey was already held in 1986, the third in 1988, etc.

4 In some analyses (see below), a combined sample of the surveys of 1990 and 1994 was used, containing respondents who were interviewed in both years. This combined sample consists of 1312 respondents and includes respondents who were unemployed in 1994.

5 We dichotomized this variable in respondents who had and who had not become unemployed in those periods. Actually, so, there were some respondents who had become unemployed more than once.

6 Of course, the respondents could have changed jobs more than once. Like the frequency of unemployement, we dichotomized our variable separating respondents who had not been promoted at all from respondents who had been promoted at least once.

7 We can not explain the decrease of younger workers in the panel (actually the mean between 1990 and 1994 rose from 34 to 38 years!). This decrease is bigger than in the 'real' Dutch labour force. So, this has probably to do with the problem with the data we refered to in note 2.

8 The declining percentage is a consequence of the fact that the labour market participation of woman has grown substantially in recent years.

9 Unfortunately, the OSA changed the way they asked this question. In 1985 and 1990 respondents could indicate that they worked as public servant or as a worker - working in an organization subsidized by the

government - whose salary is linked to civil service scales. In 1994, however, they could only indicate that they worked as a public servant. Workers in the second category are therefore in 1994 supposed to work in the private sector. As a consequence, the number of people working in the public sector has declined substantiall (from 882 in 1985 to 556 in 1994).

10 In all the following analysis we will only discuss interaction effects of gender, age and economic sector on the one hand and class on the other hand. Normally, we will only mention them if they are statistically significant in all the three surveys.

11 To give an impression of this difference: of the respondents that were thirty years or younger in 1990, 5,4% had become unemployed; of the workers older than thirty only 2,4% had become unemployed - after the effects of the other variables have been taken into account.

References

Braverman, H. (1974) *Labor and Monopoly Capital. The Degradation of Work in the Twentieth Century*, New York/London.

Berting, J. (1968) *In het brede maatschappelijke midden*, Meppel.

Berting, J. (1995) 'Het kwetsbare maatschappelijke midden. Over de veranderende principes van het samenleven', in: J. Berting, *De toekomst is altijd anders*, Amsterdam.

Crompton, R., and G. Jones (1984) *White-collar Proletariat. Deskilling and and Gender in Clerical Work*, London.

Crompton, R. (1993) *Class and Stratification. An Introduction to Current Debates*, Cambridge.

Erikson, R., and J. Goldthorpe (1992) *The Constant Flux*, Oxford.

Graaf, N.D. de, and A.J. Steijn (1996) *The Service Class in a Post-industrial Society Attitudes and behaviour of the social and cultural specialists in the public sector*. Paper for the RC28 meeting of the ISA, Stockholm, 30 May-2 June.

Glenn, E.N., and R.L. Feldberg (1977) 'Degraded and deskilled: the proletarianisation of clerical work', *Social Problems*, vol. 25, october, p. 52-64.

Goldthorpe, J.H. et al., (1969) *The Affluent Worker in the Class Structure*, Oxford.

Goldthorpe, J.H. (1980) *Social Mobility and Class Structure in Modern Britain*, Oxford.

Goldthorpe, J. (1995) 'The service class revisited', pp. 313-344, in. T. Butler and M. Savage (eds) *Social Class and the Middle Class*, + London.

Roberts, K., et al. 1977) *The Fragmentary Class Structure*, London.

Lockwood, D. (1989) *The Blackcoated Worker. A Study in Class Consiousness*, second edition, Oxford.

Steijn, A.J., and de Witte, M.C. (1992) *De Januskop van de industriële samenleving. Technologie, arbeid en klassen aan het begin van de jaren negentig* [The Two Faces of Industrial Society. Technology, Labor and Class in the Early Nineties.], Alphen aan den Rijn.

Steijn, A.J., and M.C. de Witte (1994) Class and Image of Society of Dutch Workers, in: *International Journal of Group Tensions*, vol. 24, 3, p. 219-235.

Witte, M. de (1994) 'Ongelijkheid gewogen, Rotterdams Sociologisch onderzoek naar rechtvaardigheid, de beoordeling van beroepsgroepen en maatschappijbeelden', in: De Witte, H. (ed.) *Op zoek naar de arbeidersklasse. Een verkenning van de verschillen in opvattingen en leefstijl tussen arbeiders en bedienden in Vlaanderen, Nederland en Europa*, Leuven, pp. 162-189.

Zetterberg, H.L. (1965) *On Theory and Verification in Sociology*, New York.

6

From the logic of permanence to the logic of fragmentation: Socio-productive conditions and rearticulation of the middle-class

EDUARDO CRESPO SUAREZ, FLORENTINO MORENO
AND AMPARO SERRANO PASCUAL

6.1 Introduction

The rise and consolidation of industrial societies was intrinsically linked to the ascendant ethos of modernity, in which the middle classes played a central role. This ethos entails the concept of the person as a permanent entity (consistent in various situations) in a process of linear evolution and the integrated centre of behaviour and action. This chapter discusses the internal relation between the ideological factors establishing the wage earner's condition and the normative affirmation of the middle-class ethos.

This ethos has changed profoundly in recent years. The progressive deterioration of the wage earner's condition in the last 15 years has modified the factors establishing this ideology, typical of the middle class, that links progress, stability, and agency (personal security). The new conditions of capitalism (the globalisation of the economy, the impossibility of forecasting the final product, etc.) have lead to new ideological requirements. Rather than being based on stability, agency, and the sense of individual power, these new ideologies are founded on polyvalence, capacity to adapt to different situations, and the ability to deal with uncertainty. The socio-economic conditions for an individual to enjoy and affirm personal security and stability are undergoing a deep-rooted reformulation, as insecurity and unpredictability have become the prime traits of post-industrial societies. This chapter reviews the conditions under which this ideology is being transformed in the Spanish context. They are especially acute given Spain's particular situation: its lag in industrialisation, the process of legitimising the new democratic order, the deep-rooted crisis in the labour market, and the political context which undermines the condition of the wage earner, all of which are felt particularly acutely among Spanish youth.

This process of transforming the middle-class ethos is exemplified among the young in Spain, a group that illustrates better than any other how the wage earner condition is being transformed. This group illustrates that exclusion and deteriorating

B. Steijn et al. (eds.), Economic Restructuring and the Growing Uncertainty of the Middle Class, 93-113.
© 1998 *Kluwer Academic Publishers.*

conditions, coupled with unpredictability and uncertainty, are not problems plaguing disadvantaged youths exclusively as was true in the past. Vulnerability is gradually spreading to the other social groups. This study of the Spanish context shows the processes of socialisation among young people in the new conditions of insecurity, instability, and polyvalence.

6.2 The logocentric concept of the subject of modernity

Anthropologists, historians, and sociologists at both the structuralist and deconstructionist ends of the spectrum have written extensively on individualism in Western societies. A major conclusion of these studies is that Western culture places a great deal of value on individual self-determination. Some authors[1] have described the subject model that has prevailed in our Western societies as an organised entity within a distinctive and coherent totality, a centre for experience, consciousness, emotion, judgement, and action.

The identity model grounded on security and personal stability was internally linked to 'modernity'. It essentially revolved around the following characteristics:

a. Subjective experience of power, domination, and internal control (personal security). Modern society is founded on the individual's sense of personal power and the ability to control the unpredictable. According to this belief, the individual would become sovereign if freed of the constraints of external co-actions (Arendt, 1958/83). Collectively organised work thus becomes the key to the Promethean project of human progress and control of nature: the 'Homo faber' as a subject who creates his own history. Work became the symbol of the affirmation of human power[2] (Gorz, 1988) and the foundation of the collective future (Touraine, 1966). According to these principles, human will would be the tool with which to fight the determinism that characterised life in traditional societies. Human life would be built around and guided by a vital project. The individual would emerge as the author of his own life, solely responsible.

b. Linear and optimistic notion of progress. Another factor that reinforced the institutionalisation of this identity model was a concept of progress held up as a categorical imperative, guaranteed by a sense of personal power and the ability to forecast the future. Progress would be founded on and conditioned by the transformation and domination of nature through science and technology. Through correct use of reason, individuals would be able to control their destiny and free themselves from basic needs, in other words, to overcome natural and social determinism (Touraine, 1993). Reason appeared as a guide for human emancipation. Once the traditional obstacles to the free enjoyment of human capacities were overcome, society would become open, full of opportunities and the promise of success. Society would move in continual ascension towards a goal, assisted by Reason and Science. Along these same lines, Barbara Ehrenreich[3] concluded that the leitmotif of the middle class was an incipient fear of failure, which Gergen (1991) observed as the result of the religion of progress, which in turn has laid the basis for a natural social hierarchisation of people according to how close they are to the desired objective and ads them to a frenzied struggle to achieve their objective.

This belief in progressive development became a perfectly natural notion and has been elevated to the status of a law. Humanity thus seems to witness a progressive and unlimited march towards universal progress, which in the end will reach out and include groups or countries apparently excluded from this logic.[4] This concept of development which identifies itself with a particular process of modernisation could even intervene as a mechanism for avoiding potential conflicts concerning access to and distribution of the benefits of capital.

c. Unity and permanence: continuity and exclusivity. Modernity also implies a search for unity and order imposed by reason (standardisation of time, subjects, etc.). This search and the endeavour to overcome unpredictability requires the establishment of clear and exclusive norms. The principle of unambiguous social regulation was part of a broader project to forecast, control, and model the human environment. In this sense, the predominant subject model in Western societies has presumed unity and continuity of the Ego in various situations, in other words, as individuality, liberty, autonomy, and responsibility. Potter and Wetherell (1987) stress the fallacy of a notion of identity grounded on the feeling of selfhood and permanence, and state that this line of reasoning is part of a more general search for regularity and laws in behaviour. The imperative of reason introduced by modernity produced subjects obsessed by their identity (Touraine, 1993).

6.2.1 Deconstruction of the concept of the individual: its cultural and social context

Some authors[5] have described the role played by the discursive articulation of certain classes of the Self in reproducing particular types of society. Sampson (1989) argues that the main assumptions held by modern culture on the way human beings behave are backed by an individualistic ideology in which a person is endowed with a series of internal tendencies (personality traits, attitudes, values, moral principles, etc.) that explain behaviour. This rationale for what signifies a human agent has assumed a key role in modern society, for the scope of this value system has transcended the bourgeoisie to become a collective norm. This social sector has attained a higher hierarchical status and has spread certain models of prestige throughout society.

It is in this context that we can understand the ambiguity underlying the social representation of Youth. On the one hand, Youth was the cultural model of modernity (symbol of progress, an open and progressive future, and of hope), while on the other, it was regarded as deficient (malleable, unstable, subject to suggestion, unsure, dependent, irresponsible, etc.). This representation of youth governs the transition of youths to an *adult* identity in socially valued terms (as subjects in charge of their own lives, unique and consistent in different situations, rational and independent).

6.3 Socio-productive conditions for the logocentric concept of the subject

Use of particular terms to refer to the Self implies relations of power and patterns of domination and subordination. It is in this context that this normative model of identity and its relation to forms of management may be seen. Modernity's exaltation of reason has led to an ironclad application of rational and scientific principles of organisation (standardisation of procedures and work norms). Economic rationalisation called for planning in order to achieve maximum yield and profits.

These forms of work organisation correspond to the social and political ascension of the bourgeoisie. In that stage of capitalism, companies required a certain degree of synchronisation by strictly controlling and programming production. They also had to be able to forecast and calculate their ability to function. This situation explains the strict division of labour, the decomposition of work into basic operations, and the strict controls that characterised the management of these firms. Given the employers' anxiety over insecurity and their emphasis on controlling risk factors, it was deemed that workers would be more profitable if they were obliged to work in an ordered structure. This led to categorisation, classification, and synchronisation to achieve maximum control over the workers' productive behaviour. The success of a firm was based on strictly adjusting workers to perfectly planned conditions. Modernity thus maintained a formalised and codified relation with the order of things to keep the margins of unpredictability and uncertainty to a minimum.

This form of human resource management in turn led to a parallel growth of individualism and decomposed the power of alliances at the workplace. The work force was atomised in the name of individual ambition. The ideal individual was one who fulfilled his aspirations through the power of his own actions. The industrial era thus came into being and established itself politically with a form of thinking grounded on the concept of the individual as a subject of modernity. This laid the premises for a new dominant ideology that allowed the bourgeoisie to hold a position of political and social authority and that formed the framework for the development of capitalism.

6.3.1 Other conditions establishing modernity's conditions of production

The conditions of production dominant in the 20th century were fostered not only by the extension of this ideology in a large number of Western societies, which in turn helped the bourgeoisie extend its influence and social hegemony, but also by other political and social factors. The consolidation of industrial society in the late 19th and early 20th centuries spread insecurity and dependence through broad levels of society, in deep contrast with the progress-oriented model of society grounded on modernity. The Taylorist conditions of production imposed on the majority of the working population largely undermined the belief in the relation between productive progress organised by science and technology, and social progress regulated by laws. The realm of reason (norms and standardisation), instead of leading to emancipation, tended rather to destroy the autonomy of the workers (Arendt, 1958/83; Gorz, 1988)

In many European countries, parallel networks of institutionalised solidarity developed. Protective legislation was introduced to regulate labour relations, guaranteeing a series of rights and minimum living conditions for citizens: education, health, control over work contracts, and coverage for possible risks and job security. Work conditions were improved; some firms adopted premises taken from the School of Human Relations, Group psychology, Humanist psychology, among others. Other networks for collective solidarity were also institutionalised (mutual recognition of the role of social partners).This institutionalised solidarity, through the redistribution functions of the Welfare state and the systems for collective defence of workers interests, played a role in alleviating insecurity and guaranteeing a degree of stability in situations of temporary risk.

This confluence of factors attenuated the uncertainty inherent to the condition of the wage earner. It came about in a period of strong economic growth, social well-being, noticeable stability that reinforced the utopia of progress, and the parallel extension of the social strata in the middle classes (tertiary economy, increase in the volume of white-collar work, changes in the active population's sectoral distribution and its professional qualifications, etc.). Economic growth and social progress provided a large number of households with a stable income, enabling them to plan for the future with a certain degree of security. The foundation for social stability appeared to spring from adopting behaviours to a determined set of shared values (honesty, effort, sacrifice, etc.). These conditions explain how it was possible to maintain the myths that underlie modernity: continual and infinite progress and the human being as master and controller of nature.

6.4 Rearticulating the conditions of production: redefining the individual reference model in the enterprise

At present, however, new forms of productive rationalisation require for a multicentred work organisation and co-operation among all the actors involved in order to adapt to an uncertain and variable environment. Economic development, increasing competition through differentiation, and the globalisation of capital has made capitalism highly complex and uncertainty a constant. Strict division of labour meant that production had to become increasingly rigid. Socio-economic problems and repeated crises in the Welfare state have undermined confidence in the values of unidimensional progress. At the same time, the ecological and social limits of development call into question the optimistic view of progress.

In addition to social and organisational transformations, the employment crisis heightens an individual's sense of social uncertainty. Companies also have to face increasingly open and uncertain conditions that require workers to become involved in productive transformations and require certain moral dispositions on the part of the workers (loyalty, acceptance of the objectives of production, initiative, and responsibility). Firms need to find dynamic and flexible production models which can be used to adapt the work force to variations in the volume and quality of products.

Efficient production thus demands the ability to react quickly to change, acquire a hybrid and multi-dimensional knowledge of the process, and adapt to an uncertain future. Instead of submission, employers now require performance and willing collaboration, in other words the optimalization of the objectives of production. Formal codification and regulation of workers' behaviour is unsuitable in this new situation, for uncertainty submits workers to a continuous exercise of redefinition. Informal skills and creative capacities are sought after and subsequently geared to the optimalization of productive efficiency. External control (monitoring, sanctions) is replaced by the extension of a system that promotes the worker's internal control.[6] Polyvalence and the ability to manage open-ended situations are also encouraged.

In this context, the processes of regulation can be based, not on eliminating uncertainty, but on managing it. The unidimensional individual formed by modernity and the systematisation, definition, and strict planning of earlier contexts are incompatible with the current situation that requires multi-faceted intervention. The exclusive logic of opposition and contradiction that characterised 'modernity' in Western societies is no longer relevant and is losing ground to the logic of unpredictability, fragmentation, and plurality. Rules are now contingent rather than fixed; they are ambiguous and incomplete. Faced with the impact of unforeseen events, uncertain conditions, and indefinite goals, the ability to manage insecurity and unpredictability is gaining importance.

As a result, many firms now manage, instead of suppress, informal order because they see its role in adapting to a context of economic and social uncertainty. According to Crozier (1963), rationalisation ceases to restrict itself to dictating how work should be done and places significant value on the multi-dimensional and flexible subject who can adapt rapidly to variation and change. Normative polysemy and a plurality of the Self are thus incontrovertible requirements in times of constant change such as the current period. This implies the passage from a world of explicit rules to another based on implicit rules of production (Crozier, 1963: 263). According to Terssac (1992), work organisation increasingly requires, not so much respect of rules, as the workers' involvement in order to ensure the continuity of production despite all possible disturbances.

In these new conditions, the internal relation between individual effort (personal ability to adapt to uncertainty) and the results obtained is becoming increasingly evident. This growing complexity facilitates individualisation and personal accountability, in contrast to the stability and structure that denoted the former context which fostered the establishment of social categories based on a statistical representation, and therefore social representation of the results and 'risks' of individual action.

6.5 Process of transforming the identity reference in the Spanish context: Modernisation and consolidation of the industrial society in Spain

The process described above has unfolded in a particular way in Spain. The weakness and inequality of Spanish industrialisation and the late introduction of social legislation partially explain the specific process. The development of the industrial society was characterised by the interdependent co-existence of modes of production and social relations which each belonged to different stages of economic development. The emergence of a modern sector of industrialisation, technical innovation was hampered by the weight of traditional social forces. Spanish development was thus based on late industrialisation and strong protection by the Franco regime (protectionist tariffs and subsidies), which led to a basically national orientation and little pressure to innovate. The Spanish production model has been called 'incomplete Fordism' (Toharia, 1986), given the weak development of the Social State and a mixture of Taylorist (a certain degree of differentiation in tasks and functions) and pre-Taylorist elements (Köhler, 1994). Today there is still a high degree of economic dualism: a social and labour economy in a modern capitalistic sector alongside a pre-capitalist economy which is a remnant of Spain's particular historical evolution.

In the early decades of the 20th century, Spain was a combination of pre-modern elements and structural archaisms along with signs of modernisation. Elements of *modernisation* appeared (urban concentration, lower mortality rates, increase in social unrest, feeble technological progress) without managing to introduce *modernity* as the dominant ideology (a mostly agrarian population; immobility of the State; large number of workers in traditional occupations, independent workers, craftsmen; persistence of latifundist land ownership structures in the South; lack of development in education; crucial role of the Catholic Church in defending the social order and principle of authority; inability of the armed forces to adapt after the loss of the colonial empire, etc.). Spain had yet to sever all its links with the traditional society. Until well into this century, there were hardly any salaried workers *per se*, and although a bourgeoisie was forming, it was not a modern class but one largely linked to the old regime (Tuñón de Lara, et al., 1991). The pre-Franco years were thus a period of contradiction between modernising and regressive tendencies.

Prior to the Franco dictatorship, industrial conflicts were not institutionalised, partly due to the heterogeneous social structure, but also because of the adamant refusal of employers, supported by the State, to accept labour associations. The paternalistic practices disciplining the labour force and the heterogeneity among workers explain how conflicts arising from the hard conditions of early industrialisation were often informal and weakly organised. Social legislation was introduced slowly but the process was suspended with the advent of the Franco system.

The Civil War entailed a fight between irreconcilable views of modernity, such that it ended up suffocating the Spain that was emerging and in need of a pacific form of modernisation. The Franco era ushered in a period of regression in this process of modernisation. The Catholic Church continued and even bolstered its legitimising and ideological function. Franco's political culture was characterised by political cynicism, a negative withdrawal of the individual as an active participant in society, and values founded in tradition, religion, peace and social order (Hobbesian collective security). It was also characterised by an apolitical attitude of a particular nature fostered by the military power - a passive acquiescence to the prevailing political regime. This era was marked by the obsession with abolishing the enemy within (internal ideological, linguistic or cultural divisions) which materialised in a constant promotion of an apolitical attitude, and a culture of suspicion and mistrust among individuals. This situation instead encouraged individualism and the dismantling of any form of political and social association that was not 'official'. It also fostered a deep-seated fatalism that allocated a large degree of determinism to social phenomena, thus curtailing the belief in the individual's capacity to intervene in the face of structural pressure.

The Franco system denied the existence of class struggle, and the regime's labour principles were based on situating labour authority in the enterprise with generic social legislation including, notably, the right to work and job security which restricted the freedom to dismiss workers. In return, qhe worker was offered a series of minimal advantages (a stable job and a series of seniority benefiqs). State paternalism attempted to encourage a community of producers with coinciding interests, a community which would lead to the disappearance of the class struggle (Aizpuru and Rivera, 1994). Most workers lived in a situation of dependence, in which they lacked rights, and were a part of an imposed social order in which submission and obedience played a key role. The Franco model, especially in the early phase, was based on the concept of a rural society, and was little concerned with profitability, and counted on an inexpensive labour force and a restricted job market. During this first phase, the number of industrial workers and wage earners declined, and the working population lacked technical skills and lagged behind in technology. The industrial structure was largely composed of small inefficient enterprises protected from international competition.

Although political and social isolation, together with economic autarchy, held Spain back in its economic development, it did not hinder transformations in the job structure. In the 1960s the country began to develop economically and step up its process of industrialisation. This led to vast changes from the 1960s onwards. Workers moved from the agricultural sector to the industrial and service sectors. A process of internal and external migrations entailed a degree of improvement in worker qualifications and considerable changes in living conditions (concentration of the population, and increase in schooling and professional training, etc.). From a job structure dominated by unskilled labourers, the country gradually moved towards one of specialised workers (metal and steelworkers, construction, etc.). The typical labourer became the stable industrial worker. The working class maintained its atypical attitude, merely surviving in the new conditions that reduced salaries to minimum levels.

In the 1970s, the direction shifted in favour of modernity, and the need for political and social change was made apparent. Political transition after the death of Franco followed the economic transition that had already begun in the previous decade and was accompanied by a severe economic crisis. The restoration of a modern context in society, for instance, through the reinstatement of public liberties and political pluralism, was subsequent to the process of productive modernisation. The State stepped up its social policy (old-age protection, investments in education, etc.) which increased social well-being. This led to a steep rise in public spending, in particular in the realm of social expenditures (social services, education, health, and housing, among others) in view of the need to legitimise the transition to democracy.

The development pattern in Spain over the past three decades has been one of concentration followed by contraction in periods of socio-economic and political transitions. This contrasted with the immobility of the previous decades and is reflected in the evolution in employment rates, which fluctuated much more widely than elsewhere. From 1978 to 1992, for example, Spain maintained the sharpest growth rate of any country in the European Union; at the same time, it had the highest unemployment rate (more than double the EU average).[7] The high unemployment level can be partly explained by the country's accumulated delay in restructuring its production system.

Table 6.1
Evolution of activity and unemployment rates

Year	Activity rate	Unemployment rate
1977	50.3	5.3
1978	49.8	7.1
1979	49.3	8.7
1980	48.7	11.5
1981	48.1	14.4
1985	47.4	21.9
1988	49.1	19.5
1989	49.1	17.3
1990	49.4	16.3
1991	49.1	17.0
1992	48.8	20.1
1993	49.1	23.9
1994	48.8	23.9
1995	49.1	22.8
1996	49.9	21.9

Source: Enquiry on the Active Population (EPA)

The current occupational system in Spain also shows broad regional disparity in the persistence of agricultural and non-salaried employment (in Andalusia, Galicia, and Extremadura, for instance). Spain's membership in the European Community brought new industries and foreign investment and led to the incorporation of the management models of other countries.

By the late 1970s and 1980s, the economic recession was especially acute. The government responded with protective labour legislation, initially in the form of labour contracts based on job stability. Nevertheless, measures introduced throughout the 1980s to foster economic growth gradually called into question the principle of job stability. The prevailing legislation model in the new democratic institutions is based on a tendency to erode job security (more ample possibilities to lay workers off for justifiable reasons, flexibility through temporary contracts, deteriorating job conditions, rise of an underground economy, self-employment, etc.) as is shown in Table 6.2.[8]

Table 6.2
Evolution of the wage earning population according to the type of contract

	Salaried population	Workers with permanent contracts	Workers with temporary contracts	Temporary employment rate
1988	8352	6392	1946	23.3%
1989	8880	6470	2396	27.0%
1990	9274	6453	2810	30.3%
1991	9373	6339	3027	32.3%
1992	9077	6034	3040	33.5%
1993	8686	5877	2807	32.3%
1994	8626	5708	2915	34.8%

Source: Enquiry on the Active Population (EPA), National Institute for Statistics (INE)

Two tendencies are consolidating simultaneously: fragmentation of the job structure and polarisation, with a rise in the most qualified (professionals and highly skilled technicians) and least qualified (domestic help, etc.) occupations. The Spanish productive system is defined by the volume of small production units. The processes of industrial reconversion have led to the de-industrialisation and dismantling of large sections of the obsolete manufacturing industries and a parallel growth in the service sectors, particularly finance and insurance. From the educational point of view, there has been an increase in the average level of instruction among the work force, as is shown in Table 6.3, a development which mirrors greater access to education from the 1970s on.[9]

This particular economic development makes it clear why until the 1980s the slow development of the welfare state and the structures for collective solidarity hampered the establishment of a clear link between modernity and a personal sense of power and control. Modernising elements were present alongside pre-modern elements and slow scientific and technical development. Few opportunities for social mobility were open to workers, who are mostly underskilled and had a low standard of living. The industrial proletariat and the bourgeoisie were late in establishing themselves as a social class, and the workers did not have a good bargaining position. This explains the persistence of the determinist notion of a natural order governed by laws beyond one's control, typical of traditional societies, rather than an image of the individual guided by personal will that is found in modern societies. The transition to democracy nevertheless implied the adoption of such principles, which paradoxically, the Spanish society had very little time to assimilate before they began to be profoundly rearticulated.

Table 6.3
Evolution of the education level of the active population

	Illiterate or without schooling	Primary school	Secondary school diploma or less than Higher education	Higher Education
1976	17.2	62.6	17.6	2.6
1982	13.1	54.6	28.6	3.7
1988	12.4	41.1	41.9	4.6

Source: INE (drawn up by Cachón Rodríguez, 1991)

6.5.1 Transition to the middle class society. Evolution of the job structure

The job structure has changed noticeably, as shown in Table 6.4, evolving towards a tertiary economy, with the agricultural sector now playing a less important role. In 1995, the working population could be broken down into the following categories: 61.2% in the services sector, 20.5% in industry, 9.4% in construction, and 8.9% in agriculture.[10]

Table 6.4
Evolution of the Spanish population by economic sector

	Primary sector	Secondary sector (industry and construction)	Tertiary sector
1900	68	15	17
1920	59	22	19
1940	52	24	25
1960	37	30	33
1970	23	38	40
1980	16	35	50
1990	12	33	55
1995	9	30	61

Source: INE Statistics Annual and INE inquiries among the Active Population (table drawn up by the authors)

The slow rate of industrialisation in Spain has been accompanied by a rapid movement towards a tertiary economy, without there being sufficient time for the industrial sector to fully consolidate.

As shown in Table 6.5, if we compare the Spanish social structure with that of other countries, we can see the weight of the small business owners compared to the relatively small percentage of workers who could be considered part of proletariat.

Table 6.5
Comparative structure according to Wright

	Spain	Sweden	England	USA	Australia
Business owner	3.2	5.5	6.5	7.8	5.0
Small business owner	23.8	5.4	6.0	6.9	9.0
Expert director	2.5	4.4	5.6	3.9	6.0
Non-expert director	4.7	6.5	11.1	8.5	17.0
Expert Supervisor	1.7	3.8	2.2	3.7	2.0
Non-expert Supervisor	4.4	6.3	7.2	13.7	14.0
Skilled employee	4.0	6.8	4.1	3.4	3.0
Skilled worker	18.5	17.8	14.4	12.2	12.0
labourers	37.2	43.5	42.9	39.9	32.0

Source: J.J. González (1992)

6.5.2 Socio-economic and ideological conditions in the process of change: the case of Young people

As a consequence of the weak competitiveness of the Spanish production structure, the predominance of small enterprises, which are especially vulnerable to changes in the economic cycle, technological and organisational changes (readjustment and reconversion policies) and the world economic recession, the Spanish job market has undergone a severe crisis, which was comparatively deeper than those other European countries. The younger segment of the population, had been hardest hit, as is shown in Figure 6.1.

The unemployment rate in Spain among young people from 16 to 24 years of age is 46%.[11] At the same time, the activity rate among youth (a high percentage have even stopped searching for work) has dropped, extending the period of unemployment[12] and creating precarious conditions for professional integration. Most young people obtain access to jobs through secondary paths[13] (unskilled activities, underemployment and temporary contracts). To explain the problems they have entering the job market, we should refer to a series of discriminatory practices, such as the greater contract flexibility and lesser protection granted young people under collective agreements, in labour legislation[14] and by trade unions, the consolidation of domestic job markets, and the assumption that young people are less productive and more costly (lack of training or experience).

Figure 6.1
Unemployment rate among youth

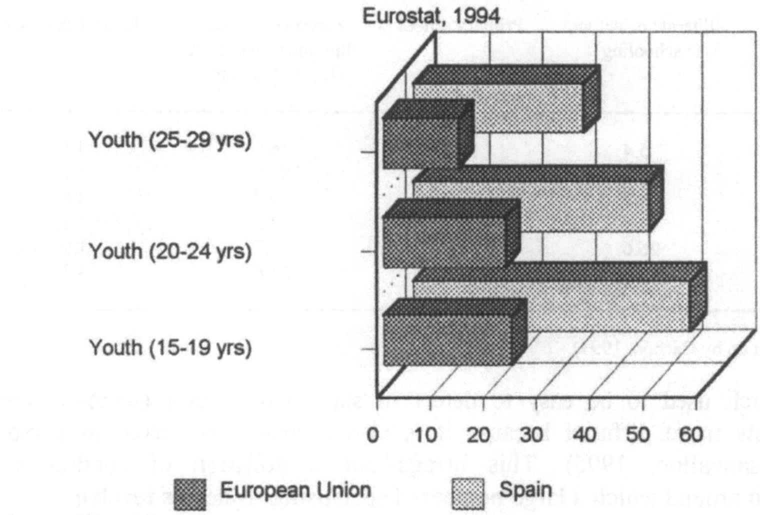

Source : Eurostat

Consequently, the job market open to young people is marked by instability and lack of job security.[15] The most important aspect, nevertheless, is that instability is no longer something provisional and it prolongs the process of youth integration into the adult world. The long postponement and late entry on the job market explain why many stay at home remaining dependent on their parents until a relatively high advanced age.[16] The family becomes the primary protection mechanism for this age group. The transitory period thus becomes a permanent situation. Prolonging what is called youth in social terms[17] has masked the structural reality of a population condemned to professional instability. The transition thus entails a high level of uncertainty, insecurity, and powerlessness. This situation explains the profound social vulnerability of youth. It may also reveal how they distance themselves from the society of modernity, as discussed, among others, by Touraine (1988). It further shows that young people are among the most active critics of development.

Precariousness and instability are distributed more evenly throughout the different social classes of young people, as compared to the adult population, for whom social class was a more discriminating factor (Tobias, 1988; Prieto, 1994). The evolution in unemployment patterns according to educational level, given in table 6.6, shows that the increase in relative unemployment among subjects with middle level studies is particularly striking among youth.

Table 6.6
Evolution of the distribution of unemployment according to educational level

		Illiterate or without schooling	Primary school	Secondary school diploma or less than Higher education	Higher Education
Youth	1976	5.4	54.5	36.9	3.1
	1982	2.6	35.8	57.9	3.7
	1988	3.1	22.4	69.7	4.8
Adults	1976	42.5	48.7	7.5	1.2
	1982	26.6	61.7	9.7	1.9
	1988	26.3	48.8	21.6	3.3

Source: INE (drawn up by Cachón, 1991)

Exclusion, which used to be easy to detect in statistical criteria (socio-economic criteria), is now more diffused because it is also increasingly linked to personal trajectory (Rosanvallon, 1995). This brings out a diffusion of conditions of indetermination around which a large number of socialising strategies revolve.

6.6 Socialisation of the Spanish population in the new conditions: The example of Young people

Leaving aside the actual weight of new management models in Spanish society, what can be seen is a set of factors which tends to stimulate a polysemous and plural approach to work, and which facilitates adaptation to the new conditions of capital. This situation is particularly prevalent among young people, because they are the most affected by this process of increased vulnerability.

6.6.1 The role of new strategies to promote employment: Representation of pressures considered to be legitimate and tolerable

In recent years, the government has dramatically increased the measures to fight unemployment and promote jobs, the most important of which are those targeting young people. Legal and employment rights reforms (changes to contractual possibilities) have been the prime measures taken. Flexibility is presented by the government as the way to escape from the model of social regulation, which has been stigmatised as the source of all our problems.

Jobs programmes directed towards young people actually present the worst conditions for stability in the job market. These measures promote precarity and diversification in their conditions for access; as a result, the first contact most young people have with the professional world is completely different from that of adults. Thus, most young people begin their careers through 'atypical' paths (part-time work,

work-training programmes, temporary jobs, home work, etc.). Their contracts are almost always temporary, leading to an increased mobility within the professional and contractual context. The mobility promoted between the different statuses keeps the young workers immersed in the logic of the job market.

These measures to lower labour costs also alter the statistical borders between categories, generating alternative statuses. As a result, even though these measures have led to a few stable and permanent jobs, they have played an important role in creating an alternative space between working and not working (apprenticeships, trainingships, fellowships, part-time or daily contracts, etc.). This diversification and fragmentation has made it possible to adapt the labour force to a market demand that is heterogeneous, ever-shifting, and unpredictable. Creating all these transitional statuses for young people has embedded them in a fragile and temporary way of life. The precarious and transitory nature and lack of autonomy of most of the jobs offered generate instability and impermanence. The professional socialisation of youth in the new conditions of uncertainty, open-endedness, and complexity can have a significant impact on the types of professional identities they value, thus encouraging the internalisation of a certain work ethic. In fact, young people may end up turning the connotations of adaptability, instability and uncertainty into professional qualities, features which were traditionally rejected by most of the Spanish population.

This flexibility on the job market (which promotes temporary, part-time work) has an impact not only on labour costs, but also on the socialisationprocess.[18] Flexibility and mobility, along with the job crisis itself have had all the indirect effect of preparing youth for new management requirements such as new behavioural skills[19], in particular the ability to adapt to different situations. In a climate of generalised indetermination and movement, adaptability and professional 'plasticity' are in high demand as they can be instrumental in disciplining the work force and encouraging the management of insecurity and instability.

Unlike the insecurity of life in the 19th century, which was caused by the wage earner's dependence on the employer and was a source of social conflicts, the new conditions of insecurity in today's Spain are rarely grounds for potential conflict. Today's situation fosters acceptance of the new conditions for occupational development.

This situation is accompanied by a process of constructing of this target group. Young people (especially those with few qualifications or who are long-term unemployed) are conceptually represented in terms of 'deficiency' (in training, skills, culture, and personality) which weighs considerably in determining responsibility for a situation of dependence. A vision of the condition itself in terms of deficiency can make the differences and dualities caused by the jobs crisis be seen as natural (Serrano, 1995).

This objectifying of youth unemployment[20], however, contrasts with the reality of the job market. According to INEM[21] data, the highest number of employment contracts in 1995 were for jobs requiring no qualifications at all. Forty-one percent of the individuals signing contracts had not obtained a primary school diploma

(*'Graduado Escolar'*) or the Grade 1 Professional diploma (*'FPI'*). Among those with the highest educational levels (*FPII, BUP, COU*[22] or university diplomas), the number of contracts was relatively low (10%). This contrasts with the substantialist explanation that youth unemployment is due to a lack of qualifications. Once an individual is described as lacking something, of being somehow deficient, the authority of the intervening actors is enhanced, and this tends to reproduction of the dominant structures of authority. The social representation of this category explains the paternalistic tendencies of policies affecting young people implicitly based on the notion of 'maturity'. Given the self-exclusion of young people and the lack of motivation to adopt a combative attitude, this situation also serves to dissuade potential conflicts. On the other hand, this analysis, approaches that of a moral diagnosis as it is linked to personel deficiencies rather than social organization. Representing youth in terms of deficiency has fostered a growth industry in supplementary training courses catering to all levels of qualification. Large numbers of young people with secondary school or university diplomas continue on this circuit through expert and master courses, and training modules for substantial periods of time.

Although this neo-liberal approach to the job market can be to some extent explained by the high level of unemployment in Spain, it can also be imputed to the need for alternative legitimisation required by the government deregulation policy. It was facilitated by the search for identity by a country wishing to distance itself from a dictatorship that offered a protective attitude towards workers in exchange for their submission to the government and subjection to cultural and economic misery. The categorical imperative of flexibility is imposed as a condition for modernity and participation in a progress-oriented Europe. Indeed, full integration into Europe was a strong point in the identity of the post-Franco governments. The insistent references to requirements for convergence with Europe in order to legitimise the deregulation of the job market is spawning an ambivalent attitude towards the modernity presented by integration into Europe.

In this context, criteria developed to manage, evaluate, and recruit the work force are based not only on whether the potential employee has a diploma or not, but also on a series of general skills an individual must have in order to continually adapt to new situations. It appears, therefore, that we are moving away from the context of earlier decades involving the consolidation of the Welfare state, as described by Rosanvallon (1995). From the objective notion of risk (which implies a probabilistic notion of 'risk'), a shift is taken place to the subjective notion of personal behaviour (notion of 'deficiency').

All these factors are calling into question the prototype of the 'modern' identity and at the same time fostering a plural and heterogeneous vision of work, as illustrated by many studies.

6.6.2 Example: the approach to work (the realm of institutionalised mutual recognition)

Several studies have shown how the younger generations have transformed their approach to work, and more specifically how they have adopted it to the cult of profit and personal commitment that characterised the industrial societies. Some studies have concluded that the contemporary approach is polysemous and multi-centred. Lalive d'Epinay, for example, mapped out an ambivalent, plural, and multi-poled attitude towards work. In Spain, Crespo (1994)[23] demonstrated the dilemmatic nature of significant nuclei (pleasure/pain, submission/liberty, etc.) around which current work ideologies are structured. Characteristic of the present, according to Crespo, is the plurality and the number of diversified moral theories on work, as well as the co-existence of different systems which legitimise the work ethos. Thus, we cannot speak of one single ethic prevailing in society. Today's complex approach to work and its polysemous structure has also been brought out in a qualitative study conducted among youth in Madrid.[24] The fluid and atomised nature of work situations and the many ways one can belong to the world of employment are so varied and fluid that the frontier between work, unemployment, and inactivity is becoming increasingly vague and the categories of labour increasingly diffuse. The fragmented, plural and multiform nature of the new identities lead to the revision of earlier referential dichotomies which previously articulated the ideology of work (work/leisure, private/public, etc.). Compared to the earlier notion of work which consisted of antagonistic poles, we now see a hybrid and complex approach.

This complexity, indetermination, and plurality of references exposes the individual to a vast range of situations. The individual is faced with a multiplication of the Self, implying experiences of variation and confrontation with his/her own Self, and the acquisition of multiple and disparate possibilities of being (Gergen, 1992). Cultural and social heterogeneity, social fragmentation and the increasing speed of information exchange all place young people in a differentiated social universe, submitting them to a perpetual axiological reconstruction in which they become the arbitrators among different intrinsic norms. Individuals carry with them a wide range of possibilities, and they harbour a multitude of contradicting expectations, values, and opinions about what would normally appear obvious in certain situations. With the growing complexity of points of view, the individual can no longer assume a coherent position in rational terms. Young people are forced to manage several autonomous registers (Dubet, 1994) and are submitted to contradictory and paradoxical socialisationprocesses due to the multiplication of reference models and cultural codes (Bajoit and Franssen, 1995). These situations revive the questioning of modernist concepts and the nature of progress.

The normative polysemy of their approach to work enables young people to deflect the contradictions inherent in the unitary normative model of modernity. This normative plurality and fragmentation of identities in turn provides them with an opening to interpret themselves in different ways, without needing to restrict themselves to the exclusive and unambiguous definitions offered by the society of modernity.

6.7 Conclusion

The complexity and diversification of the potentially significant references explains the multi-centred vision most young Spanish people have towards work. It also explains the plurality and normative polysemy that characterises their approach to it and the heterogeneity of their own normative principles. Rather than posing a threat to the new social order that arises from this advanced stage of capitalism, this normative polysemy affirms it. It indirectly prepares young people and makes them more adaptable to the polyvalence and flexibility currently required by the conditions of capital and Spanish employers, which in most cases are transformed into precariousness.

This confluence of factors is thus advantageous to a multi-centred management organisation that fosters polysemy and referential plurality as well as the ability to manage one's contradictory and precarious work situation. Organising and regulating work patterns in a centralised, unambiguous, and monosemous manner would only be counterproductive in the present context of social, economic, and organisational indetermination and uncertainty. This unilateral approach to work would only spawn an attitude of opposition to the precariousness of the situation and the need to change it. The new market requirements encourage differentiation, adaptability, and a disposition towards precariousness, approaches which are hard to structure through collective intervention.

While this does not mean that the organisational order loses legitimacy, it does call into question the model formulating modernity because it casts doubt on a large number of the references that provide its foundation (such as the sense of individual power, belief in progress, dominance of the personal and social project); this takes place to such a degree that indetermination, the individual's sense of powerless, and polyvalence become the notions that co-ordinate the new social order. This situation acts as a source of socialisation that prepares young people to adapt to working conditions they might otherwise reject.[25] It also prepares young people of different social classes to face indetermination, polyvalence, and the ephemeral and changing nature of this advanced stage of capitalism. In this context of economic fluctuation, unstable employment, and an unforeseeable future, all of which favour the indetermination of social processes, the principles that legitimise work would no longer be based on the affirmation of a sense of personal power and control but on the ability to manage uncertainty.

This social group could, thus, be acting as a precursor of a new society based on the principles of insecurity and unpredictability. Indeed, uncertainty and insecurity may no longer be signs of alienation or loss of sense, but could be tools in fostering a process that values incompleteness, the transitory, and indecisiveness, notions that are linked to youth. We are thus witnessing a rearticulation of the very ethos of modernity which held up security and stability as the keys to articulating a valid identity. This process is especially remarkable in Spain, because of both its ambiguous relation to the modernist ideology and its particular historical evolution.

Notes

1 See for example Sampson (1989); Potter and Wetherell (1987); Gergen (1992).

2 As stated by Gorz.. "*The utopia of industrialisation promised us that the development of production forces and the expansion of the economic sphere would free humanity from injustice and malaise, and that, in addition to dominion over nature, it would also endow us with full power to determine our own lives.*" (Gorz, 1988: 27) .

3 Ehrenreich B (1989); cited by Gergen (1991).

4 An example is the popular use of the term 'developing countries' (países en vías de desarrollo) in the 1960s.

5 Gergen (1992); Parker (1989).

6 In line with the reflections of Foucault, Ibañez and Parker on the link between power and norms. These authors discuss the different ways to wield power based on outside pressures compared to those based on internal pressures (there is no need to force decisions because the conditions and criteria that form the reality of the decision are controlled; rather than leading to obedience this cancels out the possibility of repressing resistance). As opposed to human resource management policies based on authority and coercion that supervise and control, the new strategies require an exercise of responsibility that implies the subject's own self-vigilence and cancels the very possibility of resisting. The most subtle exercise of control thus comes about through the absence of control. See Foucault (1975/1990); Ibañez (1982); Parker (1989).

7 This situation is particularly alarming when you consider that Spain has the highest rate of inactivity in Europe.

8 Representative in this respect is the Royal Decree of 1992 (popularly called the 'decretazo' - the Big Order) which was rooted in the old culture of suspicion and thus contained anti-fraud elements, and imposed a series of measures that cut unemployment benefits, by increasing the period of time of employment required before being eligible, by reducing the amount of the regulatory base, and by shortening the duration which one had the right to receive an unemployment allowance. In a country where most work contracts are temporary, excluding workers with less than a 12-month contract had a profound impact.

9 This increased access to the education system is the result of various economic factors (economic growth, improved living conditions, and access by a greater number to better paying jobs), social factors (urbanisation and migration of the population to cities with more educational facilities), and educational factors (education reform, compulsory school attendance, and the raising of the minimum school-leaving age from 14 to 16).

10 EPA (Encuesta de la Población Activa - Enquiry on the Active Population), 1995.

11 INE (National Institute for Statistics), 1994.

12 In 1994, 24% of the total number of young people under 25, had been out of work for more than two years, and 48% for more than one year (EPA, 1994).

13 In 1992, 23% of young people with job experience were working on an informal basis, while 29% had a temporary job (Navarro López and Mateo Rivas (1992). In 1992, 61.5% of temporary contracts were held by young people (Prieto, 1994). In 1985, two thirds of the young adults and 37,7% of those between 20 and 24 were subjected to underemployment. That is employment under irregular contracts in which contracters recieved unemployment benefits or paid their own social security payments or for wich no social security payments were made whatsoever.

14 Representative in this respect is the latest reform of the Spanish market, which introduced new types of contracts that integrated elements of deregulation. The most polemical of these, directed towards under-qualified youth, is the 'apprenticeship contract' which lowers the interprofessional minimum salary, excludes these young people from social security and unemployment coverage, and introduces temporality in a job market al..ready plagued by high unemployment and job instability. It does not guarantee any training and is not linked to any certificate or diploma. These contracts, theoretically aimed at helping young people obtain qualifications, are being used as strategies to discipline the work force. According to a study by the trade union, Comisiones Obreras, one year after the start of the apprenticeship contract most of the young people under contract were in jobs that required no qualification - waiter, unskilled labourer, cleaning, etc - either they had already held similar jobs or (90%) were working (for a minimum 6-month period) without any parallel training, etc. (Gaceta Sindical, nº 127, 1994). At the same time these contracts have a considerable effect in staffing jobs with a cheaper and more disciplined work force. It is calling on solidarity among the generations as they are often being used ideologically to undermine the Welfare state.

15 Three-fourths of the young people in employment work in unskilled jobs (Gutiérrez, 1993).

[16] Few young people under 25 were living on their own outside the family, and in the age group of 19 to 29 only 20% were economically independent (Navarro López and Mateo Rivas, 1992).

[17] In Spain there is a frequent tendency to raise the age of the group termed as young people, so that the category currently considered statistically and socially as youths can include those up to 30 years of age.

[18] As shown by an ivestigation conducted between October 1995 and May 1996, *Regionalisation des politiques de l'emploi et logiques d'intervention sociale,* Serrano. Research promoted by the Brussels-Capital Region Programme *Research in Brussels.*

[19] In the sense given by Alaluf (1993).

[20] The problems of job integration are meshed with a debate on youth training.

[21] National Institute for Employment.

[22] Formación Profesional II (FPII) - Grade II professional diploma, Bachillerato Unificado Polivalente (BUP), the Spanish equivalent of the French *bacalaureate* or the British O-Levels Curso de Orientación Universitaria (COU)- diploma received before the first cycle of university study.

[23] Crespo (1994) *Significados del trabajo.* Unpublished work. Qualitative research (analysis of open-ended questions and discussion groups) on the meaning of work in contemporary Spanish society, undertaken by Alvaro, Bergere and Torregrosa, together with the author.

[24] Serrano (1995) *Inserción laboral como transición social* Doctoral thesis

[25] As shown by data from the Injuve enquiry (1992), the meritocratic culture of adaption is fairly common among young people with differing opportunities and experiences. (Navarro López and Mateo Rivas, 1993, op.cit).

References

Aizpuru, M., and Rivera, A. (1994) *Manual de historia social del trabajo,* Madrid.

Alaluf, M. (1993) Enseignement et emploi. Lorsque le succès de l'un règlement entraine la dévalorisation de l'autre, in: *Point d'Appui. Travail, Emploi, Formation,* 3, pp. 3-11. Nivelles (Belgium).

Arendt, H. (1958/83) *Condition de l'homme moderne,* Paris.

Bajoit, G., and Franssen, A. (1995) *Les jeunes dans la compétition culturelle,* Paris.

Cachón Rodríguez, L. (1991) Segmentación del mercado de trabajo y niveles educativos. *Sociedad, cultura y educación,* Madrid, pp. 111-135.

Crozier, M. (1963) *Le phénomene bureaucratique,* Paris.

Dubet, F. (1994) *Sociologie de l'experience,* Paris.

Ehrenreich, B. (1989) *Fear of Falling. The Inner Life of the Middle Class,* New York.

Foucault, M. (1975/1990) *Vigilar y castiga,* Madrid.

Gutiérrez, R. (1993) Los jóvenes y el trabajo, in: Navarro López M. and Mateo Rivas, M. J. (eds) *Informe Juventud en España,* Madrid.

Gergen, K. (1991) *The Saturated Self. Dilemmas of Identity in Contemporary Life,* New York.

Gorz, A. (1988) *Métamorphose du travail. Quete du sens,* Mayenne (France).

González, J.J. (1992) *Clases sociales: Estudio comparativo de España y la Comunidad de Madrid, 1991,* Madrid.

Ibañez, T. (1982) *Poder y libertad. Estudio sobre la naturaleza, las modalidades y los mecanismos de las relaciones de poder,* Barcelona.

Köhler, C. (1994) ¿Existe un modelo de producción español ? Sistemas de trabajo y estructura social en comparación internacional, *Sociologia del Trabajo,* 20, p. 3-33.

Navarro López, M., and Mateo Rivas, M.J. (1992) *Informe Juventud en España,* Madrid.

Parker, A. (1989) Discourse and Power. *Texts of Identity,* in: Potter, J. and Wetherell, M. (1987) *Discourse and Social Psychology. Beyond Attitudes and Behaviour,* London.

Parker, I. (1989) *The Crisis in Modern Social and how to end it,* London.

Potter, J., and Wetherell, M. (1987) *Discourse and Social Psychology. Beyond Attitudes and Behaviour,* London.

Prieto, C. (1994) *Trabajadores y condiciones de trabajo,* Madrid.

Rosanvallon, P. (1995) *La nouvelle question sociale. Repenser l'Etat de providence,* Paris.

Sampson, E. (1989) Foundations for a textual analysis of selfhood: The deconstruction of the self, in: Shotter, J., and K.J. Gergen, *Text of Identity*, London.
Serrano, A. (1995) Procesos paradójicos de construcción de la juventud en un contexto de crisis del mercado de trabajo *Revista Española de Investigaciones Sociológicas* 71-72, pp. 177-201.
De Terssac, G. (1992) *Autonomie dans le travail*, Paris.
Tobio, C. (1988) El paro juvenil : ¿Socialmente transversal? *Politica y Sociedad*, 1, p. 89-96.
Toharia, L. (1986) Un fordisme inachevé, entre transition politique et crise économique, in: *La flexibilité du travail en Europe*, Paris.
Touraine, A. (1993) *Crítica de la modernidad*, Madrid.
Tuñón de Lara, M., Valdeón Baruque, J., and Domínguez Ortiz, A. (1991) *Historia de España*, Barcelona.

7
Social change and the risks of social exclusion in Greece: How do the middle classes fare?

MARIA PETMESIDOU

7.1 Introduction

As a late industrialising country of the European periphery, Greece has a number of social structure and social stratification characteristics which sharply distinguish it from Northwest Europe. Moreover, significant historical legacies of an eastern origin[1], combined with the dominance of Christian Orthodox religious values, also set Greece apart from the socio-cultural patterns of the Latin Rim countries, i.e. Portugal, Spain, and Italy (Petmesidou, 1996c: 96-103). It is no accident, for instance, that various comparative studies of European social structures, e.g. the comparative studies by Titmus (1974), Castles (1989 and 1993), and Esping-Andersen (1990) of welfare regimes, have so far ignored Greece. Characteristics such as the maintenance and reproduction of a large agricultural sector, a huge informal economy, and large-scale self-employment, together with the extensive practice of holding multiple jobs, tax evasion on a massive scale, the important role of the family in a social system characterised by welfare and planning policies of a very rudimentary level, and the predominance of political integration modes based upon clientelist relations and statism/paternalism are its main feature. These significantly affect stratification patterns and, more particularly, the size and composition of the middle classes.

Under these conditions, the relevance of analytic tools (i.e. class concepts)[2] and the explanatory themes developed in the class stratification debate concerning Northwest European societies (e.g. the trend of proletarianization of some sections of the middle classes)[3] to the Greek case are highly questionable. The social fluidity of class boundaries, the low degree of change in employment and occupational structures, and the predominance of traditional middle classes are inherent in Greece's social stratification pattern.[4] Owing to the rigidities of statist/paternalistic forms of social and economic organisation, which are linked to petty capitalism, the trends of change in social stratification and the risks created for various social groups (including the middle classes) differ significantly from the trends characterising Northwest Europe.

After a brief discussion of the idiosyncrasies of Greece's social structure and pattern of stratification, an empirical investigation of the socio-professional structure, the changing composition of the middle classes, and the risks of social insecurity/social

B. Steijn et al. (eds.), Economic Restructuring and the Growing Uncertainty of the Middle Class, 115-133.
© 1998 *Kluwer Academic Publishers.*

exclusion is presented. The main argument is that, although changes in occupational structure show an improvement in the socio-professional position of large sections of the middle class, the distinctive characteristics of socio-economic structures in Greece create serious risks of social insecurity, which, however, remain hidden. These risks are mainly linked to the deadlock created by the statist forms of social and economic organisation coupled with the effects of European integration and global economic changes.

7.2 The idiosyncrasies of Greece's social stratification pattern

In Greek society, where almost half of the economically active population are employers or self-employed (47% in 1991, a quite high percentage even compared to Italy, Spain, and Portugal)[5], the middle classes are made up mainly of traditional petty bourgeoisie: self-employed professionals, small business owners, and craftspeople. Salaried employees also form a large part of this group: white-collar workers in the private sector, sales personnel and service workers, as well as civil servants (employees in public administration and public enterprises constitute more than 50% of salaried workers). Further more, middle-class strata in Greek society are characterised by a high degree of fragmentation, as we shall see below, and it is for this reason that the term plural 'middle classes' is used here.

A new middle class (or service class) resulting from the expansion of the welfare state and the ranks of managers and professionals in big businesses in Northwest Europe and North America (under the conditions of what is variously defined as 'Fordism' or 'organised capitalism')[6] has only began to emerge in Greece. Fordist forms of economic organisation and attendant corporatist arrangements of welfare capitalism have never achieved prominence. Instead, we can define Greece's economic structure as petty capitalism combined with statist/paternalistic forms of socio-political organisation. Further more, owing to particular socio-historical conditions going back to the period of independence from Ottoman rule (1830), a strong hegemonic class, in economic and political terms, has never really formed in Greece, though in various historical periods, particular strata and alliances of social strata succeeded in gaining power and ruling the country. Also, given the absence of a fully-fledged Fordist system of production, the working class has always been very weak, both in size and political power. Technicians and workers employed on a salary or wage basis[7] constituted 21% of the economically active population in 1971; that figure increased to 22% in 1981 and decreased to 19% in 1991. Moreover, of the total number of technicians and workers, were only 15% employed in manufacturing amounted to only 15% throughout the seventies and early eighties; that figure decreased to 11% in 1991. Given the fact that a large number of them are employed in very small family businesses (the average size of manufacturing enterprises being about 5 persons) or that many of them have an undefined occupational status, since they are self-employed as well, it is obvious that a proletariat has never been consolidated and working class boundaries remain highly diffuse.

Weak class closure also characterises the middle classes, a large part of which are first-generation rural immigrants. The massive wave of rural to urban migration during the fifties and sixties constituted the main channel of social mobility. The acquisition of educational credentials by the upwardly mobile sections of the agricultural strata and the availability of occupational opportunities under the conditions of comparatively high rates of economic growth facilitated is rural exodus. The strong desire of agrarian and urban lower middle-class strata to seek educational credentials (and eventually a job in the public sector) for their offsprings as a vehicle of social mobility is extensively documented in the literature (see, for instance, Lambiri-Dimaki, 1974 and Tsoukalas, 1977 and 1986).

The brief discussion of the main aspects of social and economic organisation in Greece that follows highlights the peculiarities of its pattern of social stratification and the relative importance of the middle classes.

7.2.1 The leap from pre-Fordism to post-Fordism

During the fifties and sixties, the industrialisation process proceeded at a rapid rate. However, since the early seventies, the economy has de-industrialised, even before industrial employment peaked as high as in Northwest Europe (not as high as in northern Italy or northern Spain). Since the eighties, the rapid expansion of tourist activities and related services, and trade and personal services has kept the growth rate of the tertiary sector elevated in comparison to manufacturing, while other kinds of services which are central in the post-industrial employment structures of Northwest Europe (such as welfare and production) have failed to develop. Agricultural employment has also shrunk, though Greece still has a large agricultural sector (21% of the labour force) compared to the other southern European countries (employment in agriculture amount to 8% in Italy, 10% in Spain, and 12% in Portugal).

The shift from agrarian structures to a service-oriented economy contributed to an expansion of the traditional middle-class strata and reinforced such phenomena as informal economic transactions; the predominance of small businesses with informal labour relations; subcontracting and flexible forms of work resulting from the practice of multiple employment by a wide range of social groups. In the late eighties, informal economic activities in Greece amounted to about 40% of the GDP produced in the formal economy (Provopoulos, 1987). A recent study by the Centre of Planning and Economic Research in Athens concluded that 90% of the GDP produced by manufacturing remains unregistered, i.e. it constitutes part of the informal sector. This usually concerns small units, especially in the clothing and footwear industries, since, for instance, more than two hundred thousand workers (mostly women) employed in the garment industry work at home, remain unregistered, and contribute to the growth of the hidden economy (Petmesidou and Tsoulouvis, 1994b: 14).

This situation in Greece favours the expansion of social strata of mobile workers, that is, workers with no fixed employment status, who cross the boundaries between self-employment and employee status, between the private and public sector, and the formal and informal economy. Examples of these phenomena abound: peasants (smallholders) who are often employed as seasonal workers in industry or services (mainly tourism), public employees who run their own private business in their off hours or help in the family enterprise, craftsmen who are partly wage workers and partly self-employed, and so on. Undoubtedly, these phenomena render social boundaries highly fluid, increase social heterogeneity and fragmentation, and limit social integration based on collective social action and solidaristic values. The weakness of civil society in Greece testifies to this.

7.2.2 Statism, familialism, and the middle classes

Greece's most significant feature, which so strongly influences its tradition and culture, social stratification, and the very distinctive model of development and modernisation that Greece has been following for quite some time, is the social legitimation of the state as a huge apparatus of creation and distribution of value, wealth, income, and benefits by extra-economic, i.e., political means and criteria (Petmesidou and Tsoulouvis, 1990: 183). This function of the state, in relation to the widespread ideology that 'everything is a matter of politics', often orients individuals and social groups to the open use of political means to appropriate resources and other economic benefits (for a detailed examination of this statist/paternalistic model of social organisation and its historical roots, see Petmesidou, 1987 and 1992; Tsoulouvis, 1987).

This condition points at a crucial dimension of social inequalities (that of access to clientelistic networks and political power as a means of getting revenue) which seriously fragments the middle classes and makes class boundaries even more difficult to define. Let me briefly stress, socio-political conflicts have always cost strong ideological confrontations on how legitimate credentials of access to the state and clientelistic networks should be defined. Ideological-political confrontations of this type have always been at the forefront of social struggles. Some of the most striking examples include, the strong ideological-political confrontation between nationalists (i.e. those who had access to the state) and outcasts (i.e. those denied access by being branded 'communists' or 'leftists' in the two decades after the Second World War; or between progressives (with a left connotation) and conservatives, an ideological confrontation which, in the period following the fall of the junta, reshuffled the legitimate credentials of access to the state in favour of those segments of the middle classes that were excluded from the clientelistic networks of the right for more than two decades. What is more, these struggles transform social conflicts into individualistic power feuds and, thus, do not favour collective solidarity either of an occupational-corporatist mode, characteristic of central Europe, or of a universalist mode, as is the case in Scandinavia and the UK (Petmesidou and Tsoulouvis,1994a).

The extensive reproduction of the socio-professional groups that constitute the traditional middle classes is highly dependent on the conditions of statism. The weak concentration of capital, the low degree of rational competition (through market mechanisms), and great opportunities for windfall profits and state support even for inefficient businesses on the basis of political criteria create favourable conditions for small-scale businesses and self-employed people to survive. Similarly, an 'overbloated' public administration has historically been the basis for the formation and socio-political integration of large sections of the middle and lower middle classes (Petmesidou, 1991: 40; see also Tsoukalas, 1983).

Another side of this mode of social organisation is the central role of the family/household (especially among the middle classes) as a strategic unit of decision-making regarding the employment opportunities of its members and as an important redistribution unit providing individuals with the means to overcome distress, unemployment, and bankruptcy. Given the inability of society to work out compromises and a social consensus for a wide redistribution of resources on the basis of universalist social citizenship rights, family and kin are the main support units in Greek society. Families and households attempt to combine a variety of activities in the formal and informal economy, along with employment in the public sector for at least one of the family members as a source of secured income and a means of access to clientelist networks. Familialism further contributes to an individualistic culture by upholding discretionary rights to benefits and services, secured on the basis of particularistic-clientelistic criteria, and thus severely limit the full maturation of collective social solidarities and universalist values. The highly fragmented social insurance system, with huge inequalities in the structure and organisation of social insurance funds as well as in the level of contributions and the types and levels of benefits provided, is a clear example of this model of discretionary entitlements, which also creates huge inequalities within the middle classes (Petmesidou, 1991: 38 and 1996b: 335-338).

Familialism is closely linked to statist/paternalistic forms of social organisation, since family and kin would hardly be in a position to play a key role in welfare in Greek society if state intervention did not make it possible for households to derive revenue by extra economic means and distribute it to their members. Familialist values and strategies, combined with statism, create favourable conditions for individuals, households, and enterprises to pursue what could be called 'soft budgeting' practices, particularly for those segments of the middle classes which can secure access to the state and political power. 'Soft budgeting' consists of an accounting practice in which *"the strict condition that earnings must always be greater than or, at least, equal to expenses is not obeyed, simply because someone else is paying the difference"* (Petmesidou and Tsoulouvis, 1994b: 22). The ensuing imbalances are transferred to the state and are dealt with through the creation and distribution of value, income, and wealth, by political means. Various examples of such a discretionary appropriation of resources and benefits by various sections of the middle classes can be given: trespassing on public land and large-scale illegal building of houses in particular localities (including villas, hotels, and other buildings and not only accommodation for the poor), large-scale tax evasion and informal economic activities tolerated by the state, the abuse of disability pensions, etc. These examples illustrate some aspects of a wealth-generating and redistribution process which is unthinkable by the standards of the very strict system of social planing and welfare policies of north European countries. These features make it clear that conceptual tools of class analysis are highly inadequate for explaining social inequalities and attendant stratification patterns in Greece. The same holds for interpretations stressing the social insecurity faced by various segments of the new middle classes (or service class) in the post-modern era, resulting from: (a) extensive restructuring of the welfare state, e.g. through significant changes in social security, health care, education, etc., which affect occupational opportunities, careers, and incomes of large sectors of the population (including large sections of the middle classes, which were formed by the expansion of the welfare state); (b) changes in technology and job structure and, most importantly, the diminishing range of the managerial hierarchy in both the private and public sectors, combined with strategies of downsizing and flexible work conditions, which threaten job security and established career paths among the middle classes.[8] Given the fact that Greece skipped the industrialisation and Fordist patterns of production, social transformation has a different character and orientation. Consequently, forms and processes of social exclusion in Greek society and growing risks of social insecurity for the middle classes also differ significantly from the above phenomena.

7.3 Changes in occupational structure and the synthesis of the middle classes

As stressed above, the distinctive characteristic of Greece's labour force is the high percentage of self-employed and non-paid family members who work in family businesses (table 7.1). Hence, the percentage of the salaried and wage earners is only slightly over 55%. Between 1981 and 1991 Greece's labour force increased by 9.7% (342,360 workers). The number of female workers in particular increased very fast (by almost 30%), while the number of male workers increased by only 2.6%.

Table 7.1

Constitution of the labour force with reference to position in the job hierarchy (1981-1991)

Positie in the job	1981			1991			Rate of change 1981 - 1991 (%)		
	Total	Men	Women	Total	Men	Women	Total	Men	Women
Employers	3.0	3.7	1.0	7.3	8.6	4.4	159.2	132.1	441.9
Self-employed	4.4	42.1	12.9	30.4	35.6	18.7	-5.95	-15.2	78.0
Employees	51.00	49.2	56.1	55.9	52.0	64.6	16.3	6.0	41.3
Helping and unpaid members	11.60	5.0	30.0	6.4	3.8	12.4	-41.3	-23.7	-49.4
Total active population (in thousands)	3.543	2.584	959	3.886	2.650	1.236	9.7	2.6	28.8

Source: Elaboration of census data of the National Statistical Service of Greece (ESYE), 1981, 1991.

Another important observation is that the number of salaried and waged workers increased very slightly, while the number of employers almost doubled. This means that despite the economic crisis, the number of firms in the country is growing and, thus, there are many opportunities for small entrepreneurs to start a business are high. Moreover, female workers in this category increased by 441.9% (male workers by only 132.1%), reflecting the increasing opportunities for women to hold top positions over the last decade. However, this may not be an accurate picture of the present situation, given the existence of a large number of women working at home on a subcontract basis (often in the black economy).

The number of self-employed workers decreased slightly, while unpaid workers decreased by 41%. The decrease in this category (especially women) is closely linked to the shrinking of the agricultural sector. The increase in the number of employers and employees, and the decrease in the self-employed (along with the family unpaid members who could be merged with the self-employed) indicates that there may be a trend towards polarisation, as far occupational stratification is concerned, negatively affecting the lower middle classes. However, as shown in table 7.2, this trend is developing along with an improvement in job status for a large part of the labour force.

To examine Greece's occupational structure between 1981 and 1991, the 86 two-digit-code occupation categories defined by the National Statistical Service of Greece (ESYE) were for the sake of simplification merged into 14 groups. The merging of the initial categories was based on the principle of classifying occupations according to status, skill level, and industry. However, because ESYE does not provide detailed skill descriptions, separating skilled from unskilled workers is very difficult in some occupations (i.e. white-collar workers, service workers, etc.). Occupational categories 1 to 9 (table 7.1) encompass the various sections of the Greek middle classes. Part of category 12 can also be regarded as middle class, as it includes technicians and artisans who may be own account workers or small employers.

Tertiary sector employment (mainly in trade, tourism, and personal services) has always been high in Greece owing to the low degree of industrialisation, but it has grown even more in the last decade. The expansion of liberal professions and high-status service jobs creates the impression that Greece is following Europe in the rise and growth of new middle-class strata. However, this is happening only to a very limited extent, given that the percentage of workers in tertiary occupations are generally considered crucial to further growth and post-industrial development (transport and communications, finance and insurance) is still very limited.

Table 7.2
Occupational structure (1981, 1991)

	Occupational categories	1981	1991	Rate of change (%) 1981-1991
1.	Higher grade professionals	7.28	10.18	53.28
2.	Lower grade professionals	2.10	2.55	33.42
3.	Administrators and managers	1.74	1.67	5.17
4.	Higher grade clerical workers	1.98	2.89	60.05
5.	Lower grade clerical workers	7.49	8.25	20.71
6.	Employers and managers in wholesale and retail trade	5.57	7.11	40.00
7.	Sales personnel	2.93	3.77	41.32
8.	Employers and managers in services	1.14	1.52	45.56
9.	Lower grade service workers	6.70	7.80	27.54
10.	Farmers and fishermen	26.61	16.54	-31.83
11.	Agricultural workers	0.85	0.84	7.44
12.	Technicians, artisans, foremen and skilled workers	30.37	26.11	-5.73
13.	Unskilled workers	1.22	1.63	47.46
14.	Young persons entering the labour market first time	2.51	4.33	89.15
15.	Non-classifiable	1.51	4.82	250.59
	Total	100.00	100.00	9.66

Source: As in Table 7.1
[The fourteen categories are based on the 86 two-digit occupational groups defined by ESYE. The names of occupational categories constitute short descriptions of the two-digit-code occupational groups included in each one of the fourteen categories.]

Changes in occupational structure reflect an increase in the number of non-manual jobs in both the public and private sectors, that is, of all middle-class occupational categories in Greek society. The crucial issue is whether this change is being accompanied by any social polarisation, that is, a concentration of workers at the two ends of the socio-professional hierarchy, i.e. in high-level and low-level non-manual jobs. Such trends of social polarisation and labour market dualism, which affect the various sections of the middle classes differently, have been observed in some north European countries and in North-America in the post-modern era, for instance, through the expansion of high-level business-related and private welfare services, on

the one hand, and low-paid unskilled service jobs (mainly in the recreational or 'fun' industries) on the other (Esping-Andersen et al., 1993: 45-52 and Hamnett, 1994). We can hypothesise that if social polarisation continues, it might be accompanied by a lowering of education level, diminishing skills, decreasing opportunities for self-employment, and increasing unemployment for a considerable part of the labour force.[9]

Figure 7.1
Changes in the constitution of the male and female labour force (by occupational groups, 1981-1991)

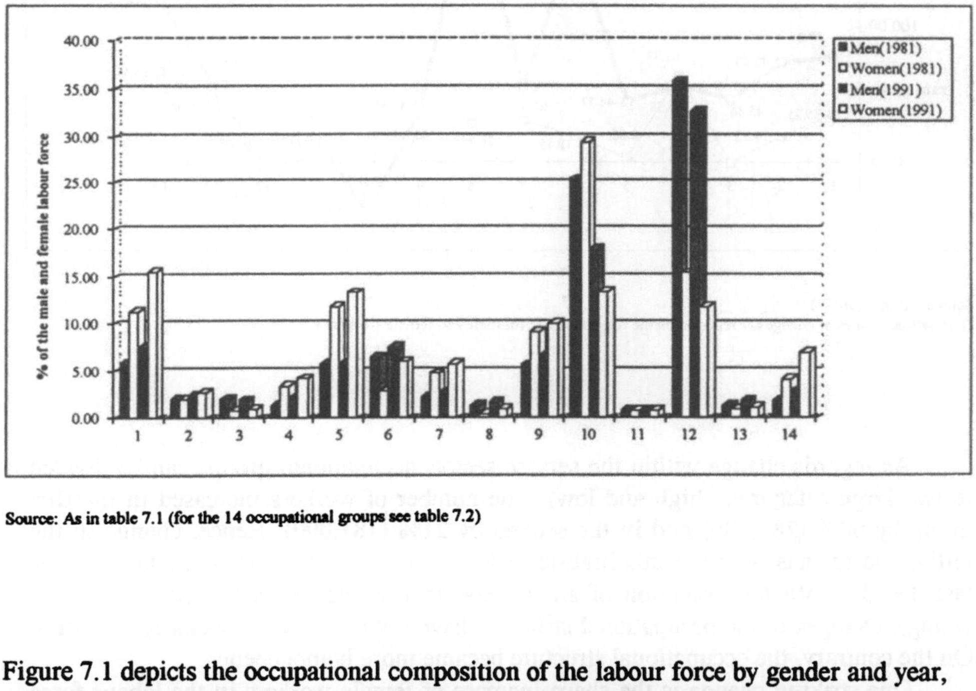

Source: As in table 7.1 (for the 14 occupational groups see table 7.2)

Figure 7.1 depicts the occupational composition of the labour force by gender and year, while the two lines in Figure 7.2 give ratios of change for the number of workers by occupational group and gender between 1981 and 1991. The growth of the labour force has not been uniform across occupational groups. Farmers (employers and self-employed) decreased by three hundred thousand, while salaried land workers increased by only two thousand. For technicians, artisans, foremen and skilled workers there has been job decline (by sixty-one thousand), while unskilled workers increased by twenty thousand. Thus, the general trend has been one of decline in the primary and secondary sector and growth in services. An increase in the number of unemployed workers seeking a job for the first time has also been observed. Their number almost doubled in one decade, to 4.6% of the country's labour force in 1991. In the same year, the rest of the unemployed amounted to 3.4%.

Figure 7.2
Rate of change of the numbers of workers by gender and socio-professional group (1981-1991)

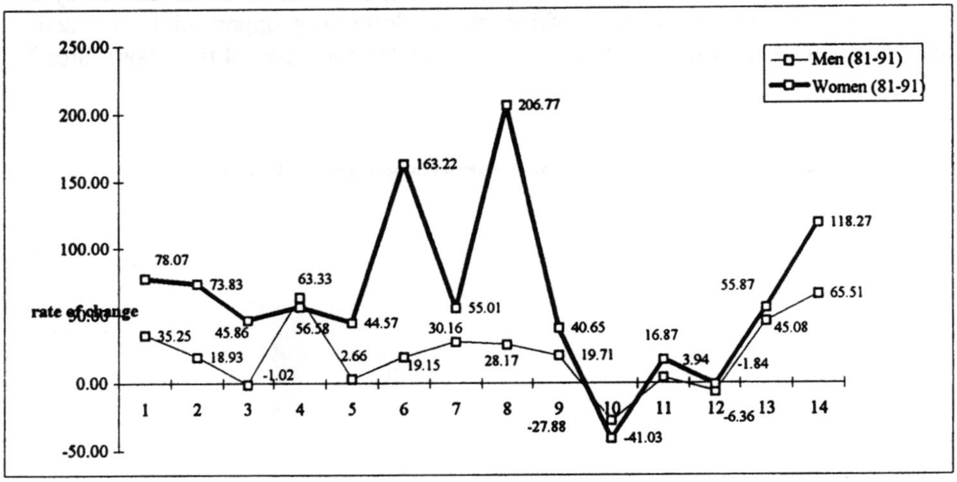

Source: As in figure 7.1
[The values of rates of change are reported on the respective line for male and female workers.]

As regards change within the service sector, occupational groups can be divided to two large categories (high and low). The number of workers increased in the first group by 60% (287,000) and in the second by 21% (181,000). Hence, change in the tertiary sector has been towards high-level jobs. Thus, it can be argued that, over the last decade, with the exception of an increase in the unemployed (especially of the young), changes in the occupational structure have not exacerbated social inequalities. On the contrary, the occupational structure became more homogeneous.

One striking change is the sharp increase of female workers in the labour force during the eighties (from 27% in 1981 to 31.8% in 1991). Rates of change by gender and occupational group show that, in many occupations, the number of female workers increased by a much higher ratio than the corresponding number of male workers. Thus, the number of female professionals increased by 78%, directors or owners of shops and other commercial businesses by 163%, and female directors or owners of restaurants, hotels and other similar establishments by 207%, while the corresponding rates for men are 35%, 19% and 28% respectively. The only occupational group in which the numbering of male workers increased faster than female workers is that of high-level clerical workers (see figure 7.2).

Further more, high-grade tertiary sector jobs for women increased faster than low-grade ones. Thus, there is no evidence of deterioration of the position of women in the Greek labour market. Nevertheless, among new entrants in the labour market women face more difficulty in finding a job than men do, as the sharp increase in unemployed 'new' female workers indicate (see figure 7.1).

The positive trends in occupational change are further supported by the fast rise in the educational level of the labour force, especially female workers. In 1981, male and female workers with university degrees comprised 5.2% and 2.3% of the workforce respectively; these figures increased to 7.6% and 5.3% in 1991 (the increase for women being faster than for men). On the other hand, in 1981, male and female workers who were illiterate or had not completed a primary education constituted 5.9% and 10.4% of all workers, while the corresponding percentages for 1991 were 5% and 2.6%, respectively, again indicating a rapid progress for women (see figure 7.3).

Figure 7.3

Changes in the level of education of the male and female labour force (1981-1991)

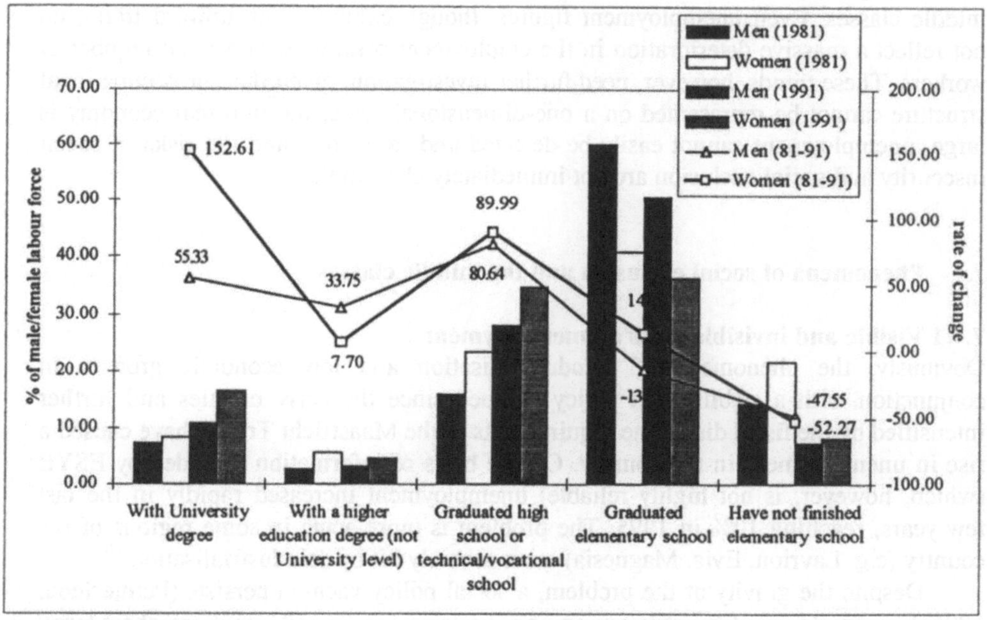

Source: As in Figure 7.1

[The right hand sight y-axis depicts per cent constitution of the labour force with regard to level of education, while the left-hand sight y-axis depicts rates of change.]

During the eighties, Greece's economy, labour market, and occupational structure undoubtedly underwent significant changes linked to the economic crisis, de-industrialisation, and related restructuring trends at the international level (Petmesidou and Tsoulouvis, 1994b). This accounts for the shift to tertiary sector activities, the decreasing number of manual jobs, and rising unemployment especially among the young and the educated. However, these changes were counterbalanced by a remarkable stability in the position of the workers in their jobs, and particularly by the maintenance and reproduction of a large number of self-employed workers who make up the bulk of the Greek middle classes; an increase in their level of training and education; and expansion of high-grade jobs (scientists, professionals, administrators, and managers). In addition, the growth in the number of female workers was accompanied by a considerable improvement in the position of women in the labour market. These observations indicate that economic decline and restructuring in Greece have not been accompanied by increasing social inequalities, labour market dualism, and social polarisation that would intensify social insecurity for some segments of the middle classes. Even unemployment figures, though exhibiting an upward trend, do not reflect a massive deterioration in the employment conditions of a great number of workers. These trends, however, need further investigation, given that the occupational structure cannot be represented on a one-dimensional scale, the informal economy is large, unemployment cannot easily be detected and measured, and the risks of social insecurity and social exclusion are not immediately observable.

7.4 Phenomena of social exclusion and the middle classes

7.4.1 Visible and invisible risks of unemployment

Obviously, the phenomena of deindustrialisation and low economic growth, in conjunction with a stabilisation policy pursued since the early nineties and further intensified by the fiscal discipline requirements of the Maastricht Treaty, have caused a rise in unemployment in the country. On the basis of information provided by ESYE (which, however, is not highly reliable) unemployment increased rapidly in the last few years, reaching 10% in 1995. The problem is more acute in some regions of the country (e.g. Lavrion, Evia, Magnesia) more severely hit by deindustrialisation.[10]

Despite the gravity of the problem, a social policy vacuum persists (Petmesidou, 1996a), unemployment benefits are among the lowest in the EU, and are short-term, while any income support schemes for the long-term unemployed (who amount to 51% of all unemployed, Eurostat, 1995) are lacking. Equally rudimentary are any active employment measures (i.e. vocational training, subsidised employment), amounting to only 0.4% of the GDP in the early nineties (see Petmesidou, 1996b: 341). Consequently, we can assume that unemployment, particularly when it is long-term, creates a major risk of social exclusion.

The relationship between unemployment and level of education exposes the risks facing the middle class strata. Unemployment percentages for those with a higher education were 5.9% in 1981, 8.5% in 1985, and 26.6% in 1994, while the corresponding percentages for women were higher. Unemployed female workers with post-graduate degrees comprised 7.1% of all female workers with this education level in 1994, while the corresponding percentage for male workers was 6.5%, indicating that educated male workers can find a job more easily than female workers with the same education. Furthermore, the Ministry of Labour questioned the reliability of the ESYE surveys, stressing that there are about 120,000 unemployed with university degree (of them 20,000 being medical doctors).

These observations contradict the remarks regarding the positive trends in the Greek occupational structure and indicate some rather subtle processes of social exclusion threatening not only the most deprived groups, but also parts of the middle-class strata. The contradiction between an apparent upward mobility to higher level jobs for a large part of the labour force and increasing risks of unemployment among the educated (most of them self-employed) can be explained by Greece's idiosyncratic economic structure and the labour market. First, because of the very small size of entrepreneurial activities in the country and the very low start-up capital required, there have been literally no economic barriers to entrepreneurs establishing new firms even in a period of economic crisis. This is particularly true for tourism, trade, and artisan activities. Thus, between 1988 and 1994, there were 354,534 closures; yet their negative impact was counterbalanced by the establishment of 747,519 new firms. As we can see, not all entrepreneurs are successful in their ventures, but those who fail seldom register as unemployed. The same holds for self-employed professionals, whose number increased significantly in the last decade. Consequently, unemployment or underemployment in middle-class strata (as well as among self-employed peasants) remains hidden, which accounts for Greece's low unemployment rate compared to other European Union countries.

Second, given the fact that a large part of the labour force are mobile workers with no fixed employment status, it could be argued that not all those in the middle class who claim to be self-employed, actually merit this status. Some of them may work on a sub-contract basis, as quasi-employees who, however, are uninsured by their employers and, when unemployed, cannot claim any benefits. This mainly relates to women working at home as sub-contractors; it is also true for an unspecified number of professionals and scientists who declare themselves self-employed but in practice are quasi-salaried workers employed in private companies under precarious conditions.

The above analysis of Greece's occupational structure mainly concerns Greek workers and a small number of registered foreigners, and ignores the increasing number of unregistered refugees and migrants who entered the country after the collapse of the communist regimes in eastern Europe and the former USSR. According to unofficial estimates by the Ministry of Labour, the number of foreign workers in Greece was 120,000 in the early nineties, 80% of whom had no work permit. Estimates by other agencies give a much higher number: up to 600,000 in 1996 (the majority of them without a work permit). Foreign workers constitute about 9% of Greece's population, or 15% of the salaried and wage earners, a high percentage by European

Union standards. There are various reasons for this new migratory pattern, which we will not elaborate here. However, one explanation is the changing demographic structure of the Greek labour force, particularly the decreasing number of young unskilled Greek workers which creates space for workers from ex-communist countries of the Balkan area or other east European countries, southern Mediterranean countries (e.g. Egypt), or Third World countries (Petrinioti, 1993). In light of the above analysis, it is evident that there is increasing competition in the ranks of the Greek labour force for higher-status positions, while lower-status jobs are left to underprivileged groups, mainly immigrants and refugees. Although official statistics do not show any observable polarisation trends, a significant percentage of the labour active population (about 9%) includes the most underprivileged and, thus, socially excluded strata.

7.4.2 Fragmentation of social protection and the risks of social exclusion

Phenomena of social exclusion linked to visible and invisible unemployment are further exacerbated by the highly dualistic social protection system in Greece. First, social insurance very much depends upon a full and uninterrupted work career, which leaves the most vulnerable groups of the labour force (the long-term unemployed, immigrants, and refugees) totally unprotected. Also, because immigrants lack a family and kin safety net, which has traditionally been the most effective means for dealing with problems of hardship and impoverishment, they become the most deprived and exploited social groups.

Furthermore, dualism in social insurance also increases the risk of social exclusion for parts of the indigenous population, including some middle-class strata. A striking example of this concerns the fact that the 'theoretical' earnings replacement rates for a person with a full working career even surpasses the net average wage in manufacturing (107% in 1992, while the EU average was 75%); on the other hand, the minimum benefit for an elderly person with no contributive entitlements and no other means of support is extremely low, amounting to only 8% of the net average wage in manufacturing (the EU average being 36%, Commission of the European Communities, 1994: 54-55). The minimum benefit for a disabled person who cannot work and has no other means of support is equally low (16% of GDP per capita in 1992, the lowest rate among EU countries), while an unemployed person with no contributive entitlements and no other means of support cannot claim any benefits.

Moreover, Greece lacks an institutional framework enabling regional/municipal and voluntary agents to play a significant role in social protection, as is, for instance, the case in Italy and Spain where regional and municipal authorities implement various social assistance schemes, and a number of voluntary organisations offer a wide range of social services and minimum income assistance to disadvantaged groups (Rossell and Rimbau, 1989: 115-117; Saraceno and Negri, 1994: 22-23).

Similarly, fragmentation in social insurance schemes is also very high. In 1995, there were 86 social security funds administering compulsory and supplementary pension schemes, and 236 institutions (under the control of six different Ministries) providing health care and social welfare benefits. These vary enormously among occupational social insurance funds creating great inequalities in per capita social expenditure. For instance, per capita expenditure for medical care, drugs, hospital treatment, and other care services for the social fund of tradesmen, technicians, and craftsmen (who are employers or self-employed), TEBE , is the lowest, amounting to only one fourth of per capita health care expenditure of the funds of bank employees (in a number of private and public banks). The total per capita health care expenditure and cash benefits by IKA (the largest social insurance fund for blue and white-collar workers) is equally low. Moreover, inequalities exist not only between the different occupational categories, but even within them (as is manifested by the inequalities in per capita health expenditure in the different social funds of lawyers; Petmesidou, 1996b: 335). As shown elsewhere (Petmesidou, 1991 and 1996b), fragmentation of social protection reflects the particularistic, discretionary appropriation of welfare resources by social groups on the basis of their access to clientelistic networks and political power structures. Inequalities in social protection are kept high among the various middle-class strata, depending upon the differential access to the state enjoyed by each socio-professional group or segment.

Legislative innovation (i.e. the establishment of a national health care system, which, however, is still far from becoming a universalist system) and the expansion of social expenditure in the early eighties (giving rise to a short glimpse of a welfare state), are closely linked to the socio-political changes which set in motion a process of political democratisation in the late seventies. The increasing social and political weight of middle-class strata added momentum and, under the political slogan of *allaghi* (change), established a broad social alliance of those social groups that had been excluded from the patronage networks of the right-wing political forces which, in one form or another, ruled the country for more than two decades after the Second World War.

A detailed historical analysis of the transition to democracy in Greece is beyond the scope of this chapter, however it should be stressed that this transition was beset by a number of contradictions. On the one hand, the increasing social and political weight of the middle-class strata promoted a political debate that acknowledged the necessity of expanding social protection to confront problems such as rudimentary welfare provision, huge inequalities in income maintenance, the absence of a universal minimum income safety net, etc. On the other hand, the very nature of social conflicts, centering on a redefinition of the 'political credentials' of access to the state, and, thus, on a realignment of clientelistic networks, hindered solidaristic values and blocked any effective solutions to the above problems (Petmesidou, 1991: 41-45). The intensification of intra-middle-class conflicts for ensuring access to the state machinery cancel out any attempt of developing consistent and efficient redistribution policies. This also explains why the response by the successive socialist (PASOK) governments to these problems was limited to rhetoric about the need of decentralisation and the development of the welfare state. The biggest obstacle to the exercise of social policy and social planning has been the lack of social consensus among middle-class strata about policy goals and, at a more fundamental level, about how the cost of social and economic development would be distributed. These conditions maintained and perpetuated fragmentation in social protection, increasing the risks of social insecurity for some of the most vulnerable parts of the middle classes (i.e. various categories of own account workers running the risk of hidden unemployment and small businessmen facing bankruptcy).

Soon a number of crises (e.g. a growing public deficit, a huge public debt (reaching 125% of the GDP in 1995) and a fiscal crisis involving social insurance funds, linked to demographic changes, as well as technological advancements in medical practice, limited the further expansion of a rather weak welfare state. Legislative reforms were passed in the early nineties to reduce the public deficit and manage the social security crisis, but they only increased social polarisation. Thus the number of pensioners receiving the minimum pension (well below the poverty threshold) increased significantly, amounting to 600,000 in 1996 (a large number of them belonged to the occupational group of white-collar workers, service workers, and self-employed craftsmen, artisans, and tradesmen). Indeed, in the last couple of years, inadequate minimum pensions and rising unemployment have become the most hotly debated issues leading to serious confrontations between pensioners' associations and trade unions, on the one hand, and the state, on the other.

7.5 Conclusion

The above analysis shows the risks of social insecurity among the Greek middle classes, linked to the conditions of petty capitalism and statist/paternalist forms of social and political organisation. The path of social transformation in Greece differs markedly from the trends characterising Northwest Europe. Since the seventies, global restructuring trends have reinforced various traditional aspects of Greek society and have accelerated the shift from pre-Fordist to post-Fordist structures. These conditions supported the extensive reproduction of traditional middle-class occupations, especially within the tertiary sector, including tourism, trade, and personal services.

Further more, changes in the occupational structure do not show signs of social polarisation of middle-class jobs; rather, an improvement in the job position of a large part of the middle classes is evident in the relatively sharp increase in high-level tertiary jobs (combined with an increase in education and skill levels for a large part of the labour force, particularly for female workers), and in the opportunities for entrepreneurs to start new businesses even under conditions of economic crisis.

However, due to the unique character of the Greek society and economy, these improvements in the socio-professional position of middle-class strata are more apparent than real. Social insecurity, unemployment, and social exclusion threaten not only the most deprived groups of the population (i.e. legal and illegal immigrants, workers in areas hit by deindustrialisation, deprived agricultural areas), but also some sections of the urban middle classes, especially the traditional petty bourgeoisie and those strata of mobile workers who fluctuate between formal and informal economic activities.

The statist-clientelist mode of social organisation led to serious deadlocks, as conflicts about access to the state intensified antagonisms and social fragmentation among the middle classes to an unprecedented scale in the last decade (large-scale corruption is an indication of this crisis). Closely linked to these deadlocks is the diminishing effectiveness of traditional modes of tackling social deprivation and hardship through family/kin support due to changing trends in family patterns (e.g. increasing participation of women in the labour force, growing rates of divorce, and one-parent families), and diminishing opportunities of 'soft budgeting' strategies under conditions of economic stagnation and the exhaustion of the model of production of surplus income and wealth by political methods. The social fabric has started to corrode, which may lead to a deterioration in the standard of living for a great many social groups.

The serious socio-political deadlocks, compounded by the fiscal crisis of the state, make the need for large-scale institutional change in Greece urgent. An expanding national debate on the necessity of large-scale modernisation bring this into relief, while pressures on Greece to harmonise its institutions with those of the European Union and improve economic performance, so as not to become marginalized in the new international economic order, make this need even more pressing. Undoubtedly, modernisation will have significant negative effects on the size and constitution of the traditional middle classes, yet it is difficult to foresee and assess the gravity of these effects. Suffice it to say that, if not backed by the development of universalist citizenship values of civil society, large-scale reforms in economic structure (i.e. restriction of the informal economy and tax evasion, measures of fiscal discipline as stipulated by the Maastricht Treaty, privatisation, etc.), combined with changes in technology and skill structure (required for economic development), will exacerbate the phenomena of social marginalization and impoverishment and will cause extreme social tensions.

Notes

1. Having their roots in Ottoman autocracy.
2. For a comprehensive review of class and social stratification analysis, see Crompton (1993).
3. A view strongly supported by Braverman (1974) and debated further by Roberts *et al.* (1977), Abercrombie and Urry (1983), Crompton and Jones (1984).
4. Indeed, various aspects of social structure which have emerged in Northwest European countries since the seventies (in the context of 'isorganized capitalism' or 'post-Fordism', see Lash and Urry (1987) and Crook et al. (1992), such as the decline of collective forms of social action and class voting, development of cross-cutting forms of social division, and political conflict are more or less indigenous characteristics of Greek society.
5. Employers and own account workers in these countries amount to 29%, 26%, and 27% of their labour force respectively.
6. See Lash and Urry (1987). For an examination of the size, profile, and constitution of the service class in Britain, see Goldthorpe (1980).
7. Detailed data distinguishing between salaried and waged technicians and craftsmen are not available from the national Statistical Service of Greece.

8 For the extent to which these processes generate social insecutiry among the middle classes in the Netherlands, in Britain and in Germany, see in this volume the chapters by Berting, Steijn and Houtman, Savage, Crompton, and Kronauer.

9 Reliable income data (collected over a time period) are not available for examining changes in income inequalities. Incomes recorded in the tax registers are highly unreliable (especially as regards incomes acquired through self-employment), because of the large size of the black economy.

10 For an analysis of the spatial dimension of social inequalities and social exclusion in Greece, see Tsoulouvis (1996 and forthcoming).

References

Abercrombie, N., and J. Urry (1983) Capital, labour and the Middle Classes, London.

Braverman, H. (1974) *Labour and Monopoly Capital. The Degradation of Work in the Twentieth Century,* New York.

Castles, F. (ed.) (1989) *The Comparative History of Public Policy,* New York.

Castles, F. (1993) *Family of Nations. Patterns of Public Policy in Western Democracies,* Hants.

Commission of the European Communities (1994) *Social Protection in Europe,* Brussels (in Greek).

Crompton, R. (1993) *Class and Stratification,* Cambridge.

Crompton, R., and G. Jones (1984) *White-collar Proletariat. Deskilling and Gender in Clerical Work,* London.

Crook, S., J. Pakulski, and M. Waters (1992) *Postmodernization,* London.

Esping-Andersen, G. (1990) *The Three Worlds of Welfare Capitalism,* Cambridge.

Esping-Andersen, G., Z. Assimakopoulou, and K. van Kersbergen (1990) Trends in Contemporary Class Structuration: A Six Nation Comparison, in: G. Esping-Andersen (ed.) *Changing Classes,* London, pp. 32-57.

Eurastat (1995) Population and Social Conditions, *Statistics in Focus,* no 6, Luxembourg.

Hamnett, C. (1994) Social Polarization in Global Cities: Theory and Evidence, *Urban Studies,* vol.. 31, pp. 401-424.

Goldthorpe, J. H. (1980) *Social Mobility and Class Structure in Modern Britain,* Oxford.

Lambiri-Dimaki, I. (1974) *Towards a Greek Sociology of Education,* Athens (in Greek).

Lash, S., and J. Urry (1987) *The End of Organized Capitalism,* Cambridge.

Petmesidou, M. (1987) *Social Classes and Processes of Social Reproduction,* Athens (in Greek).

Petmesidou, M. (1991) Statism, Social Policy and the Middle Classes in Greece, *Journal of European Social Policy,* vol. 1, 1, pp. 31-48.

Petmesidou, M. (1992) *Social Inequalities and Social Policy,* Athens (in Greek).

Petmesidou, M. (1996a) Greece, Turkey and Cyprus: Poverty Research in a Policy Vacuum, in: E. Øyen, S.M. Miller, and S.A. Samad (eds) *Poverty, A Global Review,* Stockholm, pp. 287-324.

Petmesidou, M. (1996b) Social Protection in Greece. A Brief Glimpse of a Welfare state, *Journal of Social Policy and Administration,* vol. 30, 4, pp. 324-347.

Petmesidou, M. (1996c) Social Protection in Southern Europe, Trends and Prospects, *Journal of Area Studies,* 9, pp. 95-125.

Petmesidou, M., and L. Tsoulouvis (1990) Planning Technological Change and Economic Development in Greece, *Progress in Planning,* vol. 33, 3, pp. 175-262.

Petmesidou, M., and L. Tsoulouvis (1994a) Aspects of the Changing Political Economy of Europe, Welfare state, Class Segmentation and Planning in the Postmodern Era, *Sociology,* vol.. 28, 2, pp. 499-519.

Petmesidou, M., and L. Tsoulouvis (1994b) Labour Market Restructuring and Pressures for Modernizing Social Policy in Greece, Chapter presented in the Conference on *Greece: Prospects for Modernization* held at the London School of Economics and Political Science, pp. 1-28.

Petrinioti, X. (1993) *Immigration in Greece,* Athens (in Greek).

Provopoulos, P. G. (1987) *The Informal Economy in Greece,* Athens (in Greek).

Roberts, K., F. G. Cook, S. C. Clark, and E. Semeonoff (1977) *The Fragmentary Class Structure,* London.

Rossell, T. and C. Rimbau (1989) 'Spain - Social Services in the Post-Franco Democracy,' in, B. Munday (ed.) *The Crisis in Welfare,* London, Harvester, Wheatsheaf, 105-123.

Saraceno, C., and N. Negri (1994) 'The Changing Italian Welfare state,' *Journal of European Social Policy*, vol. 4, 1, pp. 19-34.
Titmus, R. M. (1974) *Social Policy*, London.
Tsoukalas, K. (1977) *Dependence and Reproduction*, Athens (in Greek).
Tsoukalas, K. (1983) The Social Meaning of State Employment in Postwar Greece, *Greek Review of Social Research*, 50, pp. 20-52.
Tsoukalas, K. (1986) *State, Society and Work in Postwar Greece*, Athens (in Greek).
Tsoulouvis, L. (1987) Aspects of Statism and Planning in Greece, *International Journal of Urban and Regional Research*, vol. 11, 4, pp. 500-521.
Tsoulouvis, L. (1996) Urban Planning, Social Policy and New Forms of Urban Inequality and Social Exclusion
Tsoulouvis, L. (forthcoming) Planning, the Urban System and New Forms of Inequality in Greek Cities, *Progress*

[illegible] (19[illegible]) 'The [illegible] Italian Welfare State', Journal of European Social Policy, [illegible]

Pinker, R. (19[illegible]) Social Policy, London.

Tsoukalas, [illegible] (19[illegible]) Dependence and [illegible], Athens. (in Greek).

Tsoukalas, [illegible] (19[illegible]) 'The Social [illegible] of State Employment in Postwar Greece', Greek Review of Social Research, 5[illegible], pp. [illegible]

[illegible] (19[illegible]) [illegible] Athens. (in Greek).

[illegible] (19[illegible]) 'Aspects of [illegible] and Planning in Greece', International Journal of Urban and Regional Research, [illegible], pp. 560-5[illegible]

[illegible] (19[illegible]) Urban Planning, Social Policy and New Forms of Urban Inequality and Social Exclusion, [illegible]

[illegible] (19[illegible]) [illegible] the Urban System and New Forms of Inequality in Greek Cities, [illegible]

8
Notes on neocapitalism, unemployment and social exclusion: The case of Greece

ZISSIS PAPADIMITRIOU AND GEORGE HADJICONSTANTINOU

8.1 Remarks on the global economy

An important feature of post-war period is the globalisation of economic and political structures. As Paul Kennedy remarked today's globalisation differs from that of previous periods by the sheer quantity and extent of multinational firms (Kennedy, 1993). The decision of the United States to abandon the gold standard in the seventies, led to a general liberalisation of capital investments, *as companies invested abroad without constraints imposed by central banks.* By the end of 1990, foreign direct investments, that is, investment in manufacturing, real estate, financial institutions, extractions of raw materials, etc., reached over 1.5 trillion Dollars. This figure is significant not only in terms of size but also the unprecedented speed with which it has grown in the last two decades: the amounts directly invested in foreign countries nearly tripled in the eighties alone.

Another effect of financial liberalisation is the increasing separation of financial flows from trade to manufacturing and services. "*More and more, foreign currency transactions took place not because a company was paying for foreign goods or investing in foreign assembly, but because investors were speculating on a particular currency or other financial instruments. This surge in global capital flows beyond those required to finance the boom in world industry and commerce is intimately connected with two further occurrences: the deregulation of world money markets, and the revolution in global communications as a result of new technologies*" (Kennedy, 1993). Because of these speculations, most industrialised countries are going through a period of de-industrialisation. This is causing great concern about the future of the world economy (see Papadimitriou, 1993: 102).

Globalisation has introduced new economic and political features in the periphery as well as in the core countries. The internationalisation and integration of the world economy has been much more beneficial for the average inhabitant of the advanced industrial economies than for people in the developing countries.[1]

One of the most important aspects of globalisation is the observed transposition of the decision centres from the national to the multinational level. Another effect is the emergence of a new multinational ruling class, which is less attached to the particular

B. Steijn et al. (eds.), Economic Restructuring and the Growing Uncertainty of the Middle Class, 135-143.
© 1998 *Kluwer Academic Publishers.*

interests and values of their country of origin. A widely accepted theory visualises the erosion of national sovereignty at the centres of the western world, presumably to be replaced by a new organisation of capital that will make and enforce the rules of international relations. This reengineering of international economic and political relations implies the gradual exclusion of the traditional middle class strata. Therefore, in Greece, for instance, the entry of the multinational capital in the field of processing (manufacturing of clothes, tourist enterprises, etc.), as well as in the foodstuff industry (foundation of multinational supermarkets etc.), resulted in a noticeable decrease in traditional occupations (see National Centre of Social Surveys, 1996: 51). This economic, and, more specifically, the industrial restructuring process, even though it offers relatively many opportunities for professional advancement, nonetheless leads to unemployment and the social exclusion of unskilled workers (Passet, 1988: 4).

8.2 International unemployment

The Keynesian approach, which mechanistically connected the growth of production to an increase in employment and wages, has been refused, owing to the technological evolution of the last two decades. Since the mid 60s, the relationship between investment and employment has been negative because investments in advanced technology dramatically reduced employment. This is the main contradiction of the highly industrialised economies. As Minc mentioned in his work *L' apres crise est commence*, the relation between investment and occupation had been positive up until 1965, but turned into negative at that point. In this manner, 100 billion DM invested in W. Germany between 1955 and 1960 created two million new jobs. This amount of capital deflationized. If it had been invested between 1960-1965, it would have created 400,000 new jobs. However, between 1965 and 1970, the same amount of invested capital augmented the unemployment figure by 100,000, while between 1970 and 1975, the figure rose by 500,000 (Fontella, 1993). In West Germany, for example, the total number working hours increased from 9 billion in 1950 to 13.5 billion in 1959 and then decreased to 12.2 billion until 1970. It reached 8.8 billion hours in 1977. Since then, a constant decrease has been observed (Papadimitriou, 1993).

According to Eurostat data, the current unemployment figure in the European Union is approximately 18 million, that is, 12% of the active population of the E.U. Sixty percent are young people (below the age of 25). These percentages are extremely high in the southern member states of E.U. Fifty percent belong to the category of long- term unemployed, which also prevents their re-entry into the workforce. The number of unemployed in the OECD countries increased from 24 million in 1990 to approximately 35 million in 1995.

The differencia specifica of this evolution, is that unemployment, in nearly all highly industrialised countries, is structural in nature. This results in high levels of unemployment, even during periods of economic growth, since the increase in productivity has more to do with technological innovations than the human labour factor. It is worth mentioning that the application of new technologies, both in the primary and the secondary economic sectors, mainly results in the substitution of skilled labour, which causes radical changes in the constitution of the labour force. These changes are primarily reflected in the exclusion of traditional specialisations from the working process. Thus, technological developments have increased the uncertainty and anxiety of work, especially among lower middle-class skilled workers.

8.3 The reorientation of welfare policies

Since World War II, Fordism has been the dominant model of production. It's main components are: a) mass production and consumption of standardised products; b) policies aimed at full employment using a large number of semi-skilled and unskilled labour; and c) the intervention of the state implementing welfare policies (Keynesian welfare state). Because this model of development was not sufficient, the industrialised countries have been in a phase of economic and social reconstruction, since the beginning of the 80s. Transition from a Fordist to a post-Fordist model of production is accomplished by implementing radical changes in the organisation of production as well as in state policy, especially welfare programs (Storper, 1988: 273-305). The core of the economic reconstruction process is *flexible specialisation*, since international competition forces the diversification of production, as well as continual improvements in the quality of products, which today more than ever constitute a conditio sine qua non for the survival of an enterprise (Papadimitriou, 1993).

The application of flexible production systems results in radical changes in employment. The most important changes are: a) the segmentation of the labour market into a primary market (stable employment, high salaries, good working conditions, chances of promotion, etc.) and a secondary market (unemployment, low salaries, poor working conditions, etc.); b) a rise in unemployment because of the selective use of labour power; c) the appearance of alternative forms of employment (part-time, flexible worktime, outsourcing etc.) and finally d) the upgrading of skilled labour within the production process (Ibid.).

The rejection of the Keynesian policy of full employment and the implementation of the selective use of labour in connection with the economic strategy of flexible specialisation has had an enormous influence on the development of welfare policies. Instead of attempting to balance out social inequalities, the state is trying to adjust its activities to the financial and technological needs of private capital (Ibid.). A continuous increase in public revenue which is released by cutting back welfare programs, is, for example, invested in research and development (R&D) activities for the production of new technologies and technological know-how. A feature that gives a competitive edge to an enterprise (Thomas and Tieman, 1987: 102).

The deregulation of the Fordist economy was followed by a conservative trend in political and social life. If one follows the arguments of the neo-conservatives, the task of the state is not to provide a safety net for its citizens, but to ensure the profitability and competitiveness of the private sector.

A typical development in the area of industrial relations has been the transfer of initiative in collective bargaining from trade unions to employers' organisations. Employers believe that centrally directed labour mobilisation, the unified agreement policy, and demands for unified working conditions will soon be a thing of the past. This is an obvious attempt to undermine the collective bargaining and agreement policy, and to promote the individualisation of working conditions through *free agreements* between employers and employees at the level of the enterprise without the intervention of trade unions. This policy clearly undermines the position of the trade unions (Papadimitriou, 1986: 47 ff).

These radical changes in the model of production and the conditions of competition in the local and international markets have led to the restructuring of the economic policy of the member states, so that they can meet the challenges of market globalisation. The cardinal feature of the neo-liberal anti-Keynesian economic policy is the more or less uncontrolled increase in unemployment, especially among skilled workers, as well as the significant reduction of the welfare state. The current economic of the E.U. is particularly contradictory: On the one hand, social expenses have been reduced to a minimum, condemning millions to live below the poverty line, while on the other hand, *social exclusion programs* are financed by the E.U., including the *Program for the Economic and Social Inclusion of the Non-Favoured Groups*.

8.4 Technological changes and the restructuring of work

In the post-war period, tertiarisation of the economy and technological evolution brought a lot of changes in the structure of society. The increasingly abstract function of work and the requirements of the technological production equipment can be observed most markedly in the elevation of qualifications which can no longer be described in terms of traditional skills. The traditional skilled worker has disappeared and new professions have been created, especially in the field of computer technology, e.g., programming, design, operating, etc. The erosion of skilled labour and the creation of new skilled occupations, have permanently affected the labour market. Owing to the segmentation of the job market, a newly formed regular core workforce has emerged within companies, with qualifications tailored to the technical system of the plant. In this context, the loyalty of the employees towards their company and their identification with the economic targets of the company play an important role in the relationship between management and labour. Skilled and semi-skilled workers are developing a new social orientation which has brought them economically and ideologically closer to the middle classes (Historical Statistics, 1960-1989, OECD).

Technological evolution has also influenced the development of the middle class. The appearance of new technologies in industrial administration, and in the service sector, changed its structure considerably. Though segments of the traditional category of public servants, white-collar workers, professionals, and the self-employed have disappeared, new categories are emerging. Because of the new requirements in industrial production, some categories of the working class upgraded their social position and entered the middle class. More than in the past, today's middle class has lost its coherence and is increasingly confronted with the problem of self-definition. The lack of a common consciousness is preventing the middle class from developing collective strategies in order to defend its own interests.

8.5 Economic development, unemployment, and social exclusion in Greece

The most significant structural changes in the Greek labour market in the last years have been: a) the transposition of employment from the agricultural and industrial sectors to the tertiary sector of the economy (tertiarisation of the economy); and b) the increase of women in the workforce. The tertiarisation of the Greek economy has led to a remarkable expansion of some traditional middle class strata (the self-employed in personal services, professionals, etc.) as well as to the appearance of new functions and professions , especially in the administrative and planning sectors .

The percentage of women in the labour force increased from 32% to 37%, between 1981-1993. In 1993, nearly 29% of Greek women were working. The corresponding percentages for Italy, Spain, and Portugal were 30, 40, and 26% respectively (Glytsos, 1995: 115). This increase is due to the fact that the female population moved from rural to urban areas, as social prejudice against working women faded. Another explanation for the increase is the improvement in educational level. There has been an impressive increase in the number of female University graduates (Kanellopoulos, 1990).

About 426,000 people, 10% of the labour force, are currently unemployed. More specifically, the rate of unemployed young people between 14 and 24 years of age is approximately 25% compared to 20% in the European Union (tables 8.1 and 8.2).

Table 8.1

Country totals of Population, labour force, number of employed, unemployed, in thousands

	Population	Labour Force	Employed	Unemployed	Rate of Unemployment
1975	9.046	3.280	3.230	50	1.5%
1980	9.642	3.451	3.356	95	2.8%
1985	9.934	3.893	3.589	304	7.8%
1990	10.161	4.000	3.719	281	7.0%
1995	10.467	4.245	3.819	426	10.0%

Source: Labour Force Research ESYE. During the years 1981-1983 a change in definitions took place

Table 8.2
Unemployment by sex and age

	1991	1993	1995
All Ages	301.1	398.2	427.719
Men	120.8	164.5	176.091
Women	180.3	233.7	248.629
(in thousands)			
		Men	
Age			
14-19	14.8 (12%)	15.4 (9%)	14.041 (8%)
20-29	58.9 (49%)	78.0 (47%)	79.049 (45%)
30-44	28.5 (24%)	41.2 (25%)	47.351 (27%)
45-65	18.4 (15%)	31.9 (19%)	35.116 (20%)
		Women	
Age			
14-19	24.8 (14%)	32.2 (14%)	28.665 (12%)
20-29	88.4 (49%)	112.9 (48%)	126.453 (51%)
30-44	49.4 (27%)	66.8 (29%)	67.022 (27%)
45-65	16.8 (10%)	21.8 (9%)	26.490 (10%)

Source: Labour Force ESYE December, 1995

In 1994, the number of unemployed in the 14 - 29 age group compromised 60% of the Greek labour force. Graduates are in an exceptionally difficult position, about 80,000 are without work, that is, 20% of the total unemployment figure (table 8.3).

Greece has the highest percentage of self-employment in the European Union. According to recent estimates, more than 40% of the labour force is self-employed. Employment in the so-called hidden economy is also very high. Approximately 60% of the total labour force are unemployed, hold a part-time job, or work in the hidden economy. In the early 80s, a period of economic stagnation and rising unemployment, activity in the hidden economy constituted nearly 30% of the GNP (Economikos Tachidromos, 1995). There are more people with illegal second jobs in the informal economy than those who lost their jobs.

Table 8.3
Unemployment (in percents) by education level and sex

	1991			1993			1995		
	Male	**Female**	**Total**	**Male**	**Female**	**Total**	**Male**	**Female**	**Total**
Total (in thousands)	**120784**	**180315**	**301099**	**164521**	**233679**	**398200**	**176091**	**248629**	**424719**
Education level									
• Graduate Degree	**0.8**	**0.5**	**0.5**	**0.3**	**0.1**	**0.2**	**0.2**	**0.2**	**0.2**
• University Degree	**8.8**	**10.6**	**9.9**	**9.3**	**12.1**	**10.9**	**9.4**	**10.7**	**10.1**
• Under-graduates	**2.8**	**2.4**	**2.6**	**0.3**	**0.1**	**0.2**	**0.2**	**0.1**	**0.2**
• Graduates of Technical Inst.	**7.6**	**7.7**	**7.7**	**8.1**	**10.0**	**9.2**	**8.6**	**12.3**	**10.8**
• Senior High School Dip.	**36.2**	**43.1**	**40.3**	**35.9**	**41.9**	**39.4**	**37.4**	**43.7**	**40.6**
• Junior High School Dip.	**14.2**	**• 9.8**	**11.6**	**14.5**	**11.3**	**12.6**	**13.8**	**10.2**	**11.9**
• Elementary Education	**25.8**	**23.1**	**24.2**	**29.0**	**22.3**	**25.1**	**27.7**	**20.9**	**23.8**
• One Year Elementary Ed.	**2.7**	**2.3**	**2.5**	**1.6**	**1.2**	**1.4**	**1.9**	**1.2**	**1.6**
• No Education	**1.1**	**0.5**	**0.7**	**1.0**	**1.0**	**1.0**	**0.8**	**0.7**	**0.8**

Source: Labour Force ESYE December, 1995

It is also necessary to take into account the high number of legally and illegally employed foreigners, generally Albanians, but also from other former communist countries. The number of legally employed foreigners is nearly 175,000; and about 350,000 work illegally. Foreigners constitute about 5% of the total Greek population and more than 9% of the labour force (National Centre for Social Research, 1996). The presence of these marginalised individuals is sure to create many problems as long as the government does not take the necessary actions for their social inclusion.

8.6 Conclusion

Since the beginning of the 90s, Greece has been confronted with a deep economic, social, political, and cultural crisis. The European movement, instead of integrating, destabilised Greek society, because of the economic and social burdens of the adjustment process. The current economic situation in Greece is characterised by a large national debt, budget deficits and high rate of unemployment, especially among young people .

In terms of Greece's social structure, we can observe some developments which

led to a strong segmentation of public and private interests. Its integration to the new international division of labour, resulted in the reorganisation of Greek society. Some traditional middle-class professions have disappeared, while other social groups are flourishing, for example, financial consultants who deal with the mobilisation of foreign capital.

The economic, and, in particular, the industrial restructuring which occurred early on in the western European member states, took place slowly in Greece, and in such a manner that the problems associated with integration have only recently been become manifest to their full extent. Thus, long-term unemployment is rising daily while informal types of labour continue to multiply, even though they do not provide the same security and protection as regular salaried employment.

In studying the problem of social exclusion in Greece, we naturally have to consider the idiosyncrasies of Greek society. Although the problem is very acute, especially in some social groups, the way it is dealt with by society as well as the excluded groups and individuals themselves, differs from other countries. The Greek perception of social exclusion reflects their individual conception of work and employment, which is relatively different from the work ethos of other nations. In contrast to the western perception of work, which is influenced by the Protestant ethic, the Greek orthodox tradition (monastic life) has given the Greeks a more instrumental attitude towards work. They work to live instead of living to work. This also influences their attitude towards unemployment and how to cope with it. In other words, cultural background is a relevant factor in dealing with social exclusion.

In contrast with the highly organised societies which usually promote collective solutions to social problems, Greek society is more flexible, because of the existence of informal social security networks. The Greek family, for example, functions as an informal system of social security providing a back-up to the formal system, which is organisationally and financially flawed.

However, it is assumed that these informal networks are on the decline due to urbanisation and industrialisation, as it has happened also in other countries. Given the fact that the Greek welfare state is underdeveloped, these changes could, in the long run, cause serious erosion of the Greek social system.

Notes

1 As Paul Kennedy stated: " *[...] by 1991 the capita Gross Domestic Product of Switzerland had soared to 36,300, Sweden 32,600, Japan 29,000 and Germany 27,900 Dollars . By contrast, India's per capita GDP languishes at a mere 360, and Nigeria's is only 278 Dollars [...] The qrotesqueness of this disparity in wealth, a citizen, for example of Switzerland enjoys on average several hundred times the income of a native of Ethiopia. The negative effects of this disparity in wealth between advanced industrial and developing countries is mirrored in the differential rates of child mortality, life expectancy, and access to education. After nearly five decades of unprecedented global economic growth, the world heads toward the twenty-first century with more than a billion people living in poverty.*" See also Hadjiconstantinou (1995).

References

Economikos Tachidromos, (1995), pp. 85.

Fontela, E. (1993) *Investment et Emploi*, Futuribles.

Glytsos, N. (1955) Perspectives of the Greek labor market in front of 2000, in: I. Lambri-Dimaki and N. Kyriazis, *The Greek society at the end of 20th century*, Athens, pp. 115 ff.

Hadjiconstantinou, C. (1995) *The dominant model of economic development as a reason for social exclusion and racist behavior*, chapter presented at the international conference on the economic, social and political dimension of racism, 14-18 may 1995, Thessaloniki.

Historical Statistics 1960-1989, OECD.

Kanellopoulos, K.N. (1990) The informal market in Greece, What the official data show, *KEPE, chapters for discussion*, 4, Athens.

Kennedy, P. (1993) *Preparing for the twenty-first century*, London.

National Centre for Social Surveys (1996) *The dimensions of social exclusion in Greece, Primary issues and definition of the priorities of policy*, report for the European Social Fund, Athens.

Papadimitriou, Z. (1986) Changing skill requirements and trade union bargaining, in: O. Jacobi, B. Jessop, H. Kastendick and M. Regini (eds.) *Technological change, Rationalization and industrial relations*, London/Sidney, pp. 47 ff.

Papadimitriou, Z. (1993) From Fordist full employment to Post-Fordist selective use of labor power: The degradation of the Welfare State and Trade Unions, *The Keizai Gaku, Annual Report of the Economic Society*, Tohoku University, vol. 54, p. 102 ff.

Passet, R. (1988) *Production, emploi, revenue: des liens qui se rompent*, Conference Mulhouse.

Storper, M. (1988) The transition to flexible specialisation in industry, *Cambridge Journal of Economics*, 9, pp. 273-305.

Thomas, K., and H. Tieman (1987) Neoconservatismus und gewerkschaftliche Zukunftsaussichten, *Gewerkschaftliche Monatshefte*, 2, p. 102 ff.

9

Impoverishment of the Russian population and the problem of middle-class formation under market transformations

NATALIA RIMASHEVSKAYA AND GALINA VOITENKOVA

9.1 Introduction

The transition of Russia to a market economy has been accompanied by radical changes in the social structure, intensification of social mobility, disintegration of the existing social strata, and the emergence of new social strata. The analysis of these developments is complicated by the character of the period, as the formation of the new social structure is still underway. This also exacerbate the usual problems with the of empirical data: their comprehensiveness, comparability, and reliability. Despite these shortcomings, the available information does allow us to observe certain trends in the social structure in general and the position of the middle class in particular.

This chapter was prepared on the basis of the following data sources:

1) Official statistical data published by the State Statistical Committee of Russia (Goskomstat), including the results of the annual Family Budget Surveys of 50,000 households.

2) Findings of the surveys conducted by the Institute for socio-economic Populationstudies, of the Russian Academy of Sciences (ISESP/RAS):
   - The most interesting of these surveys is the study of the level of well-being among the citizens of Taganrog. This long-term project, headed by the first author, provides information on changes in the conditions, level, and quality of life in a typical Russian industrial centre over a period of three decades. The study was carried out in a series of surveys conducted in 1968, 1978, 1988, and 1993, and the next phase will start in 1998. The sample size was reduced during the period of observation from 20,000 to 10,000 households for financial reasons.
   - The results of the surveys of separate social groups undertaken by the ISESP researchers in recent years: the investigation of 'the rich' headed by Professors Rimashevskaya and Ovsyannikov in the spring of 1995; 1130 city residents, experts, and the wealthy individuals were interviewed in six industrial cities (Moscow, Saint-Petersburg, Yekaterinburg, Nizhny Novgorod, Irkutsk and Voronezh). In the

B. Steijn et al. (eds.), Economic Restructuring and the Growing Uncertainty of the Middle Class, 145-155.
© 1998 *Kluwer Academic Publishers.*

spring of 1996, a survey of 'the social bottom' was conducted which polled 1400 city residents, experts, and people from the underclass in these same cities. Outcomes of public opinion monitoring carried out by the Russian Centre for Public Opinion Research (VCIOM) since 1993 in different regions of the country (sample size about 2,000 respondents).

9.2 Social changes during the 1992 - 1995 reform period: General context

Russia is now experiencing profound socio-economic transformations, unprecedented in scope and depth. They have a very complex and controversial nature. These changes are civilizational in character with respect to altering the models and regulators of social activity. They embrace all domains, spheres and aspects of social life on both the macro- and micro - levels; they reflect remarkable changes in ideology and politics and affect the economic system, the social structure, and the ethnic and cultural composition of the country; they have lowered the living standard of individuals and of the population as a whole.

The reforms are changing the fundamental relationships between Society, Market, and State and have had both positive and negative affects. The positive affects include the following:

- rising economic activity due to the institutionalisation of private property and free enterprise. Under the centrally planned economy their potential was not realised;
- formation of new social values focusing on freedom of thought, civil rights, individual initiative, and upward social mobility;
- emergence of a new type of on the foundation of private property person (real estate, enterprises, banks, shares and securities) and a certain social status.

At the same time, the profound socio-economic transformations, undoubtedly progressive in nature, have been carried out 'from above' without taking into account their possible negative social consequences. There was no preliminary estimate of the permissible limits of the supposed deterioration in living standards, or of the possibilities, duration, and character of the peoples' adaptation to these radical changes. This entails not only adjusting to new social relations, but also to new social, material, psychological, and physical conditions of the population.

The social costs of the reforms have been so enormous, that doubts are emerging about their positive effects. Continuation of the socio-economic transformations initiated five years ago has brought no improvement in the position of the majority of the population, and has even had deleterious effect, particularly with respect to material conditions. Many groups have exhausted the expectations in relation to the ongoing developments. The standard of living is steadily declining compared to pre-reform times.

The transition from the strict statist structure characterised by unitarianism, totalitarianism, paternalism and bureaucratism to market relations and civil society has been accompanied by the destruction of the existing framework of social relations and the entire social structure. It has become a serious trial for the people left to themselves and feeling lost and insecure. Most are unable to adapt to the new conditions. In addition, the state seems unprepared to handle these social developments and has little control over the situation. There is neither a well grounded understanding of the transformations, nor a clear-cut social policy. As a result, individuals are vulnerable to the arbitrary power (or lack of power) of the authorities, illegal actions, corruption, economic decline, poverty and ecological and technological catastrophes.

Russian society is adrift and disoriented which adds to the growing social tension and instability.

9.3 Impoverishment of the population

The social and political transformations and the implementation of the so-called economic 'shock therapy' that resulted in a momentary liberalisation of prices in January 1992, ended in a disastrous fall in the standard of living and rapid income polarisation. The average income dropped in the first half of 1992 by a factor of 2-2.5. Not only was current income affected, but especially savings, which were actually 'expropriated' from the majority of the population.

Eventually 'restoration' of current income took place, but 1995 was again marked by a 13% fall in real income. During the reformperiod, the average real income decreased to 50% of its 1991 value and consumption to 40%, equalling its 1997 level - a 20-year setback.

Poverty became acute. As a result of the 'shock therapy' approximately 80% of the population were living below the official poverty level, the minimum consumption budget, including large segments of society who formerly belonged to the middle income groups. In 1992, the poverty level was redefined and set at a minimum subsistence level that barely satisfied the physiological needs for sustaining life. Food made up 70% of the new minimum consumption basket. The new poverty line was only half the previous one. It was supposed to be a temporary measure, but has not changed, (except for the indexation to price increase) even though it is outdated both in the calculation methods and in real value, and cannot even ensure survival. Unfortunately even that minimum is not guaranteed by the state.

It is no wonder that a family cannot acquire sufficient consumption within the framework of the official minimum subsistence pattern. The growth in low-elastic expenses for housing and communal services, transportation, medical services, the need for new clothes and footwear (especially for children) as well as saving for a 'rainy day', inevitably, entails undernutrition of low-income families. The situation is extremely grave, certainly with respect to food products of high nutritional value. In 1995, the per capita consumption of meat fell by 5 kg (it took 10 years, from 1975 to 1985, to attain an increase) and milk by 56 kg. The consumption of animal proteins declined 6% and approached the minimal permissible limit (32 g per household member per day against the limit of 30 g).

Table 9.1
Population with per capita income below the subsistence minimum as % of the total population

	1990	1991	1992	1993	1994	1995
Goskomstat estimates	-	-	33.5	31.5	24.4	24.0
ISESP estimates	1.8	3.8	22.5	31.7	36.7	48.9

The number of people below the official poverty line continues to grow. According to our estimates, it is now over 40% of the total population. These data sharply differ from those of Goskomstat. The decrease in the poverty rate, reported by the Goskomstat, is hard to believe.

The categories most affected are children and elderly people. Two-thirds of the children and one-third of the elderly live below the poverty line. The elderly have earned a decent living in old age and deserve a better standard of living. Impoverished children, means a decline in the quality of life of future generations and a deterioration of the human genofund.

In evaluating the consumption of families living below subsistence level we should take into account that the burden of inflation is not equally distributed over all social categories: a rise in the cost of consumer goods and services affects first and foremost those goals which satisfy the basic vital needs and constitute the majority of the consumption of poor families. Consequently, the poorest people suffer most from inflation.

Two kinds of poverty have emerged: 'stable' poverty and 'floating' poverty, when a family, as a result of circumstances, temporarily rises above or falls below the poverty line. The former is connected with the fact that poverty, as a rule, produces poverty. Low income levels entail deterioration in health, loss of professional skills and employment, and ultimately, human degradation. Poor parents reproduce potentially poor children, as a consequence of poor health, lower educational attainment, limited professional skills, and a lack of upward social mobility.

Floating poverty is rare. It refers to people who, after much effort, succeed in 'breaking out' of their exclusive social circle with its culture of poverty and adapting to the new conditions, thus securing a better life. It goes without saying that such a move depends not only on subjective conditions (on the part of an economically active person), but also on objective elements (on the part of the state and society) that are not provided.

In addition to the traditionally poor categories - single mothers and families with many children - a group called 'new poor' has emerged. This social group includes those categories of the population, which, because of their social status, education, occupational position, and income levels, have never belonged to the lower social strata before: e.g., professionals, military officers, highly skilled workers, etc. Many of them were made redundant. The work of those who retained their jobs was reduced to the levels of low-paid unskilled workers. This can be illustrated by the following figures. In 1989, only 12 % of highly skilled workers were in the low pay category, but in 1993 this proportion grew to 41%; among highly skilled professionals, these figures were 27% and 64%, respectively at present, the situation is close to that of 1993.

9.4 Pauperisation of the population and social exclusion

Poverty, unemployment, economic and social instability, and ruined hopes and plans, all contribute to the process of marginalization and the formation of a stable 'social bottom' or underclass, which appears as a result of social exclusion and rapid downward social mobility. The outcasts include beggars, vagabonds, the homeless (who have lost their dwellings owing to 'market' reasons), homeless and abandoned children (left by their parents or runaways), alcoholics, drug addicts, prostitutes etc. Of course, these categories also existed in pre-reform Russia, but were far less prevalent, and the authorities tried to reduce their number.

The 1996 survey revealed the following characteristic of the Russian underclass:

1. The size of the social bottom is impressive: the number of people excluded from society and deprived of all civil rights (including the right to life) amounts to 14-15 million or 10% of the total population. There are 4 million homeless, 4 million abandoned children, 3 million beggars, and 3 million prostitutes.
2. The intensity of the downward movement and the large scale of the underclass have external causes, that have nothing to do with individual will. The main causes are economic, political, social and psychological: alienation of an individual from society. People belonging to the lowest social stratum believe that society is responsible for their misfortunes. At the same time, they indicate the flaws in personal character (vicious inclinations, bad luck, fate, a taste for criminal romance). This personal component of social exclusion seems to be ineradicable, as world experience shows. However, the social component of downward mobility dominates. Mass social exclusion is clearly the responsibility of a society that pays for a seeming advance to the 'world civilisation' with millions of broken lives.
3. Domination of the social component of downward mobility determines the fall of quite sociable sections of the population. These include single elderly people (probability of ending up at the bottom, 72%), pensioners (61%), disabled persons (63%), families with many children (54%), the unemployed (53%), single mothers (49%), refugees (44%), resettlers (31 %). Numerous teachers, engineers, technical staff, and unskilled workers are also likely to become destitute (24-32%). Our experts are of the opinion that there is little chance of reascending the social scale. Educational attainment and professional skills do not ensure upward social movement.
4. People have little confidence in the stability of their social position. Only 24% of the population are sure that they will be able to avoid poverty. Especially alarming is the position of those verging on the underclass. They constitute a specific social section at risk, the 'pre-bottom', which is marked by a high degree of fear, despair and hopelessness. They still belong to 'normal society', but are, nevertheless, doomed to social exclusion.

The reasons for the formation of the 'pre-bottom' are more objective (the after-effects of the reforms) than subjective (idleness, lack of initiative, bad habits). In 1996, 66% of the population indicated that their sense of security had deteriorated, and 49% stated that their confidence in the future had decreased. In the spring of this year, 52% of the Russian population feared for their lives and felt threatened. Fifty-seven percent did not feel safe anywhere, even at home.

The 'pre-bottom' comprises 3-3.5% of the total population (4.5-5.2 million people). It is the lowest step on the social scale and one step away from the social bottom, where one is no longer part of 'normal' society. The 'pre-bottom' is the area of social depression and social catastrophes, where people are discarded from society.

9.5 Stratification of the present Russian society

The transformation process is still going on and a new social structure is emerging. The developments are closely connected with the complex process of adapting to market conditions: new social orientations and rules of co-operation as well as active initiation of market structures and participation in economic life. Some people quickly adopted the liberal-democratic system of values; others rejected the old views, but found themselves unable to adjust to the new values, and thus lost their orientation; still others have consolidated their old outlook. As a result, the society has split into 3 segments.

According to our estimates based on special surveys carried out by the Institute, at present, about one-fifth of the population have adapted to the new conditions, and approximately one-fourth have not and cannot adapt due to personal factors (social orientations, mentality, age, state of health, etc.). Over half the population (55%) are in a state of uncertainty. Some are making attempts to participate in the new structures, but for the most part have failed, forcing them to return to their previous position. However, the success of the reforms depends to a considerable extent on the behaviour and orientations of this 'intermediate' group.

Our evaluation of those who have 'adapted' correlates well with the results of the surveys carried out by the Russian Centre for Public Opinion Research (VCIOM). They claim the 'gainers' from the reforms in the last three years was about 20-23% (with a certain downward trend).

The social structure in Russia is undergoing dramatic changes. Old classes are disappearing and new classes are replacing them. According to the official view, there were two main classes in Soviet society workers and collective farmers, plus a vast social strata of intelligentsia (intellectuals and professionals). The actual social structure was more complicated and based on occupational status rather than social class. Professionals and administrators enjoyed certain privileges, influence, and public esteem, although their nominal income was not higher than that of skilled workers. From their position on the social scale, they could be compared to the 'service class' in Western European countries. Many of them lost their former social status during the transformation process.

At the same time, a new social class of proprietors emerged as a result of the privatisation of state property and the liberalisation of economic activity. Many people from various social groups tried to avail themselves of the new opportunities and engage in entrepreneurial activity. Most did not succeed. Those who did succeed were mainly officials and administrators with the necessary business connections and access to the right kind of information. They sometimes used illegal means and criminal support. They became owners of enterprises and firms. A small percentage of them made great fortunes. This group of extremely rich people accounts for about 5% of the total population.

Intensive social mobility, the unstable social position of the overwhelming majority of the population, do not allow us to apply the set of criteria used for class schemes in countries with stable social structures to Russian. Such indicators as professional skills, occupational status, education, job security and prospects of promotion cannot be applied. The most reliable criterion of social stratification is income differentiation.

Against the background of the disastrous decline in the standard of living of the majority of the population and their slow adaptation to market conditions, we can observe a sharp polarisation of income. It is evident that the formation of market relations can only result in a growing differentiation in income and material well-being. However the extent of the differentiation has exceeded the resources of an average individual for normal adaptation. None of the East European countries, undergoing similar transformations have experienced such a dramatic differentiation. Our country is unprecedented in this respect. This income polarisation is determined by a number of factors.

First, is the rapidly growing differentials in payment: between regions, industries, enterprises of various forms of ownership, and separate groups of workers. As a result, the decile coefficient of wage differentiation nearly quintupled over 10 years (from 3.4 in 1985 to 10.4 or even to 20.2 by various estimates in 1995). According to Goskomstat, in 1995 the average income in the upper decile was 26 times that of the bottom decile (in 1991 this ratio was 8:1). Twenty percent of the best paid workers received half the work payment fund. These disparities can be observed in enterprises, where the salaries of administrators are 20 times higher than the wages of the majority of workers. It is well known that the income of over 40% of workers is below the subsistence level. Industries can differ by a factor of 10. The highest incomes are in the financial sphere, extracting industries, and transport and trade; the lowest are in the manufacturing industries, the social sector, and agriculture. There are enormous differences in income between the state and private sector, especially joint ventures run by foreign administrations. Junior clerical staff in private international banks, for example, receive more than university professors who are paid from the state budget. Minimum wage in the state sector make up less than 20% of the official subsistence minimum (regional differences come up to 10 times).

Additional employment also plays a part in income differentiation. According to the VCIOM data, only 8% of the active population have regular additional employment; 12-14% have odd jobs. Our surveys in Taganrog show that workers with higher earnings and occupational status are more likely to have other jobs. On average, these extra jobs account for about 15 hours a week, but remuneration is higher than that of the primary job. Growing unemployment and part-time employment the huge differences in family incomes. By expert estimates, both open and hidden unemployment account for 15% of the economically active population.

Arrears in wages and pensions also contribute to income inequality. They affect millions of people and can last up to 8 months. According to the Goskomstat data, the amount of non-payment exceeded 40 billion rubles in mid 1996. Reduction in the levels of social transfers also adds to income inequality. Thus, in October 1995, the minimum old-age pension made up only 26% of the official subsistence minimum; child benefits in the last 3 years ranged from 8% to 18% of the subsistence minimum; minimal student stipends in 1995 only made 11%-16% of it.

A very significant factor in income polarisation is the emergence of new sources of income, primarily entrepreneurial activity. Entrepreneurial income accounts for 30% of the total annual income of the population. About one third of families have this source of income, but it is a main source for only 6% of the economically active population. Most entrepreneurs run their own business and work as employees. Other new sources of income are possession of real estate, enterprises, shares, and securities.

The following table 9.2 presents the economic stratification of Russian society based on the available information.

Table 9.2
Economic stratification of the Russian population

Main social strata	As % of the total population	Per capita money income a month, $
Rich	5	over 3000
Well-off	15	1000 - 3000
Intermediate (would-be middle class)	20	100 - 1000
Underprovisionised	20	50 - 100
Poor	40	below 50
Social bottom	12	

The 'shock therapy' of 1992 significantly intensified the problem of income differentiation. According to various estimates, the decile coefficient now ranges from 10 to 25. However, sociologists claim that income differentiation is fraught with social degradation, which is actually observed in Russia. The ISESP calculations of income distribution sharply differ from the official statistics, since Goskomstat does not take into account the richest part of the population ('new Russians') and the poorest people ('social bottom') who are not covered by the family budget surveys. By our estimates, the decile coefficient of income differentiation in 1995 was 27.8.

According to the Goskomstat data, in 1995, the average income of the top 20% was 8.5 times higher than that of the bottom 20% of the distribution. In 1991, this ratio was 2.6:1. The Gini coefficient grew from 0.260 in 1994 to 0.381 in 1995.

9.6 The problem of middle class formation

The figures in Table 9.2 show that there is actually no 'middle class' in current Russian society. The society is divided into a relatively small social section of the rich and well-off and a vast stratum of the poor with a wide gulf in income levels between them. The intermediate part of the population, in the middle of the distribution cannot be regarded as a real middle class, but as a combination of several social groups with very different income levels (to say nothing of their occupational positions and orientations). The income of people in this section who comprise only one-fifth of the total population, ranges anywhere between $100 and $1000 per capita per month, a spread with a ten-fold difference in income levels! Some people in this stratum border on the category of the 'well-off', but most are closer to the 'underprovisioned' group.

Social stratification in Russia differs sharply from that in most industrial countries where the middle class makes up the majority of the population and tends to be homogeneous. In our case, there is a clearly discernible erosion of those social groups which are equivalent to the West-European 'service' class, and a clear tendency towards social polarisation. In fact, there are two Russian now, sharply differing in the standard of living, life style, value orientation, and behaviour.

The former soviet 'middle class', the professionals, highly skilled workers, and military officers have suffered most of all the social groups as a result of the reforms. This mainly concerns those employed in the manufacturing industries, science and technology, the social sphere, and agriculture. Restructuring and demilitarisation of the economy plus a sharp decline in industrial production made highly skilled professionals and workers redundant. The same is true for military officers as a result of reduction in the armed forces. Their position is very dramatic: Most have been marginalised and are now living in poverty.

Nevertheless, these segments of the population have a better chance of adapting to the new conditions using their intellectual potential and mobility. Some of the former 'service class' have retained their social status and have adapted to the new structure. They are mainly employed in the financial sphere, extracting industries, trade and services, and administrative field. The majority works in the private sector. They also constitute a significant part of the emerging social categories connected with proprietorship and market relations and corresponding to the traditional European middle class (small and mid-size enterprisers, the self-employed, and farmers) actually being recruited from different social strata. They have not yet formed a stable social group owing to the absence of certain conditions and the lack of the state support in this period of economic decline and social mobility. Their position is also insecure.

Entrepreneurial activity engages about 11% of the economically active population. Only 22% of them are fully concentrated on their own business; 53% of them combine running their own business with employment in big companies as managers, professionals or workers; the rest 25% are directors of state enterprises or joint stock companies having sharers in them. 48% of entrepreneurs are engaged in trade and services; 27% in manufacturing, construction and transport; 13% - in agriculture, 5% - in culture and education. The number of those who started their own business have recently reduced - most of them are already insolvent due to the disparity in prices, the tax burden, the lack of the necessary infrastructure, corruption and racket. The position of these self-employed is even more dramatic.

Russia's entering the road of stable development and economic growth seems impossible without the formation of a real middle class. But, despite all difficulties of the transition, we still have people with high intellectual potential, education levels and professional skills and social dynamism. They can be classified as a potential middle class. The 'socio-dynamic' conception of the middle class defines them not so much by social status of individuals, as by the character of their socio-economic orientations, strivings and activities, their ability to adapt themselves to new market conditions using their potentialities. In this sense, we can rank among them all those who are ready to work actively in the current situation, to take advantage of the given opportunities without breaking the generally accepted norms of moral and business ethics. We can include in the 'dynamic' middle class the following categories of the population: small and middle- scale enterprisers, self-employed workers and farmers, professionals, administrators and managers, military officers and also skilled workers.

Under the appropriate conditions ensuring the necessary social status positions, income levels, and legal guarantees of economic activity for the socio-dynamic middle class, it can develop into a real middle class - the core of the modern social structure, the classic stronghold of social stability and order.

9.7 Conclusion

Formation of the middle class in Russia is the necessary prerequisite for society at large to advance into a market economy with its corresponding social structure. This requires a strong support of the State and active social politics aimed at the creation of favourable conditions for the transformation of the potential middle class into a real one.

This implies:

- stimulation and protection of industrial and agricultural production to ensure economic growth and general rise in the standard of living of the population on the whole;
- support of small- and middle- scale enterprisers and farmers (legal regulations, reasonable taxation and crediting conditions, liquidation of disparities in prices, development of infrastructure, etc.);
- strengthening the position of the 'service' middle class, raising the status of the professionals employed in manufacturing, social sphere and science;
- ensuring social adaptation of those who have lost their position in the course of the historic transformations, their incorporation into new market structures.

References

Goskomstat statistical yearbook (1994) *Russian Federation in 1993*, Moscow.

Goskomstat statistical yearbook (1996) *Russian Federation in 1995*, Moscow.

Goskomstat (1995) *Socio-economic situation in Russia*, Moscow.

Goskomstat (1996) *Living levels of the Russian population*, Moscow.

Goskomstat (1996) *Labour and employment in Russia. 1995*, Moscow.

Project Taganrog III (1992) *Socio-economic study of the well-being, ways and levels of life of the city population*, Moscow.

Project Taganrog three and a half (forthcoming) *Family well-being and health*, Moscow.

Russia - 1993. Socio-demographic situation, Moscow.

Russia - 1995. Socio-demographic situation - Moscow: ISESP RAS, 1996.

N.Rimashevskaya, A.Ovsyannikov, and A.Iudin (1996) in: Literaturnaya gazeta., *Social bottom: drama of reality and reality of drama*, 4 december 1996.

N.Rimashevskaya and A.Ovsyannikov (1995) People who are in love of money. Social status of the rich in view of experts in: *Social stratification of the present Russian society*, Moscow, Centre for complex studies and marketing.

N.Rimashevskaya (1995) in: *Delovoy mir, Not everybody becomes rich. Some people cannot, others do not wish*, 2 march 1995.

T.Zaslavskaya (1995) Structure of the contemporary Russian society; The monitoring of public opinion, in: *Economic and Social Change*.

L.Khakhulina, and S.Stevenson (1996) Entrepreneurial activity of the population: conditions and prospects,.in: *Economic and Social Change, The monitoring of public opinion*.

10
Middle class uncertainty: A synthesis and a research agenda

MART-JAN DE JONG

10.1 Introduction

Any article about middle-class uncertainty should be clear about two things. First, who belongs to the middle class or middle classes, and, second, why are its members uncertain? Since the first question is debatable and the second will not be answered within the foreseeable future, it might also be of interest to add an outline for a research programme. Therefore, I will divide this chapter into three sections. The focus of the first section is on the historical transformation and current composition of the middle class. The social factors that might explain current middle class uncertainty are dealt with in the second section. The third section contains a preliminary scketch of a research programme.

10.2 The expansion and composition of the middle class

10.2.1 The historical expansion of the middle class

In the nineteenth century, Marx predicted that the middle class would wither away. He was convinced that the dynamics of capitalism would create a polarisation of society into two antagonistic classes. As a consequence of fierce economic competition only a small fraction of the self-employed could move into to the class of the rich and the powerful, that is, the owners of the means of production. The large majority of the self-employed would lose this competitive struggle. They would slide down the social status ladder and become impoverished and frustrated members of the working class. So, in the end, there would only be room for a large underclass of poor and powerless workers and a small category of capitalists who own all the factories, shops, land, and machinery. Despite Marx' strong conviction that this polarisation and marginalisation thesis was a central part of a really scientific and valid theory about the evolution and inevitable demise of capitalism, we have not witnessed anything of the kind in the twentieth century. Instead, industrial societies have created a growing service class of managers, the self-employed, civil servants, and white-collar

B. Steijn et al. (eds.), Economic Restructuring and the Growing Uncertainty of the Middle Class, 157-170.
© 1998 *Kluwer Academic Publishers.*

workers. Later, modern welfare states created an elaborated system of social assistance and social security that serves as a safety net against poverty.

We have also witnessed the decline and disintegration of the labour class. Its numbers shrank by the thousands because of the introduction of technological innovations. These innovations were welcomed by factory owners and managers because they would speed up production and decrease labour costs. This innovation process made much manual work obsolete. Thus, the marriage between the capitalist drive for profits and technological modernisation changed the whole pattern of available jobs. The distribution of jobs over lower, middle and top level occupations has modified its pyramidical shape. Traditionally, the broad basis of the pyramid was filled with the largest number of unskilled and semi-skilled workers. In the middle was a somewhat smaller number of people working as skilled labourers, shop assistants, and the lower ranks of civil servants and office workers. The top of this pyramid contained a relatively small group of people in management and the professions. Now, the pyramid has turned into a diamond or onion-type figure. The broad basis of the pyramid has become very small because many of its inhabitants have become redundant or have been upgraded to middle level jobs.

Moreover, many social scientists observed that a growing number of skilled blue-collar workers got immersed in a process of embourgeoisement and moved into the (lower) middle class (See Berting, chapter 1). Even those who are still performing manual labour in industry, construction, or small craft shops have altered their attitudes towards politics and society. As a consequence, the labour class declined and class consciousness faded away.

10.2.2 The reconceptualisation of class

The marked transformation of the class structure demanded a new theoretical approach. Already in 1958 Nisbet expressed severe doubts about the usefulness of the term social class. He stated that "it is nearly valueless for the clarification of the data of wealth, power, and social status ..." (Nisbet, 1959, quoted by Steijn, 1997). Nevertheless, many social scientists interested in social stratification did not lose their belief in the value of marxist or weberian class theories and produced scores of studies which proved that social inequality integenerationally was reproduced alongside class borders. Later, the study of the persistency of social inequality was complicated by introducing gender and ethnicity. However, near the end of the eighties a growing number of former defenders of class theory lost their belief in the relevancy of the concept. They encountered too much trouble in explaining political attitudes and various forms of behaviour with the help of social class as an independent variable.

One way of coming to terms with the new situation was broadening the conception of the middle class. For instance, this was done by Jan Berting, the initiator of the project and book on middle class uncertainty (Berting, 1968). In his view, the expanded middle class currently covers about 80% of the total population of high-tech societies. Of course, this broad midfield of society is very heterogeneous. There are great differences in income, education, status, and lifestyle, which, again, raises doubts about the relevancy of class for modern societies.

Evidently, this new and complex reality confronts social researchers with difficult problems of conceptualisation and operationalisation. That's why new class schemes have been constructed, reconstructed, and tried out in empirical research. Van Parijs (1989, 215-216) assumes that any class concept has to be:

a. *hierarchical*, in the sense that one can meaningfully say that one class is `superior' to another (*Italics* by Van Parijs);
b. *discrete*, in the sense that belonging to a class is not just a matter of degree; there must be some nonarbitrary border.

Furthermore, a marxist or materialistic conceptualisation of class must
c. be concerned with the distribution of *material advantages*, that is, of income and work, but also of the exercise of (or submission to) power,
d. or rooted in the *property relations* that characterise the current mode of production.

In addition, the class concept has to be useful for the explanation of *consciousness* (ideology, values, attitudes) and/or *action* (lifestyle, political behaviour, social conflict), otherwise it is irrelevant for social scientists.

The (neo)marxist class scheme of Wright (1985; 1989) meets all these criteria. It certainly is discrete and hierarchical, and tries to determine specific class positions on the basis of different forms of exploitation or authority. Besides a fundamental distinction between owners and non-owners, Wright differentiates classes according to the type of assets they control: vz. production assets (bourgeoisie, small employers, petty bourgeoisie), organisation assets (managerial, supervisory, non-supervisory workers), and educational assets (experts, semi-credentialled, and unskilled workers).

Figure 10.1: Wrights revised class scheme

Owners	*Non-owners*		
Bourgeoisie	Expert managers	Semi credentialled managers	Uncredentialled managers
Small employers	Expert supervisors	Semi credentialled supervisors	Uncredentialled supervisors
Petty Bourgeoisie	Expert non-managers	Semi credentialled workers	Proletarians

Conceptually, Wright's class scheme is very clear. The scheme is based on three dimensions. First, the old marxist division between owners and non-owners is still present. However, in our day and age it has lost much of its theoretical and empirical power. No longer, all owners are 'superior' to non-owners. Now, owners and non-owners form two separate columns, each of them subdivided in three hierarchical levels. To differentiate the large category of non-owners, two new dimensions are added. To date, level of organisational control and educational credentials are at least as important as ownership of economic assets.

If we follow Bertings view on the expanded middle class in modern western societies, based on the big expansion of the service class and the embourgeoisement of large parts of the labour class, then only Wright's class of proletarians seem to fall outside the expanded middle class. The proletarian class is characterised by the fact that its members control no valuable assets. Proletarians are the archetypical have nots: they have no material assets suchs as land, shops, shares, bonds or other securities; they have no power to supervise anybody, and they have no educational credentials of any value (Steijn, 1997).

To readers who have studied all the preceding chapters it is evident that this scheme is less appropriate for southern European countries. Petmesidou (chapter 7) reports that 21% of the Greek workers are employed in the agrarian sector. Nearly half of the active population is self-employed, mostly as owner of a small one-person business. Half of the salaried employees is working in the public sector. Many people combine ownership of a small business with a job in the public sector. Of course, they are hard to fit in Wright's or any other class scheme.[1] Furthermore, it is interesting to learn that technicians and workers employed on a wage basis constituted only 19% of the economically active population in 1991. Maybe, the most striking phenomenon is the huge expansion of the informal sector. Many people have a job that is unregistered. No taxes are paid on these wages. In the late eighties, informal activities amounted to about 40% of the Greek GDP. According to Petmesidou, it is no accident that various comparative studies of European social structures have so far ignored Greece. She defines the Greece's socio-economic structure as petty capitalism combined with statist/paternalistic forms of socio-political organisation. Greece never has been a class society, because it never had a strong hegemonic upper class, and, given the absence of a full-fledged industry, the working class has always been weak.

Nevertheless this is easy to see that Wright's scheme is very useful for empirical descriptions of modern western societies, but also very awkward to use in multivariate analysis. For statistical analysis a unidimensional model would be more convenient. Perhaps that is one of the reasons why the class scheme of Erikson, Goldthorpe and Portocarero (1979) is more popular. The EGP-class scheme separates classes on the basis of differences in sources and level of income, economic security, career opportunities, and location in the system of authority. There are several variants of this scheme. The most elaborated version consists of eight classes:

Figure 10.2 The Erikson, Goldthorpe and Portocarero class scheme

EGP I	Higher controllers
EGP II	Lower controllers
EGP III	Routine non-manual workers
EGP IV	Self-employed
EGP V	Manual supervisors
EGP VI	Skilled manual workers
EGP VII a	Semi/unskilled workers
EGP VII b	Agricultural workers

Pierre Bourdieu has presented quite a different approach to the analysis of classes. Although his work is not mentioned in this volume, I think it is relevant for this topic. In his most famous book, *Distinction*, he sketches a very complex picture of society. He has left the idea of a system of only a few discrete classes and introduces the idea of class fractions (Bourdieu, 1979). On page 332 he presents a table in which the chances of access to the dominant class are calculated for 19 class fractions for which data were available, such as farm workers, unskilled workers, farmers, semi-skilled and skilled workers, foreman, craftsmen, office workers, small shopkeepers, junior executives, technicians, primary school teachers, industrial employers, big commercial employers. engineers, senior executives, secondary and higher-education teachers, and professions. Given in this order, the probabilities monotonously rise from only 2 % for boys whose father is a farm worker to 55 % for boys whose father is working in one of the professions. On the one hand these data show how inequality is reproduced. On the other hand they also show that society is open, at least to some degree. Clearly, children from lower classes only have a slight change of reaching high status jobs, but it is also evident that not all children from the middle classes will have a good career and acquire a high status position. This, accounts for an important aspect of middle class uncertainty.

Splitting up the traditional class scheme in a long hierarchical list of class fractions is not enough. The pièce de résistance of *Distintion* is shown on page 340. There two complicated pictures are printed over each other, representing the outcomes of two correspondence analyses[2] of the distribution of the variants of petty-bourgeois tastes and values of a great many of class fractions with different levels of economic and cultural capital, combined with their level of upward or downward mobility, representing a form of social capital, that is, social ties with high status families.

Bourdieu devotes much of his analysis of the struggle for cultural distinction and upward mobility, which is central to his studies of social reproduction, to fights that go on within social fields, that is, within social spaces in which there is a clear division between between 'players' who occupy a dominant position and 'players' who do not have a dominant position. On these battle-fields, cultural capital in the forms of a high level of education and, even more important, an upbringing in a family with a lot of cultural capital, such as the possession of works of art or a great knowledge of art and literature, has become an important source of power in the fight for social status.

According to Bourdieu, the one great, international class struggle is replaced by thousands of 'local' fights between different class fractions within specific sub-classes or or social fields. But all these struggles within restricted social fields will not alter the social structure in significant ways. This structure will be reproduced with only slight shifts between some class fractions. Only a relatively small number of successful social climbers will feed the illusion of an open society, thereby helping its reproduction. Here, exceptions disprove the rule. So, all classes are highly fragmented and the class struggle is transformed in hundreds of thousands of minor, but mean fights over field dominance. In Bourdieu's view, it is a general law of sociology that people who dominate their field always want to retain a significant social distance from the rest of the field, who are desperately fighting for upward mobility. But they fight an uphill battle because they always strive to become somebody else, whereas the people who have inherited cultural capital as a young child can maintain a head start, simply by being who they are. Nevertheless, these continuous fights within and between old and emerging class fractions create a lot of unrest and insecurity in all the fractions of the middle classes. They can never be sure of their position, nor whether their children will have a good career, which is of great importance for members of the middle classes.

After this short introduction of three different 'schemes' to describe class structures, the reader might wonder which approach is best. The answer is: it depends. It depends on the range and quality of the data and also on the facts or processes we want to describe or explain. Clearly, every class scheme has its pros and cons. So, why not try all of them? With modern computers it is quite easy to try different schemes and types of analyses. I am fairly sure that she various outcomes produced in this way will give us more insight in the topic under study.

10.2.3 The ascent and domination of middle class values

Berting (chapter 1) observes that the middle class as a whole is not integrated socially. There is no class consciousness in the middle classes. Therefore, they are no classes in a Marxist sense. They constitute no 'Klasse für sich.' Of course, their members share a common set of typical middle class norms and values, but the core of this value system centres around individualism and social mobility. Certainly, this does not create much class solidarity. Especially in times of economic growth, as was the case in the first decades after the World

War II, the orientation towards individual achievement became highly dominant. The upwardly mobile from the former labour class also adopted these social objectives. They wanted a better deal for themselves and for their children. Education was viewed as the golden gate to better jobs and higher incomes. They also started to believe that society was quite fair and offered equal opportunities to everyone with the right abilities and motivation. However, this view of an open society is seen as one of the great myths of modern times by many sociologists (See also Eduardo Crespo Suarez et al. in this volume). Of course, modern society is more open than the societies of Ancient History or the Middle Ages (Lenski, 1966), but, as we all know, it still is not completely open in that it really offers equal opportunities to everyone irrespective of one's gender or one's social, cultural, or ethnic background.

In our expanding and modernised economy, many new jobs are created that could be considered better jobs, that is, jobs that demand less physical energy and provide the workers with more income, autonomy, and variation than many jobs in the first stages of industrialisation. Of course, some of the new jobs created by industrial and technological innovation are very boring too. But, as long as the number and quality of new jobs equalled or surpassed the loss of unchallenging, low income jobs made obsolete by technological progress, everything was right. That machines and computers also make some interesting and challenging jobs redundant simply is the price we have to pay for modernisation. As long as industrial society is booming there seems nothing to complain about.

Thus, the massive and continuous introduction of technological innovations in industry and services gave rise to a whole new range of jobs, while at the same time driving out a huge number of traditional jobs. Most of these new jobs require more education than the old jobs. Acquiring a higher level of education and working in these new types of jobs goes hand in hand with an exposure to middle-class norms and values. So, the middle class boomed and its individualistic culture and lifestyle became more dominant than ever before.

In this volume, Berting as well as Eduardo Crespo Suarez et al draw attention to the individualistic core of the middle-class culture, which by now has become a fundamental tenet for the culture of modernity. More than ever before, the emphasis is on individual self-determination. The modern individual is seen as a person with a stable identity, who is very rational and can control his environment thanks to the many discoveries and innovations of science and technology.[3] In this view, modern people are the authors of their own lives, able to create their own history, their own world. In addition, they have a linear and optimistic notion of progress, fed by an impressive past performance of science and technology. They expected society to present us with ever more material wealth, freedom, and opportunities, and also more richness and social opportunities for their children. Alas, in the eighties and nineties sharp rises in unemployment undermined career prospects and job securities. It also blocked many young people at the start of their career. The middle-class dream was shattered. Its self-confidence and its concomitant belief in social and individual progress were severely dented.

10.3 What went wrong with middle-class careers and prospects?

10.3.1 Globalisation, rising unemployment, and cuts in private and public spending

Various contributors to this volume have come up with theories and data about deterioration in the social and economic position of the middle classes. However, Steijn and Houtman (Chapter 5) present data that give less rise to alarm. In their analysis of Dutch panel data they find significant increases in net income for all classes in the period from 1985 till 1994. What is more interesting is that the increase in net income of the upper middle class is substantially higher than that of the lower class. However, this does not prove that there is no reason for feelings of uncertainty in the middle classes, because the possibility of being fired does not significantly correlate with class. This might indicate that the situation of the middle class has worsened in comparison with the period before 1985.

Savage (Chapter 2) mentions the rearrangement of the income distribution at the expense of some segments of the middle classes, but other segments seem to have improved their relative position in the income distribution. Again, this could indicate why at least some fractions of the middle class have lost confidence in the future.

Other contributors to this volume refer to drops in the economic growth rate that affect large numbers of people negatively. Since the middle classes form such a large part of society, they cannot shield themselves against the negative effects of economic depressions. If businesses periodically make less profit or are more and more confronted with fierce international competition, then they simply have to cut down on production costs. Otherwise they will not survive. This will generally lead to the firing of a large number of employees. Sometimes the workers will accept lower salaries in exchange for a better chance to save their jobs. As we all know, many businesses have indeed cut the number of their workers by hundreds. In the eighties and the beginning of the nineties, some big multinationals have cut even tens of thousands of jobs. Downsizing is still going on. Worldwide, millions of jobs have been removed.

Furthermore, in times of economic decline, governments receive considerably less tax money. Therefore, they also have to cut their budgets. Since salaries make up at least 80 per cent of their budgets, a decrease in the number of civil servants or their salaries is unavoidable. Other measures that have been taken are lowering the outlays for state pensions and social assistance.

In this volume, various authors have mentioned a neo-conservative move towards significant budget cuts in education, social security, and social assistance in their country. This is being done not only to make ends meet, but is legitimised by the ideology that the state has to retreat wherever possible to make more room for market processes. A less expensive government bureaucracy lightens the tax burden and make national industries and services more competitive within the framework of the globalised economy. Thus, in years of economic decline, large segments of the population will be hit by sharp cuts in private and public budgets.

This volume gives ample evidence of the erosion of career prospects and economic security of the labour force at large. The simple statistical fact that the middle classes now make up about 80 per cent of the population must lead to the conclusion that every severe blow that has to be faced by the economy, will have repercussions on the middle classes or large parts of the middle classes. It is impossible to imagine that a serious slowdown of the economy will not be felt by the middle classes, but only by the reduced underclass.

Another important objective change concerns organisational aspects of the economy, such as the rearrangement of bureaucratic organisation structures as a consequence of new theoretical insights and soaring global competition. In a globalised economy, a growing part of the work in industry and the service sector is transferred to countries with low labour costs. Intensified global competition and a growing demand for higher profits from shareholders are forcing managing directors to take drastic measures and make organisations as lean as possible. This strategy puts thousands of jobs at risk, not only the jobs of low-skilled manual workers, but also the jobs of skilled workers, office workers, middle management and even parts of top management.

Organisational hierarchies are levelled off and ever more jobs are made `flexible.' Permanent jobs are changed into temporary jobs, and full-time jobs are changed into part-time jobs. Pension schemes are trimmed. This puts individual pensions at risk, because most pension schemes are based on full time jobs in long, uninterrupted careers. Managers will have to agree that part of their salary will depend on their success in reaching specific targets, such as cheaper production, higher sales, and higher profits. All this is affecting a growing number of middle-class people. This constant reorganisation of economic businesses, as a consequence of globalisation and further technological innovations is creating a lot of insecurity. Moreover, this feverish climate of continuous reorganisation is also affecting the managers of government bureaucracies. There it decreases the job security and worsens career prospects too.

At the subjective level we are forced to turn our minds to phenomena such as the fear of a further reduction in the number of jobs available to middle-class youngsters and to a deterioration of their career prospects and that of those already in the workforce for many years (Eduardo Crespo Suarez et al., Chapter 7.)

Also, there is a growing angst that the demographic build-up of society and the economic outlook for the future no longer seem to warrant a secure pension scheme for those who now have passed half their working lives and who do not have financial reserves to build up a solid private pension scheme. It is clear that the number of old-age pensioners is growing rapidly in many countries, whereas the number of young people has decreased as a consequence of a sharp decline in the birth rate. On the basis of simple calculations, many people will think that this must lead to markedly lower state pensions. And this makes them very pessimistic about their financial situation during the years of retirement.

10.3.2 Consequences of the feminisation of the labour market

In recent decades the level of unemployment was aggravated by the marked rise in the proportion of women who wanted to stay in the labour market after their marriage, and even after childbirth. Young women with children also wanted to return to the labour market as soon as their children reached the age of compulsory education. This belated feminisation of the labour market, especially at the middle level of administration, sales, and other services, was a consequence of higher educational levels and a concomitant need for self-actualisation.

The feminisation of the workforce was supported by a feminist ideology that stressed the equality of women in every respect. It is now generally accepted that women have paid jobs. This is especially true for the middle class. The extra family income helps them keep up a middle-class lifestyle. Less educated women also want to maintain their jobs, even jobs as office cleaners, jobs in sweat shops, and assembly line jobs. In their case, it is also the need or the strong desire for money to keep up their living standard and, in cases of a double income, even acquire material goods for imitating a middle- class lifestyle.

In Chapter 3, Mary Crompton reports that the number of female judges, advocates, barristers and solicitors in England rose from 4 to 27 per cent in two decades. In the same period the proportion of female local government officers rose from 20 to 51 per cent. Other categories of typical middle- class jobs and professions showed similar rises. Once more, this underlines that the middle classes are very heterogeneous. The professions are much more feminised than management jobs in banking, insurance companies, and other commercial businesses. Similar trends can be observed in the rest of western Europe. All this is related to a sharp decline in the birth-rate. Having fewer children is one way of `solving' the difficulties of combining a job and a family.

But problems of domestic chores and child care have to be solved. A large number of studies show that women get the worst part of the deal. Many women content themselves with a less demanding job to have enough time for the traditional task of mother and house-wife. Women in managerial functions are not in a position to opt for a career with somewhat limited responsibilities. There, it is all or nothing. In their case, a man that is prepared to take on the role of `houseman' and child carer would be very convenient. If they have married the wrong type of man, this situation will lead to severe marital conflicts. The fight over a just and fair sharing of domestic work is an important reason for divorce in many families, especially in middle-class families, because the upper level of middle-class jobs tend to be more demanding than lower-class jobs.

So, the belated, but by now massive entrance of women on the labour market has set living standards at a higher level, so that more people can have a middle-class lifestyle, i.e. buy their own house, have a car, and go on holiday at least once a year. The flip side of the coin is that the combination of a job and domestic work and caring puts too much stress on women and also on their husbands. If this problem cannot be solved, it puts stress on family life, and might be one of the reasons why divorce rates have soared in modern times. Divorce almost always creates new hardships and uncertainties, especially in the middle classes were it will mean a sharp reduction in financial resources.

Also, feminisation is affecting the men in jobs that by now have become highly feminised. This has lowered their status as well as their career prospects, thus feeding middle-class uncertainty.

10.4 A first sketch for a research programme

In their respective chapters, Savage and Kronauer, make it that in their countries middle class uncertainty was first highlighted by the press. Important national papers in England and Germany drew attention to it by using alarming headlines for strong worded articles, partly supported by their own research or research commissioned by them. Obviously, in some countries, journalists were ahead of the social scientists in detecting major social trends. Maybe this is because many social scientists still have much more concern for the plight of the underclass. Perhaps they think that the middle class is capable of solving its own problems and can easily regain lost ground. This seems plausible, since, in general, they are better educated and have more financial resources and social capital in the form of the right social networks than members of the lower class. Well, of course, this remains to be seen, and should be studied before we arrive at this conclusion. For the time being, it does not seem sensible to direct all our research efforts at the plight of the underclass. If we really are interested in major transformations of society, then we certainly must study those classes that seem to uphold the core structure and dominant culture of society. Expanding this metaphor, we can easily see that the whole of society will be in danger as soon as the broad mid-section of society becomes uncertain and vulnerable.

There are still many questions about middle-class uncertainty and vulnerability which have to be answered. What is the degree of middle-class uncertainty or even anxiety? Why and to what extent have they become more vulnerable in recent periods? Will this uncertainty and vulnerability disappear as soon as the economy recovers, or will it become more permanent, because labour market conditions will never return to the old situation with fixed jobs for the large majority of workers and good career prospects in many sectors of the economy? Will the psychological damage remain and even be passed on to the next generation? Or will new generations quite easily adapt to the new economic and political paradigm?

To what extent are societal and economic changes harming the status and position of the middle classes objectively, or is it mainly a subjective phenomenon? Does it make a difference whether the members of the middle classes have experienced real losses in income or only relative losses? And, if so, did this affect all the middle classes, only the lower middle classes, or only certain fractions of the middle and lower middle classes?

The contributions from southern Europe and Russia direct our attention to totally different aspects. The social structure of countries such as Greece and Spain is quite different from that of northern welfare states. In the South, industrialisation did not take off as quickly as in the rest of Europe. As a consequence, they still have a very large agrarian sector and a very large category of self-employed. In Greece, there is also a hugely expanded black economy. Nevertheless, processes of urbanisation and individualisation are taking place fast in these countries. This brings us to another aspect of middle- class uncertainty. What will happen if the market economy collapses, government bureaucracies shrink, and there is no extended family or flourishing family business to fall back on? This problem can be generalised to all countries. Where can people go if markets and welfare systems collapse, and family networks have fallen apart or vanished, as is the case with people who have no children, nor parents, or those who have broken with their family long ago?

Quite a different set of questions pertains to the impact of middle-class uncertainty on society as a whole, on the dominant work ethos, and on social cohesion. To what extent does it matter whether setbacks experienced by members of the middle class seem less salient than the setbacks that are experienced by members of the lower class? Is a temporary setback enough to destroy the work ethos and the belief in social progress and upward mobility for good?

It is not very difficult to think of many research questions that still need to be studied in depth. Even this short list makes clear that Berting is right when he asserts that a research agenda for the social exclusion paradigm has to be broadened to the social, psychological, and even medical consequences of social exclusion. The same could be said about a research programme that is focused on middle-class insecurity and vulnerability. It is not enough to know the volume and social composition (of the fractions) of the middle classes that really or `only subjectively' have undergone a worsening of their economic position and social status.

Let me try to systematise this handful of assorted questions. In order to arrive at a clear description and explanation of middle-class decline, we have to make a distinction between objective and subjective aspects. Furthermore, we have to distinguish between causes and effects. We must also identify various economic, social, and political causes and effects. First, I will formulate three main questions related to objective facts about or causes of middle class uncertainty and vulnerability.

1. Which macro-economic factors, including globalisation, reorganisations, budget cuts,

international transfer of jobs, flexibilisation, etc., damage the economic and social position of middle-class employees? Which of these factors has the most negative impact on the middle classes? Are there fractions of middle classes that profit from these macro-economic transformations in the short or the long run?

2. Which cultural, social and demographical factors, such as the individualisation and the greying' of society, create middle-class uncertainty and vulnerability, or exacerbate middle-class uncertainty and vulnerability when produced by other factors? Under what conditions can middle-class uncertainty and vulnerability be counteracted by intermediate structures such as voluntary associations, labour unions, churches, community centres, etc.?

3. Which political factors, such as policies to privatise large parts of the collective system, policies to restructure the welfare state into a more sober one or policies to make further and higher education more expensive for students, increase middle-class uncertainty and vulnerability? How can this reorganization of welfare make people less dependent on welfare and more autonomous and responsible for their own social condition? Which fractions of the middle classes will profit from these political changes?

This short list still leaves open important questions about the integration or disintegration of society as a whole. What will happen if large numbers of people belonging to the middle classes become frustrated? Berting asserts that the individualisation of the middle classes is so strong that they will not unite to fight the economic system nor the government. However, at the moment they constitute the core and the bulk of the nation, not only in terms of the bearers of core values but also as the people who earn the cost of living for society as a whole. What will happen if they lose trust in society? What happens if they lose morale because their future looks very bleak and their present has already greatly deteriorated in comparison with their past?

This leads to the fourth cluster of research questions:

4. What are the social, economic and political consequences of different degrees of middle-class uncertainty and vulnerability? Will this lead to more individualisation, loneliness, and alienation? Will this lead to an exacerbation of economic decline because of a loss in work motivation and work ethos? Will this lead to more alienation from politics or to more political extremism?

Of course, these questions have to be refined and placed in a more solid theoretical framework. Some of the building blocks for this theoretical framework can be found in this volume, especially in chapters by Berting (Chapter 1) and by the trio of Spanish contributors

(Chapter 7). One thing is clear: there is a challenging, interesting and highly relevant research programme waiting to be addressed.

Notes

1 Wright is aware of this. Therefore , he introduced the concept of 'contradictory locations within class relations'. (Wright, 1989; pp.270).

2 Outside France correspondence analysis is known as homals analysis.

3 Nowadays, more and more people are aware of the huge risks involved in the production and use of some forms of modern technology.

References

Berting, J. (1968) *In het brede maatschappelijke midden*, Meppel.

Bourdieu, P., and J.C. Passeron, (1977) *Reproduction in education, society and culture*, London. (Orig. La réproduction. Élements pour une théorie du système d'enseignement, Paris, 1970).

Bourdieu, P. (1984) *Distinction. A social critique of the judgement of taste*, Cambridge (Mass.). (Orig. La distinction. Critique sociale du jugement, Parijs, 1979).

Lenski, G. E., *Power and Privilege, A Theory of Social Stratification*, New York.

Nisbet, R. (1959) The Decline and Fall of Social Class, *Pacific Sociological Review*, vol. 2, nr. 1, pp. 11-28.

Steijn, B. (1997) Post-industrial Society: The End of Class, in: Mart-Jan de Jong and Anton C. Zijderveld, ed. *The Gift of Society*, Amersfoort.

Parijs, Ph. A. van (1989) A Revolution in Class Theory. In: E.O. Wright (ed). *The Debate in Class*, London, pp.213-242.

Wright E.O. (1985) *Classes*, London.

Wright, E.O. (1989) A General Framework for the Analysis of the Class Structure, in: E.O. Wright (ed.), *The Debate on Class*, London, pp. 3-46.

Subject Index

A
Achievement orientation 1; 9; 11
Alienation 12; 110; 149; 169
Anxiety 15; 19-21; 62; 96;137; 167
American job machine 70
Automation 2; 7

B
Blue-collar workers 10; 39; 63
Bourgeois 15
  bourgeoisie 95-97; 110; 159
  petty bourgeoisie 116; 130; 161
Britain 25-27; 29; 39; 42; 46; 48; 50; 76; 80; 157

C
Capitalism 7; 64; 87; 93; 96; 97; 110; 115; 116; 130; 160
Capitalist 7; 157; 158
Capitalist society 7
Career 1; 13; 15; 20; 25; 28; 33; 35; 37; 39; 42; 48; 53; 128; 163-166
  ladders 33
  opportunities 20; 21; 79; 86; 160
  prospects 29; 41; 74; 86; 163-165; 167
Civil rights 146; 149
Civil society 118; 131; 146
Civil servants 10; 11; 63; 76; 116; 157; 164
Class 157; 158; 161; 162
  antagonism 9;18
  closure 117
  concepts 115
  conflict 12
  consciousness 10; 12; 162
  differences 69
  intermediate 77; 78
  reproduction 42
  scheme 75; 77; 78; 151; 158-166
  service class 26-28; 42; 77; 78; 116; 120; 153
  struggle 9; 11; 100; 162
  theory 157; 158
  underclass 146; 149; 167
Collective
  action 11; 15; 23; 118
  antagonism 12
  bargaining 64; 138
Consensus 14; 26; 28; 119; 130

D
Deconstructionist 94
Deindustrialisation 126; 131
Division of labour 9; 45; 96; 97; 142
Domestic labour 12; 48
Domestic servants 49
Domestic work 45; 49; 54; 166
Dominant ideology 18; 96; 99
Downsizing 7; 27; 53; 62; 120; 164

E
Education 28; 29; 31; 37; 42; 46; 97; 103;120; 126; 130; 139; 141; 148; 159; 162-164; 166
Educational
  credentials 49; 117; 160
  opportunities 9
  qualifications 20; 47
  system 18; 20; 29; 42; 64
Egalitarian 11
Embourgeoisement 1; 2; 15; 74; 158; 160
Employment 7; 15; 17; 37; 46; 48; 53; 64-70; 109; 110; 115; 117; 126; 136-142; 148; 151; 153
Employment rights 106
England 104; 166
Ethnic divisions 25
Ethnicity 18; 27; 29; 158

Europe 46; 47; 108; 115-118; 121; 130; 166; 167
European 8; 47; 97; 104; 115-117; 120; 123; 128; 150; 153; 166
European Union 8; 101; 127; 128; 131; 136; 139; 140

F
Flexibility 8; 14; 18; 46; 54; 102; 104; 106-108; 110
Flexible specialisation 137
Fordism 99; 116; 117; 137
Fragmentation 16; 21; 46; 98; 102; 107; 109; 116; 118; 128-131
France 8; 11; 19; 46-48; 61; 66
Fraternalistic model 11

G
Gender 24; 27; 29; 75; 79-82; 85; 88-90; 124; 158; 163
Greece 115; 135
Germany 46; 47; 61-70; 76; 136; 162
Globalisation 7; 19; 93; 97; 135; 164; 165; 168

H
Household 8; 29; 42; 48; 63; 97; 119; 145
Human resource management 96
Hyperindividualism 13; 17

I
Income inequality 11; 29; 63; 70; 151; 152
Individual achievement 8; 10; 13; 15; 22; 163
    principle 13
Industrial society 1; 7; 9; 10; 19; 22; 23; 93; 96; 99; 100; 157; 163
Inequalities 7; 16; 23; 70; 118; 119; 120; 124; 126; 129
Informal care
Informal economy 115; 118; 119; 126; 131
Information society 7
Insecurity 2; 8; 9; 13; 19; 20; 47; 62; 63; 69; 75; 91; 93; 94; 96-98; 105; 110; 116; 120; 126; 130; 162; 165; 168
Insecure 91; 147
Instability 94; 106; 108; 147; 149
Integration 15; 19; 69; 105; 109; 116; 118; 119; 158; 169
Intelligentsia 150
Italy 46; 47; 115-117; 128

J
Job security 29; 33-35; 41; 42; 79; 90; 97; 100; 102; 105; 120; 151; 163 ;165
Job structure 100; 102; 103; 120

K

L
Labour class 10-12; 15; 158; 160; 162
Labour contracts 12; 14; 20; 21; 85
Labour market 7; 9; 15; 17; 20; 27; 39; 41; 42; 64-70; 75; 80; 85; 93; 126; 127; 137; 138; 139; 166; 167
    Labour market dualism 123; 126
Lean production 7; 19

M
Maastricht Treaty 126; 131
Manufacturing 102; 116; 117; 135; 153; 154
Market principle 16; 22
Market situation 2; 4; 26; 89
Mass production 137
Middle class 157-169
    lower middle class 1; 64; 78; 80; 85-90; 121
    ethos 4; 93
    heterogeneity 167
    occupations 30; 31; 46; 57

society 12; 15; 73; 103
strata 136; 139; 116; 117; 121; 127; 128-130
Modernisation 13; 15; 95; 99-101; 118; 131; 158; 163
McDonaldisation 19
Mobility 117
-downward 17; 149; 161
-intergenerational
-intragenerational 14
-upward 79; 86; 127; 146; 148; 161; 162; 168
Mobility opportunities 90

N
Need principle 11; 13; 23
Neo-liberal 64; 108; 138
Netherlands 8; 11; 14; 17; 19; 46; 47; 74; 76

O
Occupational
androgyny 57
segregation57
feminisation
structure 45; 115; 116; 120; 122; 123; 124; 126; 127; 130
success 47
Organic solidarity 14
Organisational restructuring 25; 27
Organisational career 25; 28; 33

P
Part-time 8; 19-21; 54; 106; 107; 109; 140; 151; 165
Pauperisation 149
Periphery 115; 135
Polarisation 25; 27; 30; 47; 70; 102; 121-123; 126; 128; 130; 147; 151-153
Post-industrial society 47; 48; 93
Post-modern 120
Poor; the 8; 69; 70; 148; 153
Poverty 8; 15; 130; 147-149; 158
Poverty line 138; 148; 149
Professional workers 9; 34
Professionals 14; 30; 31; 35; 39; 46; 53; 62; 107; 122; 127; 139; 148; 150; 153; 154
Progress 9; 90; 93-97; 99; 108-110; 163; 168
Proletarianization 4; 25; 73-75; 79; 80; 85; 88-91; 115
absolute 74; 75; 85; 87; 89; 90
relative 74; 78; 81; 85; 89; 90
proletarianization thesis 74; 78; 89
Proletariat 11; 40; 102; 104; 116
Proletarian situation 11; 15
Promotion 26; 29; 33; 74; 79; 86; 137; 151

Q

R
Race 18; 27; 29
Recession 27; 33; 63; 69; 102; 104
Redundancy 33; 34; 41
redundancy rates 34
Restructuration/ restructuring 8; 75; 136; 138; 142; 153; 169
Retirement 33; 34; 41; 66; 67; 166
Risk(s) 7; 11; 16; 21; 66; 70; 79; 85; 86; 89; 96-98; 108; 115; 116; 120; 126-128; 130; 165
Russia 3; 5; 50; 55; 56; 145-154; 168

S
Sector
agricultural 100; 103; 139; 160; 168
primary (economic) 103; 123; 137
private 10; 21; 31; 41; 76; 82; 85; 86; 89; 116; 118; 120; 123; 138; 151; 153

public 17; 27; 29; 33; 41; 48; 76; 82; 85; 86; 89; 117-120; 122; 160
quarternary 10; 77
secondary (economic) 77; 103; 123; 137
service 7; 100; 102; 103; ; 124; 139; 165
tertiairy 10; 77; 103; 117; 121; 124 ;126; 130; 139
Segmentation 137; 138; 142
Self-determination 94; 163
Self employment 38; 39; 102; 115; 118; 123; 140; 154
Self-employed 10; 46; 50; 62; 63; 76-78; 116; 120; 121; 126; 127; 139; 157; 160; 161; 168
Service relationship 78
Shock therapy 147; 152
Social commitment 13
Social division 70
Social exclusion 2; 8; 9; 18-23; 61; 62; 64; 65; 67; 68; 70; 116; 120; 126-128; 130; 136; 139; 142; 149; 168
Social inclusion 141
Social inequality 7; 13; 16; 67; 70; 118; 120; 124; 126; 137
Social insurance 11; 69; 119; 128; 129
Social isolation 67; 68; 100
Social polarisation 47; 122; 123; 126; 130; 153
Social prestige 10
Social protection 128-130
Social security 16; 17; 20; 21; 23; 69; 142; 158; 164
Social stability 64; 97; 154
Société éclatée 12
Socio-normative qualifications 14
Spain 46; 47; 76; 93; 99-102; 104; 107-112; 115-117; 128; 139; 168
State paternalism 100; 115
Statism 115; 118; 119
Stratification 82; 115-118; 120; 121; 151-153; 158
Subsistence level 21; 147; 148; 151

T
Trade unions 104; 130; 138

U
Uncertainty 4; 8; 9; 11; 15; 17; 19-21; 41; 61; 62; 64. 69; 70; 93; 96-98; 105; 107; 110; 137; 150; 157; 158; 161; 166-169
Unemployed 8; 17; 18; 20; 63; 65-69; 76; 78; 79; 84; 85; 136; 139; 140; 149
Unemployment 47; 61; 64-70; 79; 84; 85; 89; 136-142; 101; 104; 106; 107; 108; 123; 126-138; 130; 149; 151; 163; 164; 166
United States (USA) 8; 63; 104; 135
Unpredictability 93-96; 98; 110
Unskilled labour 11; 41; 137

V
Vulnerability 9; 15; 17; 19; 21; 167-169

W
Welfare state 7; 9; 13; 15; 19; 27; 28; 64; 66; 69; 70; 97; 102; 108; 116; 120; 130; 137; 138; 142; 157; 168; 169
White-collar workers 1; 26; 39; 63; 87; 139; 157-158
Working class 1; 2; 12; 21; 35; 41; 64; 69; 73-75; 78; 80; 81; 82; 84-90; 100; 116; 139; 157; 160
Work situation 2; 53; 88; 89; 109; 110
Women('s) employment 45; 47; 166

X
Y
Z

Name Index

A
Abercombie, N. 25; 26
Aizpuru, M. 99
Arendt, H. 94; 96

B
Bajoit, G. 109
Bauer, M. 12
Beck, U. 45
Bell, D. 7
Berting, J. 1; 2; 3; 4; 5; 12; 73; 74; 75; 78; 82; 85; 91; 158; 160; 162; 168; 169
Boli-Bennet, J. 12
Boudon, R. 16
Bourdieu, P. 161; 162
Braverman, H. 1; 2; 25; 26; 74; 87; 88
Brunetta, G. 47
Büchel, F. 69
Bulmahn, Th. 63; 69
Burrage, M. 53
Butler, T. 3

C
Castles , F. 115
Chafetz, J. 48
Crespo, E. 109; 112
Crompton, R. 1; 2; 4; 25; 26; 29; 45; 46; 50; 51; 53; 58; 74; 75; 77; 87; 88; 166
Crozier, M. 98

D
Dahrendorf , R. 26
Danziger, S. 63
Davies, C. 45; 46; 58
Devine, F. 58
Donzelot, J. 21
Dubet, F. 109

E
Ehrenreich, B. 94; 95; 111
Erikson, R. 26; 42; 77; 160
Esping-Andersen, G. 40; 65; 115; 123

F
Fagan, C. 46; 47
Fieldberg, G. 74
Finlayson, L. 48
Fontella, E. 136
Flynn, R. 29
Franssen, A. 109
Freeman, R. 70

G
Geißler, R. 63
Gergen, K. 95; 109
Gershuny, J. 13; 39; 49; 58
Giddens, A. 26; 45
Glenn, E.N. 74
Goldthorpe, J.H. 1; 26; 27; 33; 37; 38; 42; 74; 77; 82; 160
Gorz, A. 47; 94; 96
Gottschalk, S. 63
Graaf, N.D.de, 78
Gregson, N. 48

H
Haarscher, G. 12
Hagan, J. 48
Hakim, C. 46
Halford, S. 33; 35
Hamnett, C. 43
Harrop, A. 47
Häußermann, H. 65
Heath, A. 28
Hochschild, A. 49
Hutton, W. 16

I

J
Jessop, B. 26
Jodelet, D. 21
Jones, G. 1; 2; 25; 26; 29; 74; 75; 87; 88
Jong, de M.J. 17
Jordan, B. 48; 49; 58

K
Kanter, R. 53
Kanellopoulos, K.N. 139
Kennedy, P. 135; 142
Kerr, C. 1
Klingender, F.D. 25
Köhler, C. 99
Kronauer, M. 66; 67; 68; 167

L
Lash, S.
Lasch, C. 13
Lambrini-Dimaki, I. 117
Lane, R.E. 22
Laval, G. 15
Leach, E. 12
LeFeuvre, N. 53; 58
LeGrand, J. 28
Lenski, G. E. 163
Lockwood, D. 26; 82; 85; 86; 89
Lowe, M. 48

M
Maffesoli, M. 13
Massey, D. 45; 46
Miller, D. 14
Mills, C. 38; 39; 40
Moelker, R. 14
Moss, P. 47

N
Negri, N. 128
Nisbet, R. 158

O
Ovsyannikov, A. 145

P
Pakulski, J. 15
Papadimitriou, Z. 135; 136; 137; 138
Parijs, Ph. A. van, 159
Parsons, T. 52
Passet, R. 136
Paugaum, S. 18
Pennef, J. 15
Petmesidou, M. 115; 117; 118; 119; 126; 129; 160
Petrinioti, X. 128
Pond, C. 26; 27
Potter, J. 95
Prieto, C. 105
Provopoulos, P.G. 117

Q

R
Renner, K. 26
Reich, R. 70
Ridge, J. 28
Rifkin, J. 2
Rimashevskaya, N. 145
Rimbau, C. 128
Rivera, A. 100
Roberts, K. 74
Rosanvallon, P. 2; 11; 106; 108
Rossell, T. 128
Roustang, G. 2; 8; 19
Rowntree, J. 29
Rubery, J. 46; 47

S
Sampson, E. 95; 111
Saraceno, C. 128
Saunders, P. 43
Savage, M. 2; 4; 26; 27; 28; 35; 38; 39; 43; 46; 47; 58; 73; 75; 78; 80; 164; 167

Schäfer, C. 63
Schoonhoven, van, R. 17
Scott, A. 45; 46; 47
Serrano, A. 107
Siebel, W. 65
Sporton, D. 47
Stacey, M. 58
Steijn, A.J. 14; 74; 77; 78; 158; 164
Stewart, A. 26; 40
Storper, M. 137
Stovel, K. 33

T
Terssac, G. de 98
Thierry, H. 14
Thomas, K. 137
Thurow, L. 63; 70
Tieman, H. 137
Titmus, R.M. 115
Tobias, C. 105
Todorov, T. 21
Toharia, L. 99
Torstendahl, R. 53
Touraine, A. 12; 94; 95; 105
Townsend, P. 28
Tsoukalas, K. 117; 119
Tsoulouvis, L. 117; 118; 119; 126
Tuñón de Lara, M. 99

U
Urry, J. 25; 26; 27

V

W
Wacquant, L. 8; 70
Wajcman, J. 50
Wagner, A. 66
Waters, M. 15
Wetherell, M. 95
Whyte, W.F. 35
Wijmans, L.L. 11
Witte, H, de 74; 77
Witte, M.C., de 14; 15
Witz, A. 45; 46; 47
Wright, E.O. 159; 160

X

Y

Z

MIX
Papier aus verantwortungsvollen Quellen
Paper from responsible sources
FSC® C105338

If you have any concerns about our products,
you can contact us on
ProductSafety@springernature.com

In case Publisher is established outside the EU,
the EU authorized representative is:
Springer Nature Customer Service Center GmbH
Europaplatz 3, 69115 Heidelberg, Germany

Printed by Libri Plureos GmbH
in Hamburg, Germany